ROMAN DRAMA

and

ROMAN HISTORY

EXETER STUDIES IN HISTORY

General Editors:
Jonathan Barry, Tim Rees *and* T.P. Wiseman

Other paperbacks in this series include:

Roman Political life, 90 BC–AD 69
edited by T.P. Wiseman (1985)

The Administration of the Roman Empire, 241 BC–AD 193
edited by David Braund (1988)

Satire and Society in Ancient Rome
edited by Susan H. Braund (1989)

Flavius Josephus: *Death of an Emperor*
translated with an Introduction and Commentary
by T.P. Wiseman (1991)

Historiography and Imagination: Eight Essays on Roman Culture
T.P. Wiseman (1994)

Roman Public Buildings
edited by Ian M. Barton (new edition 1995)

Roman Domestic Buildings
edited by Ian M. Barton (1996)

Phlegon of Tralles' Book of Marvels
translated with an Introduction and Commentary
by William Hansen (1996)

Figuring Out Roman Nobility
by John Henderson (1997)

A Roman Life: Rutilius Gallicus On Paper and In Stone
by John Henderson (1998)

The front cover illustration shows Hercules and Mars on the Roman stage, watched by Victory, Jupiter and Minerva: appliqué relief from a second-century AD Gallic vase in the British Museum.

ROMAN DRAMA
and
ROMAN HISTORY

T.P. WISEMAN

UNIVERSITY
of
EXETER
PRESS

First published in 1998 by
University of Exeter Press
Reed Hall, Streatham Drive
Exeter, Devon EX4 4QR
UK

British Library Cataloguing in Publication Data
A catalogue record for this book
is available from the British Library

ISBN 0 85989 560 2

Typeset in Monotype Sabon by
Exe Valley Dataset, Exeter

Printed and bound in Great Britain by
Short Run Press Ltd., Exeter

For Tony Woodman

CONTENTS

ILLUSTRATIONS

Introduction

Rome as a city-state dates from about the end of the seventh century BC. That was when the valley between the Palatine and Capitoline hills was first developed as a public space (the *forum Romanum*), and when public buildings with terracotta relief decoration (the *Regia* is the first identifiable example) began to be constructed.[1]

The writing of Roman history dates from about the end of the third century BC. That was when the senators Q. Fabius Pictor and L. Cincius Alimentus, using the Greek language and the Greek literary genre of historiography, first narrated Rome's past for the Hellenistic world at the time of the war with Hannibal.[2]

The four intervening centuries had seen Rome expand from a small Latin town at the crossing-point of the lower Tiber to a major power successfully challenging Carthage for the mastery of the western Mediterranean. The indices of her power were conspicuously visible: the great temple of Jupiter Optimus Maximus on the Capitol (late sixth century), the huge circuit-wall enclosing an area of 427 hectares (early fourth century), the purpose-built road network linking Rome with her military colonies (late fourth century onwards), the aqueducts constructed to supply the needs of an ever-growing population (late fourth century onwards), and the lands marked out for Roman settlers all over Italy.[3]

Here was a highly successful polity, intensely conscious of itself and proud of its achievements. But how did the Romans conceive of their own past? How was the story of Rome remembered? Fabius and Cincius must have talked to the sons and grandsons of men who took part in the later stages of the conquest of Italy; but like Herodotus or any other pioneering historian, for events more than a hundred years or so before their own time they had no first- or second-hand evidence to go on. For at least three centuries of the history of Rome we do not know how the memory of events was transmitted.

In the first chapter of an earlier volume in this series, *Historiography and Imagination* (1994), I argued that the Roman historical tradition was largely created and perpetuated in dramatic performances at the Roman games (*ludi scaenici*)—not only the regular annual festivals in honour of the gods, but also *ad hoc* celebrations for triumphs, funerals and the dedication of temples. I developed the idea, with particular reference to the foundation legend, in *Remus: a Roman Myth* (Cambridge 1995). Both books have been generously received, and some reviewers particularly welcomed the drama hypothesis.[4]

But it is easy to object that there is no evidence for Roman historical drama before about 220 BC (Naevius' play on Marcellus at Clastidium), and no secure evidence for Roman drama at all before about 240 BC, when Livius Andronicus produced his first play at Rome. The objection is not compelling, however, for there could have been non-literary drama at the Roman games long before Livius Andronicus. Plays without texts would leave no evidence, so later historians of the theatre, like Varro in the first century BC, would not have been aware of them.

'There could have been'—but is there any reason to think there *were*? The first half of this book represents the next stage of the argument. Chapter 1 traces the history of the idea that drama may have played a part in the creation of the Roman historical tradition; I have been surprised to find how many scholars have thought of the idea before, and how often it has been forgotten again. If such plays did indeed exist, one should be able to detect the traces of them in episodes of extant historical narratives in our sources; chapters 2–6 argue for some possible examples. Several of them come from Ovid's *Fasti*, aetiological poetry being no doubt more hospitable than historical prose to the sort of material involved. But there are vestiges also in Livy, Plutarch and even Suetonius.

Chapter 7 analyses a further passage in the *Fasti*. Here the dramatic source used by Ovid created not historical narrative but the explanation of a Roman ritual. But even the mythology of Roman gods could be set in a historical context, in this case the secession of the *plebs*.

It has recently been emphasised, in a fine book by Harriet Flower, that Roman aristocratic funerals were themselves the occasion of dramatic or quasi-dramatic performance celebrating the history of the *gens*.[5] Chapters 8–10 offer three examples of the Roman historical tradition as seen from the perspective of a noble family. In the first case a systematic literary creation can be identified; but no doubt the Valerii, like the Aemilii and the Minucii, had been elaborating their ancestral story long before Valerius Antias took up his fertile pen. Drama, epic, historiography, funeral oratory, the iconography of coins and monuments, will all have played their part in that complex process.

Finally, there are chapters on two modern historians of Rome, one obscure, one world-famous, but both preoccupied in their very different ways with the creation of narrative and the relationship of history to fiction.

Chapters 1, 3 and 4 are hitherto unpublished; chapters 5 and 6 are an expanded and rearranged version of *Scripta Classica Israelica* 15 (Studies in Memory of Abraham Wasserstein vol. 1, 1996) 152–8; chapter 8, with Appendix B, is the English original of 'Valerio Anziate e il palinsesto della storia', in *Tra antiquitas e annalistica* (Eutopia, Rome forthcoming). The other chapters are reprinted, with thanks to the editors and publishers concerned, from the following sources: ch. 2, *Pegasus* 38 (1995) 2–8; ch. 7, *The Third Syme Memorial Lecture* (Wellington N.Z. 1996), minus the opening and closing sections; ch. 9, *Imperium sine fine: T. Robert S. Broughton and the Roman Republic* (Historia Einzelschriften 105, ed. J. Linderski, Stuttgart 1996) 57–74; ch. 10, *Tria lustra: Essays and Notes Presented to John Pinsent* (Liverpool Classical Papers 3, ed. H.D. Jocelyn and H. Hurt, Liverpool 1993) 181–92; ch. 11, *Qui Miscuit Utile Dulci: Festschrift Essays Presented to Paul Lachlan MacKendrick* (ed. G. Schmeling and J. D. Mikalson (Wauconda, Ill. 1998) 377–400; ch. 12, *Donum Amicitiae: Studies in Ancient History* (ed. E. Dabrowa, Kraków 1997) 235–49. I have added translations where necessary, and made a few additions to the notes (in square brackets).

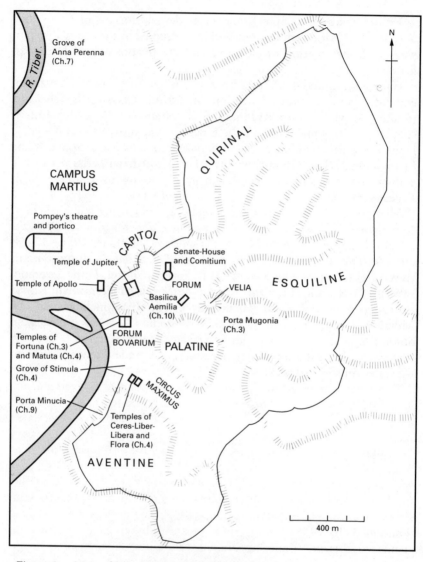

Figure 1.   Map of Rome, showing the republican city walls and some of the sites discussed in this book.

1

The History of a Hypothesis

I

On 8 January 1849, Leopold Ranke gave a paper on Dionysius of Halicarnassus to the Philosophy and History section of the Prussian Academy in Berlin.[1] At 53, the great historian was at the height of his powers. His history of the Papacy had appeared in 1834–6, and his *Deutsche Geschichte im Zeitalter der Reformation* in six volumes from 1839 to 1847. He was now working on the histories of France, England and Prussia, but evidently still had energy and curiosity to spare for the history of early Rome.

The paper was never published, but on one point at least its impact was evidently substantial. Ranke seems to have argued that Dionysius' account of the story of Romulus and Remus originated in a stage play,[2] thus contesting, tacitly or explicitly, the famous theory of Niebuhr that the traditions of early Rome were created in native oral poetry, the 'lays of ancient Rome' made famous by Macaulay's reconstructions.[3]

Although much criticised, Niebuhr's idea had a powerful hold on the minds of historians. Even after Schwegler and Cornewall Lewis had refuted it in the 1850s,[4] it still clung on as a dogma that could not be abandoned. In 1858, for instance, Gustav Linker gave a lecture in Vienna on ancient Roman historical sagas, with fulsome acknowledgment to Niebuhr's 'immortal work'; he recognised that the story of Lucretia was *tragisch*, and that the character of Tullia was like that of Lady Macbeth, but Niebuhr's authority prevented him from exploiting his insight.[5] Linker was looking straight at the evidence, but because it disproved his master he couldn't see it. It took a historian of Ranke's stature to do that.

In his later published treatment of Dionysius on the story of the twins, Ranke adduced various items as evidence for a theatrical origin: the presence of Amulius' daughter, who 'in a very effective dramatic scene' begs for the life of her friend and cousin Ilia, the mother of the twins; the 'recognition scene' when the guards find Faustulus carrying the vessel in which the twins were exposed; the brevity of the account of Amulius' fall, as if from a messenger-speech reporting what could not be shown on stage. Such techniques, along with Euripidean motifs and the tightly-organized succession of scenes, were hardly consistent with Niebuhr's ancient sagas. They betrayed the hand of a dramatist such as Naevius, who we know wrote a play on the upbringing of the twins.[6]

This later text of Ranke's owed much to the work of Otto Ribbeck, who had edited the collected fragments of Roman drama and in 1875 published a substantial monograph on tragedy in the Roman Republic. Ribbeck had pointed out that both Dionysius and Plutarch were aware of the theatrical nature of the Romulus and Remus story; he identified two plays, one on the birth and rescue of the twins, the other on their discovery of their birthright and the overthrow of Amulius.[7] Naevius' work, said Ribbeck, 'would do credit to the lost Greek tragedians of the school of Euripides'. Conrad Trieber in 1888 preferred Sophocles as the model (and denied Naevius' authorship), but no-one doubted that the story had originated on the tragic stage.[8]

Meanwhile, other dramatic plots had been identified in the Roman historical tradition. In 1859 Otto Jahn pointed to Livy's account of Sophoniba, wife of Syphax and beloved of Massinissa; her tragic story provided a ready-made plot for modern dramatists, and might well have been created by an ancient one. It was just one example, he argued, of a genre of historical drama (the *fabula praetexta*) which expressed the Romans' sense of their own identity.[9] In 1881 Ribbeck drew attention to a phrase in Livy's narrative of the fall of Veii: the Roman historian distanced himself from one particular episode in terms which clearly imply that he thought it had been invented for a play. Picking up the way Livy exploits the idea of fate in this part of his narrative, Ribbeck inferred the existence of a *praetexta* with Camillus as the tragic hero.[10]

The titles of known *fabulae praetextae*, duly registered in Ribbeck's great catalogue of the remains of Roman drama,[11] are as follows:

1. Naevius, *Clastidium* (on M. Marcellus' victory over the Gauls in 222 BC).[12]
2. Naevius, *Romulus*.[13]

3. Naevius, *Lupus*.[14]
4. Naevius, *Alimonium Remi et Romuli*.[15]
5. Ennius, *Ambracia* (on M. Fulvius Nobilior's victory in 189 BC).[16]
6. Ennius, *Sabinae* (on Romulus' abduction of the Sabine women).[17]
7. Pacuvius, *Paullus* (on L. Aemilius Paullus' victory at Pydna in 168 BC?).[18]
8. Accius, *Aeneadae uel Decius* (on P. Decius Mus' self-sacrifice in 295 BC).[19]
9. Accius, *Brutus* (on the first consul of the Republic).[20]
10. Cornelius Balbus, *De suo itinere* (on Balbus' visit to L. Lentulus in Pompey's camp in 48 BC).[21]
11. Cassius, *Brutus*.[22]
12. Pomponius Secundus, *Aeneas*.[23]
13. Curiatius Maternus, *Cato*.[24]
14. Curiatius Maternus, *Domitius*.[25]
15. Anon., *Octavia* (on Nero's rejection of Octavia in favour of Poppaea, AD 62).[26]

Two plays of unknown title and authorship may be added to the list: one attested in a disputed passage of Varro (discussed below) explaining the Nonae Caprotinae festival,[27] and one on the reception of the Magna Mater in 204 BC, with the miraculous vindication of Quinta Claudia.[28]

That was the nucleus of hard evidence to which the scholars were now adding their hypothetical new examples. The *praetexta* was a dramatic genre that flourished for nearly three hundred years, from Naevius in the late third century BC to Curiatius Maternus in the late first century AD, and Horace confirms that in his day such plays were an important part of the repertoire at the Roman dramatic festivals.[29] That is what we should expect. On the one hand, the Romans were proud of their past, and the deeds of their ancestors were a constant source of exemplary inspiration; but equally, as in Homer, recent events were a popular subject,[30] and great contemporaries like Marcellus, Fulvius Nobilior and Aemilius Paullus were no doubt glad to see themselves in glory on the stage.

II

It may not be accidental that the Roman 'national drama' was of particular interest to German scholars in the second half of the nineteenth century. Their own nation, unified since 1871 under the

3

Hohenzollern Kaisers, needed a common cultural tradition. (Bismarck's *Kulturkampf* was one expression of that need; the work of Wagner was another.) The idea of a Roman dramatic genre which brought the citizens together in the common celebration of a heroic past was naturally an attractive one.

Two scholars, one Bavarian, one Prussian, provided syntheses of what had been done so far in working out Ranke's insight. Karl Meiser ended his Munich *Festrede* on 15 November 1887 with the wish that German dramatists would turn away from antiquity and celebrate their own time, as the Romans had done. Alfred Schöne in Kiel chose the same theme for his lecture on the occasion of the birthday of Wilhelm II in 1893. 'Everyone knows,' he began, 'that our all-gracious King has a lively interest in the German stage, and encourages national historical drama in particular'; and he ended, predictably perhaps, by urging the Hohenzollern tradition itself as an appropriate theme for the German equivalent of the *fabula praetexta*.[31]

Both men drew attention to the known *praetexta* titles, and endorsed Jahn's idea of a Sophoniba play; Schöne also accepted Ribbeck's argument for a drama on the fall of Veii.[32] But they had new material to offer too. The theatrical nature of the Romulus and Remus story was common ground, but Schöne now pointed out that Dionysius had said the same thing about the duel of the Horatii and Curiatii, and about the Fabii at the Cremera; he wondered whether Caeso Fabius could have been an anti-hero like Coriolanus.[33] Moreover, both men offered a range of historical episodes as likely examples of material from drama: Tarpeia, Cloelia, the death of Servius Tullius, the conspiracy of Brutus' sons (Schöne); Pacuvius Calavius of Capua, Perseus and Demetrius, the death of Gaius Gracchus (Meiser).[34]

The enquiry they were pursuing was a combination of two strategies. On the one hand, traditional scholarship could collect all the references to, and quotations from, the known *fabulae praetextae*, and follow the grammarian Diomedes in defining the genre as a form of tragedy.[35] Ribbeck had done all that, and the result was disappointing: only fifteen titles for three hundred years of theatre.[36] So Gaston Boissier in 1893, though well aware of the importance of the *praetexta* in the traditional value-system of the Republic, was nevertheless forced to conclude that the genre never caught on.[37]

Meiser and Schöne were able to avoid that paradox by applying their other strategy, the detection of traces of *praetexta* material in historical narrative, claiming back for drama, as Schöne put it, what had previously been considered the property of other literary genres.[38] That presupposes a substantial number of otherwise unattested *praetextae*, influential enough to dictate the way historians conceived their material. But if they had such an impact, why is there no direct evidence?

One possible answer, conceded but not exploited by Boissier,[39] is that topical dramas created for a particular occasion, such as games put on for a victorious general's triumph, could influence the way people thought about an event without the text surviving to be consulted in libraries. That is, only a few *praetextae*, by the greatest practitioners, would become literary classics quoted by later writers, the necessary condition for the survival of their titles and 'fragments' in Ribbeck's collection.

An enthusiastic follower of the twin-track approach was a young scholar from Königsberg in East Prussia, Hermann Reich. In 1896, in a *Festschrift* article for a senior colleague, he combined the fragments of Naevius with Dionysius' narrative of the foundation story (Ranke's theme of nearly half a century before) to produce an adventurous reconstruction of a Euripidean drama on *The Boyhood of Remus and Romulus*.[40] It is a lively and entertaining piece, and I reproduce it in translation (Appendix A below) as the most confident statement of the 'national drama' hypothesis.

We may concede to Reich, give or take some of the details of his reconstruction, that Naevius' play may well have helped to form the Roman foundation legend. But that story is hardly typical of Roman history. Is it equally likely that the historical tradition as a whole was largely formed by *fabulae praetextae*?

Wilhelm Soltau thought it was. His book on the beginnings of Roman historiography, published in 1909, identified *die Römerdramen*—along with Ennius' *Annals* and material borrowed from the Greek historians—as one of the main sources for what passes for early Roman history.[41] He stated his position emphatically at the outset: 'This book will demonstrate that all the lively and individual characteristics of early Roman history are based on *creative literature* and *invention*.'[42] And at the end he offered a list of all the unattested *praetextae* he had argued into existence: Naevius on Coriolanus and the first secession of the *plebs*; Ennius on Horatius and the Curiatii, the capture of Veii, the surrender of Falerii, the liberation of Rome from the Gauls, the Nonae Caprotinae, and Demetrius; Accius on Porsenna, Virginia, Spurius Cassius, Spurius Maelius, Marcus Manlius, and Fabricius.[43]

As in his previous book on Livy, where he had assigned a named source for every passage in the entire text,[44] Soltau's dogmatic self-confidence was counter-productive. His case would have been a good one if presented more cautiously, but inappropriate claims to certainty made readers predictably disinclined to believe it.[45]

Historians in particular resisted the idea that the Roman historical tradition had been created so late. Naevius and Fabius Pictor were near-contemporaries; Soltau's theory presupposed that the artistry of individual dramatists was immediately accepted by the Roman people as the story of its own past.[46] Could it really have happened so suddenly? Niebuhr had posited a poetic tradition which was native, epic, and popular; Soltau's version was Hellenised, dramatic, and artistic—but no more convincing for that. After all, not everything dramatic has to come from a drama.[47]

III

So far, with the exception of Boissier, the debate had been a wholly German affair. For the next forty years it would be carried on by Americans—appropriately, since the great republic's founders had been much influenced by a play about Roman history (Addison's *Cato*).[48]

Soltau's book quickly crossed the Atlantic. At Yale, Henry B. Wright was immediately inspired to add to the list of inferred *praetextae* in a study boldly entitled *The Recovery of a Lost Roman Tragedy*.[49] Soltau had shown

> that the traditions of early Roman History, as we now know them, owe their form and in large degree also their substance . . . to the clothing of gaunt and meagre Roman family traditions with borrowings from the whole cloth of Greek drama and history by Roman dramatists of the third and second centuries BC.

But there was more to do, as he explained in another striking metaphor:

> We have discovered certain fossil bones, and can assert positively that a certain form of dramatic life once existed. We cannot, however, . . . build up the whole structure of the lost fossil, for we have no assurance that either of our possible models, classical Greek Tragedy, or the *Octavia* ascribed to Seneca, belonged to the same species. At the present time, the further study of Roman National Drama would seem to be blocked by the ignorance of investigators as to the structural anatomy of particular species.

6

That this structure so long sought after is to be found in a hitherto undiscovered *Fabula Praetexta* which lies imbedded practically intact in a chapter of the first book of Livy; and that this fossil deposit, in addition to meeting the demands of all the criteria for detection of lost plays—of external involuntary clue, of dramatic incident, of patent borrowing from Greek sources, and of compatibility with the temper of the times, can, in addition, be brought into relation with two hitherto unclassified fragments of a Roman dramatist, the present discussion strives to demonstrate.

The Livy chapter is I 46.4–9, on the two Tulliae, the two Tarquins, and the marriages that led to two murders and a regicide. The 'external involuntary clue' is Livy's comment that the Roman royal house too provided an instance of crime fit for tragedy.[50]

Here is the play Wright reconstructed:[51]

1. Prologue: the wicked Tullia has married the virtuous Tarquin, and *vice versa*.
2. Choral ode (*parodos*), thanking the gods for keeping the wicked characters apart.
3. The virtuous Tullia tries unsuccessfully to influence her wicked husband.
4. The wicked Tullia taunts her virtuous husband and expresses admiration for his brother.
5. Contrasting soliloquies by the two Tulliae.
6. Choral ode: evil will find evil.
7. The wicked Tullia and the wicked Tarquin meet and plot.
8. The bodies of the murdered spouses are brought on for a funeral, while Tullia and Tarquin 'depart to be joined in unholy wedlock'; the old king mourns, aware of his future fate.

Two unattributed lines of Accius—'One woman for two husbands', and 'I see two tombs for two bodies'—provided Wright with an author for his *Tullia*.[52]

That may have been good enough for Yale, but not for Bryn Mawr. In 1915 Eleanor Shipley Duckett dismissed the whole school of thought, from Ranke to Wright, as a dangerous virus infecting scholarship: 'no certainty can be based upon uncertain and imaginary deductions.'[53] The Romulus story was part of 'the native tradition of Rome' long before Naevius; Ennius found the source for his *Sabinae* in a 'native tale'; if Accius' *Brutus* and *Decius* influenced historiography, that was only because 'they were composed at a time when Roman writers had little feeling for historical accuracy'; in short, 'our knowledge . . . of the early Roman legends and *praetextae* cannot show that dramatic matter influenced the earliest Roman annalists.'[54] So that was that.

It took twenty-five years for the pendulum to swing back. In 1940 Cornelia C. Coulter (Mt Holyoke College) emphasized 'the splendid pageantry and dramatic power of *fabulae praetextae* in the Roman Republic'.[55] She was prepared to entertain the possibility of hypothetical dramas as the source of historical episodes (Ranke's theory 'has formed the basis of much interesting speculation'), and as evidence for it she pointed out the dramatic character of Livy's narrative of Brutus and Lucretia at I 56–60, which was surely based on Accius' famous tragedy.[56]

Eleven years later Agnes Kirsopp Michels developed the argument further. She proposed a whole trilogy on the Tarquins—a *Tanaquil*, a *Tullia*, and a *Lucretia*—which profoundly influenced Livy but was not used by Dionysius.[57] She saw Tanaquil's speech from the window and the Furies' pursuit of Tullia as indicators of drama, and wondered whether Asinius Pollio might have been the author.[58]

But still the sceptics resisted. Henry Bardon would not allow any of the hypothetical *praetextae* into his *Littérature latine inconnue*, while R.M. Ogilvie, in his magisterial Livy commentary, insisted that the drama in the Tarquin narrative was all Livy's own.[59] Jacques Heurgon did wonder about a dramatic source, but assumed it must have been Etruscan, not native Roman.[60]

Ranke's notion had now been debated for more than a century, with no clear result. It was always based on the assumption that the *praetexta* was a tragic genre, and that it had been invented by Naevius in the late third century. But what if those premises were unsound?

IV

One piece of evidence that had not been much exploited was a difficult passage in Varro's *De lingua Latina*. It comes in the section where the great antiquarian gives explanations for the names of festivals:[61]

> Dies Poplifugia uidetur nominatus, quod eo die tumultu repente fugerit populus; non multo enim post hic dies quam decessus Gallorum ex urbe et qui tum sub urbe populi, ut Ficuleates ac Fidenates et finitimi alii, contra nos coniurarunt. aliquot huius diei

8

uestigia fugae in sacris apparent, de quibus rebus Antiquitatum libri plura referunt. Nonae Caprotinae, quod eo die in Latio Iunoni Caprotinae mulieres sacrificantur et sub caprifico faciunt; e caprifico adhibent uirgam. cur hoc, togata praetexta data +eis+ Apollinaribus ludis docuit populum.

The day of the *Poplifugia* seems to be so called because on that day the people suddenly fled in disorder. For this day is not long after [the date of] the departure from the city of the Gauls, and those peoples then living nearby, such as the Ficuleans and Fidenates and other neighbours, who united against us. Some traces of that day's flight appear in the rituals, on which my books of *Antiquities* give more details. The *Nonae Caprotinae* [are so called] because on that day in Latium the women sacrifice to Juno Caprotina, and they do it under a wild fig tree [*caprificus*]. They employ a stick from the tree. The reason for this was explained to the people by the *togata praetexta* presented at the Games of Apollo.

I have marked *eis* in the last sentence as a textual problem, and left it untranslated. 'At those Games of Apollo' is unintelligible, since the *ludi Apollinares* did not exist at the time of the supposed events.

Ever since Pomponius Laetus' original edition (*c.* 1471), many editors have preferred to emend the manuscript reading *togata* to *toga*.[62] That would at least account for *eis*. The sentence would then mean: 'The reason for this was explained to the people by the embroidered toga presented to them [i.e. the women] at the Games of Apollo.' But how can a toga explain anything? What sort of presentation are we to imagine?[63] And why should the simple phrase *toga praetexta* be corrupted into the problematic *togata praetexta*? (The opposite corruption, of course, would be easily explicable, and may have happened in the manuscript Laetus used for his edition.)

On the other hand, 'to present' (*dare*) is the technical term for putting on a play, and both *togata* and *praetexta* are names for types of Roman drama.[64] So P. Drossart of Lille, in an important article in 1974, was surely right to defend the manuscript reading and keep the story of the Nonae Caprotinae as an attested Roman historical drama, as Ribbeck had long ago proposed.[65]

The story is told by various authors, most succinctly in Polyaenus' *Stratagems*:[66]

> The Latins under Postumius marched on Rome, and as their condition for making peace demanded the Romans' daughters in

marriage, just as the Romans had taken the daughters of the Sabines. The Romans feared the war, but could not endure the surrender of their daughters. Then an attractive maidservant called Philotis suggested that she and all the other maidservants who were good-looking should be dressed up as the daughters and sent out to the enemy, adding that she would hold up a fire signal at night when the enemy had taken them and gone to sleep. So the Latins slept with the girls, and she raised the signal. The Romans attacked the Latins and killed them as they slept.

The reason for the Romans' helplessness, according to Plutarch and Macrobius, was that the city had not yet recovered from being sacked by the Gauls; and the same authors tell us that the heroine raised her signal from a wild fig-tree (*caprificus*).[67] Both items are alluded to in the Varro passage as explanations of Poplifugia and Nonae Caprotinae respectively.

It's an erotic story, and as we shall see in chapter 7, it probably explained an erotic festival. It certainly could have been a play, but hardly a tragedy. Wilhelm Soltau saw it as a cheerful end-piece coming after serious dramas on Camillus and the Gauls,[68] rather as in the Athenian theatre a satyr-play followed the tragic trilogy. That is certainly a possibility, but we know too little of the conventions of the Roman theatrical festivals to be dogmatic about it. What matters more is a methodological issue.

The editor of the Budé text of Varro rules out the manuscript reading *a priori*:[69]

> On ne peut garder *togata* des manuscrits ... qu'en donnant à *togata* le sens général de pièce de théâtre, et en imaginant une représentation scénique commémorative. ... [O]n ne sait rien de telles commémorations scéniques et justement l'histoire des esclaves déguisées en femmes libres et des ruses de *Tutela* [i.e. Philotis] relève plutôt de vaudeville que de la tragédie.

Rather than declare an ancient text corrupt on the basis of a modern preconception of what was or was not possible in Roman drama, it is surely preferable to take the text seriously and allow it to modify the preconception. If the story was like vaudeville,[70] that may tell us something about the Roman stage festivals. It was entirely proper that Drossart should insist on the manuscript reading in the Varro passage; his article marks a turning-point in the history of the debate.

One unanswered question is, who played the girls? The Nonae Caprotinae story is presented as a 'return match' for the rape of the Sabines, the subject of Ennius' play *Sabinae*.[71] Each story has a single female protagonist whose initiative creates the action (the one surviving fragment of *Sabinae* is from a speech by Hersilia), and that part could have been taken by a male actor in a mask, if that was the convention. But the action itself involves in each case a number of nubile girls whose nubility is precisely the point of the drama. That makes one think of mime, and the *mimae* who were the showgirls of the Roman theatre. By pure chance, we happen to know that the story of Actaeon was featured on the Roman stage in the 70s BC; another day, the dancers who played Diana and her nymphs could have played Philotis and the Roman 'brides'.[72] Is it conceivable that patriotic drama and erotic burlesque could be presented in the same performance?

It is not helpful to assume from the start that the formal genres of tragedy and comedy in the Athenian mode were all the Romans ever saw on the stage, or that 'serious' and 'popular' drama must always have been kept strictly apart. Mime could be serious, and morally exemplary, as well as farcical and obscene.[73] One of the genres of Roman drama was the 'cheerful tragedy' introduced by Rhinthon of Tarentum in the third century BC.[74] 'Seriousness mixed with laughter' is how an authoritative source (the Sibyl herself) defined the plays shown at the Roman games.[75]

Two random bits of evidence reveal how little we really know about the genres of Roman drama. First, St Jerome's list of the works of Varro, which included six books of 'pseudo-tragedies';[76] and second, Cicero's account of the most popular items at the *ludi scaenici* in 66 BC—'banquets of poets and philosophers' featuring Euripides and Menander, Socrates and Epicurus.[77] If such works do not fit into any of the generic categories we have inherited from the ancient grammarians, that is no doubt because the grammarians' schematic classification could never adequately represent the constant innovation and creative experiment of live theatre.

It is only when we try to define those categories too restrictively that the Varro passage becomes a problem. It is true that we don't know what sort of play he had in mind when he used the phrase *togata praetexta*. We don't even know whether he meant *togata* as a description or *Togata* as a title ('The Girl in a Toga' would do well for Philotis).[78] What matters, as Drossart saw, is to argue from the received text, not from an emendation.

11

V

In the last quarter of the twentieth century the question of historical drama was attacked from a different angle. Not much more could be expected from the traditional philological approach, trying to reconstruct lost texts; on the other hand, archaeological advances and a better understanding of early- and middle-republican Rome now made it possible to imagine a pre-literary context for performance. Two Italian contributions—one from Urbino in 1977, one from Trieste in 1980—give an idea of the change of direction.

Bruno Gentili presented *Lo spettacolo nel mondo antico* as a study of the archaic Roman theatre in the light of Hellenistic drama.[79] Papyri, inscriptions and the fragmentary literary evidence combine to show how far from the classic Athenian model the fourth- and third-century Greek theatrical performers had developed their art; and in particular, vase-paintings reveal the vitality of drama in the cities of south Italy, neighbours, allies and eventually subjects of Rome.[80] The result, in the mid-third century BC, was a native Roman tradition of oral improvisation coming to terms with the sophisticated literary drama of the Greek world at a late and innovative stage of its development.[81]

Gentili emphasized the inadequacy of merely literary criteria in assessing how Roman dramatists reworked their Greek models: they were theatre people who had to satisfy the demands of their audience.[82] And the audience wanted not just entertainment but also political comment and patriotic history, the subject-matter of the *fabula praetexta*. There too, Gentili pointed out, the Greek tradition could provide a model, from the early tragedies of Phrynichus and Aeschylus on the Persian wars to Theodectes' *Mausolus*, Moschion's *Themistocles* and the *Cassandreis* of Lycophron.[83]

Nevio Zorzetti, in *La pretesta e il teatro latino arcaico*, made an even more direct attack on the kind of literary history which reduces to the status of the primitive everything prior to the introduction of literary texts.[84] There was a complex tradition behind Roman literary drama, and the *fabula praetexta* in particular can only be interpreted in the context of the festivals at which it was performed. 'The archaic *praetexta*,' wrote Zorzetti, 'is only the tip of the iceberg.' What cannot be seen are all the other means the Roman people had for expressing, maintaining or adapting their consciousness of their own tradition.[85]

Zorzetti defined the primary role of the *praetexta* as 'the celebration of *imperium*'. But since Roman success depended on the will of the gods, he also noted the occurrence of prayers in the surviving fragments, and drew attention to Polybius' analysis of the god-fearing Roman society of his time, which the Greek historian attributed to the use of 'tragedy'.[86]

An exuberant example of the late twentieth-century approach to the history of the Roman theatre was offered by Florence Dupont in her book *L'acteur-roi* of 1985:[87]

> [C]ette vérité historique a été le plus souvent méconnue: Rome a été la grande cité du théâtre et des spectacles scéniques pendant près d'un millénaire . . .
>
> Le théâtre latin, tragédies, comédies, mimes, pantomimes, n'est donc pas comme on l'a longtemps dit, l'enfant mal venu et tôt disparu d'un rendezvous manqué entre Rome et la Grèce. Les comédies de Plaute, les tragédies de Sénèque ne sont pas des exceptions, miraculeusement éclosés dans un désert d'inculture et d'héllénisme mal assimilé, ce sont des restes d'un continent immense, ayant sombré dans le temps, d'une culture véritablement populaire du théâtre chez un peuple musicien jusqu'à la folie et danseur jusqu'à l'indignité.

Dupont's continent was Zorzetti's iceberg, the lost popular culture of mid-republican Rome. Unfortunately, however, her reconstruction of it was based on a schematic binary polarity:[88]

> En fait, du point de vue du public, les spectacles scéniques romains se répartissent toujours en deux types bien distincts: le théâtre tragique et le théâtre comique, la terreur et le rire, les furieux et les clowns. Tout intermédiaire est voué à l'echec.

That dismissive final phrase applied in particular to the *fabula praetexta*:[89]

> Par conséquent, les catégories de la moralité civique, les valeurs d'effort, de courage, d'endurance et même de liberté n'ont rien à faire au théâtre dans les jeux scéniques; il ne peut y avoir à Rome de théâtre civique qui ne soit voué à l'echec. Ce sera l'histoire de la tragédie prétexte.

In her pursuit of this improbable notion, Dupont supposed that Roman historical drama was a Hellenistic genre adapted by the aristocracy merely for its own glory, a form of spectacle with no popular base at all.[90] The idea depended solely on the comparative paucity of fragments.

13

Ironically, the iconoclast was using a century-old argument, led astray by the assumptions of the very philologists she claimed to supersede.[91]

Traditional scholarship has a doughty champion in Nicholas Horsfall, whose reflections on 'problems of method' appeared in 1994. In his section on the prehistory of Roman drama, Horsfall rightly challenged the credulous assumption that information about early- and middle-republican stage practice can be obtained from late-republican antiquarian evidence:[92]

> Scholars have realised for over a century now that surviving accounts of the origins of drama in central Italy are substantially of Varronian origin and that behind Varro there stands above all the account of Eratosthenes of the origins of Greek comedy . . .
>
> Our standard texts on the origin of the Roman theatre repeat, then, what remains of a first-century BC reconstruction, heavily influenced by research undertaken a couple of centuries previously on the origins of Attic drama.

After all, what real evidence could there have been for Varro to use, of plays that had no texts?[93]

Contemporary literary evidence (what little there is of it) reveals that Rome in the fourth and third centuries BC could be thought of by Greeks as a Greek city, a part of 'Panhellas'.[94] That surely justifies Gentili's argument about Hellenistic influence on early Roman drama, and entitles us, with all necessary caution, to bring in the research of Richard Green, Oliver Taplin and others in the nineties on the archaeological evidence for Greek theatre in southern Italy in the Hellenistic period.[95] The vase-painters, mosaicists and statuette-makers reveal a wonderfully lively and varied world of stage-performance, into which our notion of early Roman drama must be flexible enough to fit.

One of its characteristics was evidently an uninhibited attitude to generic boundaries. In fifth-century Athens, tragedy, comedy, satyr-play and mime were kept carefully separate; the visual evidence suggests, however, that in the fourth- and third-century south-Italian theatre the distinctions were not observed in the same way.[96] As we saw in the previous section, Rhinthon of Tarentum's 'cheerful tragedies' may help us to understand the play about the Nonae Caprotinae mentioned by Varro. 'This use of the serio-comic form,' wrote Zorzetti in 1990, 'lies at the root of the ambiguity to be found in the *praetexta*, an ambiguity inherent in those aetiologies created as civic comedies'—of which he cited the Nonae Caprotinae play as an example.[97]

14

Meanwhile, what of the Ranke hypothesis, the attempt to identify lost drama plots from episodes in the historians? The whole idea was waved away by Harriet Flower in 1995:[98]

> Such a line of approach is both risky and subjective. It is based on the desire to recover a lost genre, which modern scholars feel must or should have existed . . . The conclusions reached have virtually no basis in the ancient sources we actually have. The result is largely a fiction created by the scholarly imagination.

That could have been written by Eleanor Shipley Duckett eighty years earlier. As then, the argument was narrowly based, tacitly assuming that the near-silence of later literary sources must be decisive, and no other considerations possibly valid.[99]

In one respect, however, Harriet Flower's article was a major contribution. In her search for the 'cultural and social context' of the *praetexta*, Flower drew attention to a neglected phenomenon, the votive games performed on the occasion of the dedication of temples.[100] She emphasized the vowing of temples as triumphal *monumenta*, and thus as part of the competitive ethos of the republican aristocracy. But a new temple was also a new cult, and the Roman people needed to know what the divinity had done to deserve it. 'Teaching the people' is what Varro says the *praetexta* did.[101]

VI

The next five chapters revisit Ranke's hypothesis, and propose some new examples. One and a half centuries have passed since he read his paper to the King of Prussia's academy, and this selective survey of the ebb and flow of scholarly opinion has shown, I think, that in all that huge span of time little progress has been made. Further examples were soon identified of the phenomenon to which Ranke drew attention; but argument raged over their validity, and no agreed solution emerged. It may seem rash to reopen the question now, and suggest some more.

As always, there are two questions to be addressed: 'What counts as evidence?', and 'What can be inferred from it?'. Classical scholarship has always, and very properly, been concerned with literature. But literature is not the only source of information about the ancient world; and the interpretation of texts, as of anything else, is inevitably affected by the preconceptions of the interpreter. If one starts from the assumption that anything not directly attested in a literary source cannot have happened,[102] without asking whether such attestation can be expected anyway (e.g. for a period long before the writer's own), then one's range of possibilities is automatically restricted.

Similarly, to assume that the Romans had no significant drama before Livius Andronicus (and no drama on historical subjects before Naevius),[103] or that any drama the Romans had must always have obeyed the same generic rules as the surviving texts of Attic tragedy and comedy, is simply to beg the question in advance. I prefer to make a different assumption: that since the *ludi scaenici* were important festivals, the performances watched by the Roman people will have touched on the matters that concerned them most—their gods, their freedoms, their victories—and presented them in whatever way they would most enjoy.

2

Tales Unworthy of the Gods

I

Was Rome a myth-free zone? Some people think so. The proceedings recently appeared of a conference in Basel on the theme 'Myth in a mythless society: the paradigm of Rome'. Among the contributors was Mary Beard, who wrote:[1]

> One of the main problems in identifying an active mythic tradition in late Republican and Imperial Rome has been the apparent lack of any arena for myth-*making* or *remaking*. In fifth-century Athens the dramatic festivals seem to fit that bill perfectly: a series of social occasions in which (at least in theory) the whole citizen body participated in the reworking and reinterpretation of the 'traditional tales' of the mythic inheritance. True, there was a self-conscious, intellectual side in the work of the tragic dramatists. But, in a broad socio-cultural analysis, that 'literariness' does not undermine the central fact of the shared, polis-wide, repeated negotiation of the repertoire of Greek myth. Rome, by contrast, seems to offer no such context for the shared re-presentation of mythic stories.

But surely the Romans had dramatic festivals too? There were regular 'theatrical games', *ludi scaenici*, throughout the year—fifty-six days of them by the time of Augustus[2]—not to mention one-off performances at triumphs, funerals and the dedication of temples. Just as in Athens, the Roman games were where the citizen body met to honour its gods with dance and drama. As another distinguished historian, Elizabeth Rawson, put it, the dramatic festivals were central to Rome's culture; they were a focal point, a unifying social force.[3] The

17

difference is, compared with Athens we know very little about what went on at them.

If we had, for Rome, thirty-two surviving tragedy texts, a philosophical treatise on the theory and practice of the genre, and eleven comedies from a satirical genre intimately involved with the topical concerns of the community, then we might understand the *ludi scaenici* as well as we do the Great Dionysia at Athens. As it is, we have the plays of Plautus and Terence. As adaptations of Greek comedies of manners, they represent just one of the many dramatic genres we know existed at Rome—and it happens to be the one that *least* directly reflected the attitudes and preoccupations of the Roman citizen body. Worse still, for the period we know best from contemporary evidence, the first-century BC Rome of Cicero and Catullus, Sallust and Lucretius, we have no dramatic texts at all. As a result, we inevitably think of the late Republic in terms of poetry and politics, oratory and war. The dramatic festivals may have been 'central to Rome's culture', but we know next to nothing about them.

If only we had the forty-one books of Varro's *Human and Divine Antiquities*! One of them, book X of the *Antiquitates divinae*, was entirely devoted to the dramatic festivals of Rome. What we do have, however, thanks to St Augustine, who argues with Varro as a worthy opponent in the sixth book of his *City of God*, is a long verbatim quotation from Varro's discussion of the nature of the gods in the introduction to the *Divine Antiquities*.[4] Varro divided theology into three types, 'mythical', 'physical', and 'civil':

> The name 'mythical' applies to the theology used chiefly by the poets, 'physical' to that of the philosophers, 'civil' to that of the general public.
>
> The first type ['mythical'] contains a great deal of fiction which is in conflict with the dignity and nature of the immortals. It is in this category that we find one god born from the head, another from the thigh, a third from drops of blood; we find stories about thefts and adulteries committed by gods, and gods enslaved to human beings. In fact we find attributed to gods not only the accidents that happen to humanity in general, but even those which can befall the most contemptible of mankind.
>
> The second type which I have pointed out ['physical'] is one on which the philosophers have left a number of works, in which they discuss who the gods are, where they are, of what kind and of what

18

character they are: whether they came into being at a certain time, or have always existed: whether they derive their being from fire (the belief of Heraclitus) or from numbers (as Pythagoras thought) or from atoms (as Epicurus alleges). And there are other like questions all of which men's ears can more readily tolerate within the walls of a lecture-room than in the market-place outside.

The third variety ['civil'] is that which the citizens in the towns, and especially the priests, ought to know and put into practice. It contains information about the gods who should be worshipped officially and the rites and sacrifices which should be offered to each of them.

The first type of theology is particularly suited to the theatre; the second is particularly concerned with the world; the special relevance of the third is to the city.

So by 'poets' Varro means *dramatists*. The mythological 'gods of the poets' were what the Romans of his day saw in the *theatre*. There can be no mistake about it: Augustine, who knew the whole of Varro's work, refers constantly to the stage as the place where these disgraceful stories were presented. Are we, the bishop indignantly demands, to ask for eternal life from 'the gods of poetry and the theatre, the gods of the games and the plays'?[5] Perish the thought! But his polemic has preserved for us a fact of crucial importance about the mythology of Rome in the first century BC.

II

Augustine's vocabulary is consistent: pagan mythology as seen in the theatre is degradation and disgrace (*turpitudo*, *dedecus*); the stories are 'slanders' (*crimina deorum*).[6] But the phrase he uses most often is 'tales unworthy of the gods', where *indigna* picks up Varro's own description of them as 'in conflict with the *dignitas* of the immortals'.[7] Varro too, for different reasons, disapproved of the undignified portrayal of gods on the stage. But his very disapproval is evidence for it.

Who would have guessed that that was what happened (among other things, of course) at the dramatic festivals of the Roman Republic? In fact, we do have one surviving play that falls squarely into Varro's category—Plautus' *Amphitruo*, in which Jupiter and Mercury appear on stage as the adulterous lover and his slave. The prologue is spoken by

19

the actor who plays Mercury, slipping into and out of character as the jokes require, and what it reveals, a century and a half before Varro was writing, adds a further dimension to our understanding of the Roman stage.

'Mercury' comes on and introduces himself, as both god and actor. At line 38 he gets serious and calls for attention: 'my father Jupiter and I have deserved well of you and the Republic.' Jupiter knows the Romans are grateful to him, as they should be. So there is no need for Mercury to give details, as he has seen other gods do in tragedies— Neptune, Virtus, Victoria, Mars, Bellona, all spelling out to the Roman audience what benefits they have conferred on them.[8] 'Tragedies' here probably means just 'serious plays', and the implication is that the plots were Roman, or at least relevant to Rome, to justify the gods' appearance as benefactors to the Republic. Again, who would have guessed that that was a regular feature of Roman drama? But it is wholly consistent with dramatic festivals as civic occasions, just as in Athens.

'Mercury' now promises to give the plot of his tragedy. Tragedy? This is Plautus! The audience frowns. No problem: 'I'm a god, I'll turn it into a comedy.' Or rather a tragicomedy, because a play with gods and kings in it must be a tragedy, but one with a part for a slave must be a comedy, and this has both.[9] That seems to imply that gods in comedy were unusual, and certainly the *Amphitruo* prologue has to explain a few lines later how it is that Jupiter is appearing in a comedy.[10] Perhaps what was for Plautus a daring innovation (*nouom*) had become routine by Varro's time, when undignified comic gods were evidently the norm.

The *Amphitruo* plot was one of Jupiter's better known love affairs, an artificially extended night to let him enjoy himself at length making Alcumena pregnant with Hercules. Jupiter's adulteries were Augustine's classic example of tales unworthy of the gods.[11] Other comic characters he mentions are Mercury as a beardless boy, Priapus with his huge erection (a favourite of the mimes), Saturn as an old man and Apollo as a youth; also, for some reason, Diana armed.[12] But the best examples come from another Christian polemicist, also arguing with Varro, a hundred years or more before Augustine.

This was Arnobius, whose *Against the Pagans* was written about AD 300. Towards the end of the fourth book, using the same phrase about 'tales unworthy of the gods',[13] Arnobius has a wonderful purple passage in which he imagines all the magistrates and priestly colleges—the *pontifices*, the *curiones*, the *quindecimuiri*, the *flamines*, the augurs, the

Vestal Virgins—sitting in the theatre with the Senate and People of Rome
and watching a ballet of Venus in love. 'The mother of the race of Mars,
the ancestress of the imperial people, is represented in shameless mimicry
as raving like a Bacchante, with the desires of a vile harlot.' Or perhaps
it was a different plot, with Cybele the Great Mother of the Gods shown
as writhing with passion in the embrace of a herdsman (Attis).[14]

Were those examples from Arnobius' own time, or taken from Varro?
We might ask the same question about Augustine's choice of the
judgement of Paris as an example of disgraceful stories; Lucian's
scenario of that story, with its emphasis on the goddesses' undressing,
gives an idea of how it might have been presented on the stage.[15]

III

In the following book, Arnobius extends his attack from poets'
inventions to stories he has found in serious historians. Fairly serious,
anyway: his example comes from Valerius Antias, whom even Livy
described as a credulous reporter of *fabulae*. Arnobius' story was in
book II of Antias' history, on king Numa.[16] It runs as follows.

Numa Pompilius, the second king of Rome, consults his divine
consort, the nymph Egeria, about lightning-strikes. How can he ward
off from his people the evil that Jupiter's bolts portend? Her advice is to
get two local gods of the countryside, Faunus and Picus Martius, to
reveal the secret. (Plutarch, who tells the same story in his *Life of
Numa*, describes Faunus and Picus for his Greek readers as '*daimones*
who may be likened to satyrs or Pans'.[17]) On the Aventine is a shady
spring where they come to drink; so Numa leaves cups full of wine by
the spring, and conceals 'twelve chaste youths' nearby, carrying fetters.
Faunus and Picus Martius come to the spring, drink the wine, and fall
asleep; the twelve leap out and bind them fast.

Thus compelled, Faunus and Picus Martius reveal to Numa how
Jupiter himself can be brought to earth. Numa carries out the appropriate sacrifices, and Jupiter duly appears on the Aventine. How, Numa
asks, can the lightning-bolts be expiated? Jupiter wants human sacrifice,
but Numa is too smart for him. Jupiter: 'Give me a head!' Numa: 'An
onion's.' Jupiter: 'Human!' Numa: 'Hair.' Jupiter: 'Living!' Numa:
'Sprats.' And Jupiter admits defeat, which is why the expiatory sacrifice
against lightning-strikes is of onions, hair and sprats.

Arnobius is outraged at this story, which he describes as written
wholly for laughs,[18] and designed to bring divinity itself into contempt.

The first part of that judgement may be right, but not necessarily the second. What about those twelve chaste youths? Chastity implies a serious religious act.

The story has a sequel, which Arnobius does not tell. It comes in Ovid's *Fasti*, at the point where the poet of the Roman calendar, discussing the Kalends of March, asks why the Salii bear the divine arms of Mars, and sing of Mamurius in their hymn.[19] March was of course the month of Mars (*mensis Martius*), and the Salii were the priests of Mars, who performed their dance in armour during the month.[20]

Surprisingly at first sight, Ovid asks Egeria to explain, since it was her doing.[21] He then tells the story of Egeria's advice, the capture of Faunus and Picus Martius, and the bargaining with Jupiter. But now the story continues. Jupiter laughs, and promises Numa an infallible guarantee of Rome's future power.[22] Sure enough, next day at dawn there descends miraculously from heaven a bronze shield, of archaic figure-eight design (*ancile*). For security, Numa has eleven identical copies made, so that no-one shall know which of the set is the divine talisman. These are the shields borne by the twelve Salii in their ritual dance. The song they sing contains the name Mamurius, in honour of the craftsman who made the copies.

Now we can explain the 'twelve chaste youths' in Valerius Antias' version: they were (or became) the Salii, their chastity appropriate to a priesthood. The whole story is a multiple aetiology—not only of the altar of Jupiter Elicius on the Aventine,[23] and the bizarre ingredients of the lightning-expiation sacrifice that was presumably carried out there, but also of the *collegium Saliorum* and the mysterious figure of Mamurius, whose festival on 14 March featured the Salii and their twelve shields.[24]

Now, aetiology was not just for learned antiquarians. It could be an integral part of the dramatic festivals, explaining to the citizen body the significance of its own rituals and institutions.[25] Was this story first produced on the stage? Certainly it exemplifies both the characteristics we have seen attributed to the Roman *ludi scaenici* in their treatment of the gods. The binding of the drunken Faunus and Picus Martius, and the way Numa is shown to be cleverer than Jupiter, surely count as what Varro called 'fiction in conflict with the dignity and nature of the immortals'. As for Jupiter's granting of the shield as a talisman of empire, that is equally clearly a benefaction to the Roman people of the kind 'Mercury' refers to in the *Amphitruo* prologue. Indeed, in one version of the story the descent of the shield is accompanied by a speech from Jupiter himself: 'Your city will be the most powerful of all, while this remains in it.'[26]

So it could have been a play: prologue, Egeria; first act, the capture of Faunus and Picus Martius; second act, the bargaining with Jupiter (including the famous dialogue reported by Valerius Antias, Ovid and Plutarch); third act, the shields and Mamurius. See how Ovid describes the granting of the heavenly shield:[27]

> Credite dicenti; mira, sed acta, loquor.
>
> Believe my words; what I tell is amazing, but it happened/it was performed.

The ambiguity of *acta* may be deliberate. Ovid uses a similar phrase after narrating the murder of Servius Tullius and the aetiology of 'Wicked Street'. As we shall see in the next chapter, that story is described by Livy as suitable for tragedy, and was quite possibly taken from a play.[28] In Dionysius' narrative of the episode, the king's murderously ambitious daughter is given a speech out of Euripides, and Ovid's own account concludes with a speech to the Roman people from the goddess Fortuna.[29]

Another Ovidian parallel for *mira sed acta loquor* is even more specific. In *Fasti* IV, reporting the miraculous vindication of Claudia by the Mother of the Gods in 204 BC, he says 'What I shall tell is amazing, but attested also by the stage'.[30] Not only is that clear evidence for a play about gods (and Cybele the Great Mother, who brought victory over Hannibal, was certainly a benefactress of Rome), but the similarity to the other passages makes it a reasonable guess that *acta* there may be taken as synonymous with *scaena testificata* here. In which case we would have confirmation that the Numa story was originally a play.

IV

It has long been recognised that plays were among the sources Ovid used for his *Fasti*.[31] Occasionally, known titles enable us to guess at likely sources for particular episodes: Accius' *Brutus* for the tragedy of Lucretia at *Fasti* II 711–852, or Laberius' *Anna Peranna* for the farcical burlesque of Mars and Minerva at III 675–96. Elsewhere, the nature of the episode itself may be revealing, as with the randy Priapus—cited by St Augustine as a mime character—and his frustrated attempt on the sleeping nymph Lotis, which ends with a sudden dénouement and laughter all round.[32] Amy Richlin has noted this general laughter as a

23

feature of Ovid's sex narratives;[33] I suggest it may represent the audience's reaction at the end of a mime or similar risqué comedy.

More significant, perhaps, is the way Ovid handles the tale of Lara the Silent Goddess, mother of the Lares.[34] Jupiter is in love with the nymph Juturna, but she succeeds in hiding from him in woods or streams. What he has to put up with is unworthy of so great a god[35]—just the sort of plot Varro objected to. Speeches follow: Jupiter's harangue to the assembled nymphs, Lara's report of it to Juturna, and above all Lara's tactless speech to Juno ('I'm sorry for you married women'),[36] which is surely condensed from a speech on the comic stage. Not that the story stays comic (in our terms, at least): Jupiter tears out Lara's tongue and banishes her to the Underworld; Mercury rapes her on the way. But there is a happy ending for Rome in the birth of the protector gods, the Lares Praestites.

A similar combination of comedy and machismo comes in Propertius IV 9, with the story of thirsty Hercules and the grove of the Good Goddess. Act one, the theft of the cattle and Hercules' killing of Cacus (as in *Aeneid* VIII); act two, Hercules' vain pleading for water at the women's closed precinct, where he utters 'words unworthy of a god'.[37] The priestess says no, but he bursts the door down anyway and drinks—and that's why women are not allowed to worship at the Ara Maximus, Hercules' altar. A link with mime has already been suggested for this poem;[38] I think the Varronian phrase confirms that here too we have an example of the undignified gods of the dramatic festivals, who are also the beneficent gods of Rome.

So it seems that the Romans of the late Republic did have a mythology after all, and that their *ludi scaenici* did indeed 'offer a context for the shared representation of mythic stories'. It is clear too that they could both laugh at the gods and at the same time take them seriously as benefactors and protectors. Just as in Greece (think of Plato's expulsion of the poets and dramatists from his ideal city), so too in Rome that free and easy attitude to the divine powers was a problem for religious purists like Varro. And it was a gift for the Christian polemicists, whose gleeful mockery provides us with so much of our evidence.

What that evidence implies, if we try to make sense of it, is a Roman citizen body which saw no conflict between piety, patriotism and cheerful entertainment, a theatre audience with a taste for humour and pathos, farce and tragedy, which became in due course an appreciative readership for the mature sophistication of Propertius' fourth book and the *Fasti* of Ovid.

3

Ovid on Servius Tullius

I

In 1937, during the later stages of Mussolini's 'redemption' of the Capitoline Hill from the medieval buildings that surrounded it,[1] a major archaeological site was identified by the church of S. Omobono in the Via della Consolazione. Careful postwar excavation revealed the existence of twin temples on a single podium, facing south across the Forum Bovarium (fig. 1). The podium had been constructed, probably in the early fifth century BC, on the site of a destroyed sixth-century temple; a combination of the stratigraphic and literary evidence enabled the twin temples to be identified as those of Fortuna and Mater Matuta, supposedly founded by Servius Tullius.[2]

The festival day of both cults was 11 June, and Ovid gives each of them a substantial treatment in book VI of his *Fasti*. His account of Mater Matuta, which will occupy us in the next chapter, is followed by this:[3]

> The same day is yours, Fortuna; the same founder, and the same place. But who is that figure hiding with togas thrown on his head? It's Servius, that much is agreed. But why he hides is uncertain, and my mind too is in the grip of doubt.
>
> While the goddess timidly declared her secret love, ashamed that a dweller in heaven should have slept with a mortal (for she burned for the king, swept away by a great desire, and for this man alone she was not blind), she used to enter his house by night through a little window, from which Littlewindow Gate takes its name. Now she's ashamed of it, and hides her lover's face under a shroud, and many togas cover the royal features.

25

Or is the truth rather that after Tullius' murder the common people were bewildered at the death of their gentle leader, there was no limit to their grief, and their distress was made worse by his image till they covered him up by putting togas on it?

There is a third reason, which I must sing on a longer course, though I shall drive my horses pulled to the inside track. Tullia, having achieved her marriage at the price of crime, used to urge on her husband in these words:

'What's the good of being two of a kind, you by my sister's murder, I by your brother's, if a virtuous life satisfies us? They should have lived, my husband and your wife, if we weren't going to dare a greater deed! My dowry is my father's head and kingdom. Go on, if you're a man, and claim what's offered! Crime is a thing for kings. Kill your father-in-law, take his kingdom, and bathe our hands in my father's blood!'

Impelled by such speeches, he took his seat in the high throne, a private citizen. The horrified people rush to arms. Hence blood and slaughter, and weak old age is conquered: Superbus holds the sceptre torn from his father-in-law. The king himself is murdered below the Esquiline, where his palace was, and falls in his blood to the hard ground.

His daughter, on her way to her father's house in her carriage, was proceeding through the streets, haughty and fierce. The driver halted in tears when he saw the body. She rails at him in these words:

'Get on, or do you want a bitter reward for your loyalty? I tell you, drive your reluctant wheels over his very face!'

There is a sure proof of what was done: Wicked Street is named after her, and the deed is branded with everlasting infamy.

Even so, afterwards she dared to enter the temple, her father's monument. What I shall tell is a miracle, but yet it happened. There was a statue seated on a throne, in the likeness of Tullius. It is said to have put its hand to its eyes, and a voice was heard:

'Hide my face, lest it should see my daughter's abominable features.'

A robe is provided, the statue is covered, Fortuna forbids the veil to be moved. And this is how she spoke from her own temple:

'The first day Servius' face is uncovered will be the first day of shame abandoned.'

Matrons, do not touch the forbidden robes (it's enough to utter
prayers in solemn voice); and may the head of him who was seventh
king in our city be always covered with a Roman cloak.

The temple burned down, yet that fire spared the statue; Mulciber
himself brought aid to his son. For Vulcan was Tullius' father, and
Ocresia of Corniculum, renowned for beauty, was his mother.
When she had carried out the rites with her according to custom,
Tanaquil ordered her to pour wine on the decorated hearth. There
among the ashes was the shape of a male organ—or it seemed to be;
but no, it really was. At the queen's orders, the captive woman
squats at the hearth. Servius, conceived by her, has from heaven the
seed of his race. The god who begot him gave a sign, when he
touched his head with glittering fire, and on his hair there burned a
cap of flame.

The account of Servius' conception in the closing paragraph is found
also in Dionysius, Pliny, Plutarch and Arnobius, though the identity of
the god who manifests himself as the phantom phallus in the hearth is
disputed in the various versions—perhaps the *Lar familiaris* rather than
Vulcan, or even the collective *Di conserentes*, the seed-sowers.[4] The
same story was also told of the conception of Romulus, by a Greek
author called Promathion whose date, though highly controversial,
could be as early as the sixth century BC.[5]

Of greater interest for our purposes are Ovid's aetiologies of the
muffled statue,[6] particularly the first and the third. The second is
comparatively banal, the sort of *en passant* aetiology that could have
come from any historical narrative of the death of good king Servius:
'so distraught were the common people that they covered his statue in
the temple with togas, and to this day . . .'[7] The stories that feature
Fortuna herself have more to offer.

II

In the first one, the goddess declares (*profitetur*) her humiliating passion
for a mortal. To whom does she declare it? And if she's ashamed of it,
why tell anybody? The commentators offer no explanation.

Perhaps the window will help us to understand what was going on.
Filippo Coarelli, in a bold and speculative reconstruction of the archaic

27

nature of the Fortuna and Mater Matuta cults, argues that the Porta Fenestella ('Littlewindow Gate') was next to the Fortuna temple, and that the chamber to which it belonged was designed for the ritual wedding of the king with the goddess.[8] There are serious difficulties with this theory,[9] but it is surely ruled out in any case by Ovid's explicit description of the window as Fortuna's way into the king's house.[10] She was making the running; she came to his bed, not *vice versa*.

The Porta Fenestella was the subject of one of Plutarch's 'Roman questions':[11]

> Why do they call one of the gates 'Window', which is what *fenestra* means, and why is the so-called 'Chamber of Fortune' next to it?
>
> Is it because king Servius, the luckiest of men, was reputed to have slept with Fortuna, who visited him through a window? Or is that just a myth?
>
> When king Tarquinius Priscus died, his wife Tanaquil, a wise lady and a real queen, leaned out of a window, talked to the citizens, and persuaded them to proclaim Servius as king. Is *that* why the place has this name?

'*The* place.' That is, two explanations for a single gate, and the second one shows us where it was. When Livy tells the story of Tanaquil addressing the crowd from the window, he is very specific about the scene of the action:[12]

> Cum clamor impetusque multitudinis uix sustineri posset, ex superiore parte aedium per fenestras in Nouam uiam uersas— habitabat enim rex ad Iovis Statoris—populum Tanaquil adloquitur.
>
> The noise and excitement of the crowd were almost out of control. From a window in the upper part of the house facing the Nova Via (for the king's house was by the temple of Jupiter Stator), Tanaquil addressed the people.

Solinus gives the site of Tarquinius Priscus' house as 'at the Porta Mugonia, above the top of the Nova Via'.[13]

It was not uncommon for Roman gates to have more than one name,[14] so 'Littlewindow Gate' must have been a nickname for the old gate on the north side of the Palatine, the Porta Mugonia.[15] The fortifications of which the gate formed a part had been obsolete for six hundred years when Ovid wrote. It is a familiar phenomenon in the growth of cities (compare Ludgate, Newgate, Bishopsgate and Aldgate in the City of London) that gates from long obsolete wall-systems survive in the urban fabric that has outgrown them. They are incorporated into the buildings that replace the old walls, and become arches across the streets of a densely built-up city centre. One good example in Rome is the Porta Flumentana, part of a wall parallel to the Tiber that was abandoned some time in the third century.[16] By Cicero's time, one could speak of someone 'occupying' the Porta Flumentana—that is, presumably, occupying the property that incorporated it.[17]

So we may imagine the ancient Porta Mugonia, originally part of the defensive wall of the Palatine, incorporated into one of the sixth-century houses that were built over the line of that wall (fig. 2).[18] The old house was identified as a royal palace, and a window in its upper floor, adjacent to the arch and commanding the highest point of the Nova Via, evidently gave the Porta Mugonia its popular name.

Two stories arose out of this visibly archaic corner of old Rome, each presupposing a royal bedroom behind the window. In one of them, it was Tarquinius Priscus' death-bed, with his queen at the window giving falsely hopeful bulletins. In the other, it was 'Fortune's chamber', where good king Servius, luckiest of men, sported with his goddess.

Basic to the second story, and to Ovid's aetiologies in the *Fasti*, is the idea of covering the head to avoid recognition.[19] The usual implication

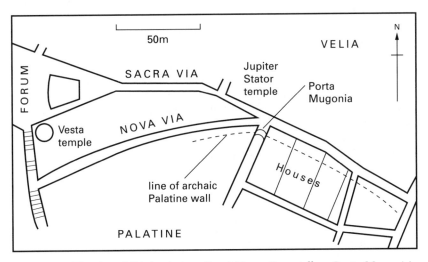

Figure 2.   The site of 'Littlewindow Gate' (*Porta Fenestella* = *Porta Mugonia*), on the north slope of the Palatine.

is that the person concerned is up to no good—frequenting a brothel, for instance, or a disreputable tavern.[20] Adulterers were particularly given to this furtive behaviour,[21] and Servius' love-affair with Fortuna was evidently adulterous.[22]

When Seneca describes Maecenas as going about in public with his head wrapped up in his cloak, he compares it to the behaviour of mime characters.[23] Adultery was the most popular subject of mime dramas in Ovid's time,[24] and many of the mime plots featured gods and goddesses.[25] Indeed, mythological burlesque, with adulterous gods climbing through windows, had been part of the south-Italian stage tradition since at least the fourth century BC, as the painted vases of Paestum clearly show.[25] Are we, perhaps, entitled to infer a farce on 'Fortuna the adulteress' in the repertory of the Roman dramatic festivals?[26]

That would at least explain the puzzle with which we began. If Ovid had in mind a story he knew from the stage, Fortuna's declaration of her secret love was no doubt to the audience, a soliloquy in the first act.

III

Ovid begins his third and longest aetiology of the muffled statue with a metaphor he often uses, of the poet as a charioteer.[27] He is going to take the shortest line, the inside track; but even so, this is a story for a longer race. Here too is a familiar Ovidian trope, the constant generic self-consciousness of the elegiac poet. Elegy is a slender genre: how can it tackle grand historical themes?[28]

The story of the house of Tarquin had been told in epic, by Ennius in the third book of his *Annals*, and in prose narrative, by all the Roman historians from Fabius Pictor to Livy.[29] It was also a subject for tragedy, as we know from the fragments of Accius' famous play *Brutus*.[30] Indeed, it may have been a tragic theme before it was a historical one, to judge by Livy's treatment of this very episode.

Young Tarquin was busy plotting against king Servius:[31]

> ... et ipse iuuenis ardentis animi et domi uxore Tullia inquietum animum stimulante. tulit enim et Romana regia sceleris tragici exemplum, ut taedio regum maturior ueniret libertas ultimumque regnum esset quod scelere partum foret.

> He himself had a burning ambition, and at home his wife Tullia incited his restless mind. For the Roman royal house too produced

30

an example of crime fit for tragedy, that hatred of kings might bring
liberty the sooner, and that the reign won by crime might be the last.

The house of Tarquin, like the house of Atreus, could provide a tragedy
plot in every generation.

In his great commentary on the early books of Livy, Robert Ogilvie
insists that the drama is all of the historian's own making. On this
passage (I 46–8): '[M]ost of the tragic features of the story in L. are due
to L. himself . . . He has not, of course, utilized an actual play as a
model. He has written his own tragedy.' On the reign of bad king
Tarquin (I 49–60): 'For him the history of the Tarquins is a tragedy with
a moral, the triumph of *pudicitia* over *superbia* . . . It is certain that L.
does not depend on Ennius or an unknown Roman tragedian. With a
profound interest in psychology he is writing tragedy not copying it.'
On Lucretia (I 57–9): '[H]e presents the sequence of events as the plot
of a tragedy . . . he has manipulated his material to secure the
impression of a play, an impression which has deceived many into
believing that he was copying or reproducing an actual play.'[32]

Ogilvie is engaged here in tacit polemic with Henry B. Wright and
Agnes Kirsopp Michels, whose work he cites in his bibliography but
whose arguments he does not confront.[33] They were both convinced,
from a close reading of the same passages, that Livy did indeed have
one or more tragedy plots in mind. Ogilvie's authority is powerful, but
it is directed, in part at least, against a straw man. The question is not
whether Livy 'copied an actual play', with all the pejorative overtones
of that verb when applied to a great creative artist, but whether the
story he knew, and told in his own way, was a story he knew from
having often seen it on the stage.

One striking element in the Tullia story is the way the preliminary
murders are handled. Tullia's sister (Tarquin's first wife) and Tullia's first
husband (Tarquin's brother) have to be got out of the way before Tullia
and Tarquin can marry and plot their murderous coup. How was it
done? Nobody tells us. A subordinate clause in Livy, a throwaway
sentence in Dionysius, an ablative absolute in Ovid, and they are
gone.[34] No comment in Ogilvie, but it is an obvious possibility that the
authors' narrative emphasis reproduced scenes on stage—soliloquy,
dialogue, dramatic conflict—and what happened off stage was out of
sight and out of mind.[35]

It matters, for our reading of Ovid, whether we prefer Ogilvie's
dramatic historian or Wright and Michels' historical drama. Normally it

is taken for granted that Ovid's source for the Tullia story is Livy.[36] But we know that he used theatrical sources elsewhere,[37] and a careful reading of the passage may suggest a different view.

'Crime is a thing for kings,' says Tullia: *'regia* res *scelus* est.' That certainly sounds like Livy—but the phrase it evokes is Livy's acknowledgement of a tragedy theme: 'tulit et Romana *regia sceleris* exemplum.'[38] In late-republican Rome, tragedy was *par excellence* the exemplary genre for revealing the ways of kings and tyrants.[39]

A couple of lines earlier, Tullia had taunted Tarquin: her sister and his brother might as well have lived, if they haven't the nerve for a greater work (*maius opus*). That is a phrase with a particular reverberation in an elegiac poet. Elegy is a little work (*exiguum opus*), but Ovid uses it for grander themes (*magna, maiora*).[40] We have noticed already how the *Fasti* constantly refers to that paradox of weighty subjects in slender verse, as the elegiac poet takes on material appropriate to other genres.[41] The first time the idea appears is in the prologue to book II, with an explicit cross-reference to Ovid's earlier love poetry, and to *Amores* III 1 in particular.[42]

What happens in *Amores* III 1 is that Tragedy and Elegy compete for Ovid's allegiance. Tragedy, a formidable lady, carries a royal sceptre. Enough of love, she tells him; it's time for something more substantial. 'Cessatum satis est: incipe *maius opus*.'[43] The seductive Elegy tempts him back, and for the moment he yields. But he promises Tragedy that his greater work (*grandius opus*) will come next—and he repeats his promise, as he signs off at the end of the *Amores*, with the very image that introduces the Tullia passage in the *Fasti*: his horses now need a bigger arena.[44]

Ovid kept his promise and wrote a great tragedy, the lost *Medea*.[45] He also gave to Medea one of the epistolary monologues of the *Heroides*, in which, after dwelling with rage and anguish on Jason's perfidy, she ends with an ominous hint of 'greater deeds' to come: 'nescio quid certe mens mea *maius* agit.' The allusion is clear. What happens next is Tragedy, by Euripides or Ovid himself. As Alessandro Barchiesi puts it, in a subtle comment on this passage,[46]

> she speaks not only as a self-conscious character, but also (by implication) as a self-conscious author ... Medea is suggesting that a new poetic kind is called for: she could not write a letter about her 'greater' actions, and this material, unspeakable for elegiacs, is reserved to the heights of a *cothurnata*.

So too Tullia in the *Fasti*. What you and I must do, she tells Tarquin, is a *maius opus*, a work for the tragic stage.

It seems then that both Ovid and Livy, the elegist and the historian, were aware of a third genre, tragedy, behind their narratives of Tullia and the death of Servius. Of course Ovid must have known Livy's account, but it is not likely to have been his only source, or even the main one. For his story goes on beyond Livy's. 'Post tamen hoc . . .': the final scene was essential for Ovid's aetiology, but it was the sort of thing a historian would avoid, 'more appropriate', as Livy put it in a similar context, 'to the stage, which delights in marvels.'[47]

What happened is described by Ovid in the same ambiguous phrase he had used for the talisman shield falling from heaven. 'Mira sed acta': amazing, but performed.[48] Tullia enters the temple of Fortuna. Inside is the founder's statue (and only now do we discover that it is a seated statue, of the king on a throne). 'A voice is heard'—the regular formula for this sort of miracle[49]—as Servius demands to have his face covered. Then comes another voice, that of the goddess herself 'speaking from her own temple'. That too was a formulaic phrase for a recognised phenomenon, guaranteeing the authenticity of the divine message.[50]

How often did Romans hear the voices of the gods in their temples? They certainly heard them in the theatre, as Neptune, Virtus, Victoria, Mars, Bellona and the rest addressed the citizen body from the tragic stage.[51] That, I think, is what happened in the tragedy of Servius Tullius. Fortuna speaks to the audience in the last act, promising Rome her favour as long as Rome deserves it. (As for Tullia, she can be left to the avenging Furies.[52])

Was Fortuna in the prologue too? She seems to be present as *Fortuna populi Romani* at the start of Livy's narrative, where the historian explains about Tarquin and his gentle brother:[53]

> His duobus, ut ante dictum est, duae Tulliae regis filiae nupserant, et ipsae longe dispares maioribus. forte ita inciderat ne duo uiolenta ingenia matrimonio iungerentur fortuna, credo, populi Romani, quo diuturnius Serui regnum esset constituique ciuitatis mores possent.

> As related above, these two young men married the two Tulliae, daughters of the king, who were also very different in character. It happened by chance that the two violent characters were *not* joined in matrimony—thanks, in my opinion, to the fortune of the Roman

33

People, so that Servius' reign might last longer and the community have a chance to establish the habit of virtue.

The purpose clause at the end implies a guiding intelligence, which can only be that of Fortuna herself. As the Prologue she could explain who was who, and why fierce Tullia was married to gentle Tarquin and *vice versa*. She has offered a breathing space, the opportunity for virtue, which will be shattered by the adultery and murderous plotting of the two villains as the drama unfolds. And at the end she will return, to lecture the audience on *mores* and *pudicitia*.

History as farce, history as tragedy. Ovid on Servius Tullius offers evidence for both. If I had to guess when the two scenarios were created, I would imagine theatrical games either on 11 June 212 BC, when the temple of Fortuna in the Forum Bovarium was rededicated after the fire, or on 25 May 194 BC, the dedication date of the temple of Fortuna Populi Romani on the Quirinal.[54]

4

Two Plays for the Liberalia

I

The Liberalia (17 March) was one of the festivals in the oldest identifiable stratum of the Roman calendar, dating back at least as far as the fifth century BC.[1] It was in honour of Liber, whose identification with the Greek Dionysus was certainly current in the late fourth century BC, and no doubt long before that.[2] The god shared the temple of Ceres, Liber and Libera on the slope of the Aventine just above the starting-gates of the Circus Maximus (fig. 1).[3]

When the temple was built is not clear. Livy does not report its construction, and though Dionysius says it was vowed in 496 BC and dedicated in 493, his narrative is suspect.

Dionysius tells the story of the battle of Lake Regillus, in a version which ultimately derived from the historian and senior senator A. Postumius Albinus (consul 151 BC).[4] He reports a long pre-battle speech by the dictator Postumius (Albinus' ancestor), followed by his vow to the gods

> that if the battle were attended with a happy and glorious outcome,
> he would offer great and expensive sacrifices and institute costly
> games to be celebrated annually by the Roman people.

Those sacrifices and games are duly reported in the post-battle narrative, but with an addition: Postumius also let contracts for the building of temples (*sic*) to Demeter, Dionysus and Kore—the Greek historian's translation of Ceres, Liber and Libera.[5]

This, we now learn, had been a vow made by the dictator before setting out from Rome, as a result of a crop failure and threatened famine. The Sibylline books had told Postumius that those three divinities must be placated, and so he had promised them temples (sic), and sacrifices to be performed every year. The gods heard his prayer, the land bore rich crops, and the dictator paid his vow. Three years later in Dionysius' narrative, the temple (now singular) is dedicated, with a cross-reference back to the dictator's vow, which is now said to have been made immediately before the battle.[6]

But there was another tradition, preserved in a Christian treatise of the late empire, which made no mention of Postumius and his epic campaign. According to this version, Rome was indeed afflicted by a famine—date unfortunately not given—and so stage games (ludi scaenici) were introduced in honour of Ceres and Liber.[7] The natural inference is that Postumius Albinus in the second century BC took an undated 'once upon a time' tradition about a famine and wrote it into the highly-wrought narrative of his ancestor's heroic command at Lake Regillus. And so the date of origin remains obscure, both for the temple and for the games.

The Liberalia came immediately after the Ides of March, and the Ides of March (the festival of the year-goddess Anna Perenna, whom we shall meet in chapter 7) was the day when the magistrates of the Republic used to enter office.[8] That is, the civil year began with the festival of Liber and Libera, whose names mean 'free'. Since the old year had ended with the 'flight of the king' (Regifugium, 24 February), the sequence is evidently ideological, representing the passage from tyranny to freedom.[9]

A similar ideological reading has been proposed for the City Dionysia at Athens, in honour of Dionysus Eleuthereus (eleutheros, 'free'): the establishment of that festival 'may have conveyed a message of political liberation . . . to celebrate the overthrow of the tyrants'.[10] According to tradition, the Tarquins were expelled from Rome at the same time as the Pisistratids from Athens; and at least one learned scholar of the late Republic identified Liber as Dionysus Eleuthereus.[11] It is not impossible that the Roman cult was introduced (added, perhaps, to an existing cult of Ceres) in imitation of the Athenian one, and for the same reason.

Certainly it was influenced by Greek ideas. The splendid new temple was adorned by Greek artists, who put up an inscription (in Greek) to record their work.[12] The sort of work it was may be seen in the antefixes and statue-groups from the early fifth-century temple of Mater Matuta at Satricum, a Latin city thirty miles south of Rome. In

36

particular, the *acroteria* or ridge-pole statues on the roof of the Satricum temple, brilliantly reconstructed from the tiny fragments by Patricia Lulof, constitute a masterpiece of late archaic Greek art. They represent the battle of the gods against the giants, and one of the groups shows Dionysus (i.e. Liber) in company with a youthful goddess (fig. 3).[13]

Who is she? The iconography of Dionysus in the sixth and early fifth centuries BC was largely an Athenian creation, and to judge by Attic black- and early red-figure painted pottery (which was very popular in Etruria and Latium at that time) the most likely identification is either Semele or Ariadne.[14] Semele was Dionysus' mother, blasted by Zeus before his birth, whom he rescued from Hades and made a goddess; Ariadne was the Cretan princess abandoned by Theseus, whom Dionysus rescued from her island and made his consort in heaven.[15] In Rome, Semele was associated with the grove of Stimula close to the Ceres-Liber-Libera temple, and Libera herself was identified as Ariadne.[16]

Dionysius identifies Libera with 'Kore'—that is, Persephone (Proserpina) the daughter of Demeter (Ceres). But it is obvious from the name itself, and from the order of names in the formula *Ceres Liber Libera*, that Libera was conceptually closer to Liber than to Ceres. There must have been a particular reason for the paradoxical identification in Dionysius, and we shall see later what it may have been. The pair whose names meant 'freedom' to Latin-speakers were evidently the Bacchic god and his consort.[17]

In particular, Liber symbolised the freedom of the city. The evidence is late, in Servius' commentary on Virgil, but it includes a clear indication that the idea was an ancient one. For Servius adds that statues of Marsyas the satyr, the servant of Liber, were set up in the forums of free cities as a symbol of liberty.[18] The original was certainly the Marsyas statue in the Roman Forum, which is convincingly attributed to the period around 300 BC and the freedom of the *plebs* from debt bondage; it was probably erected by one of the Marcii Rutili, prominent members of the new plebeian élite, who claimed descent from Marsyas.[19]

The temple of Ceres, Liber and Libera stood at the foot of the Aventine, a plebeian quarter from the fifth century BC, and it served as the headquarters of the aediles of the *plebs*.[20] In 241 or 238 BC, two plebeian aediles with the appropriate name Publicius fined wealthy landowners for occupying public land; with the proceeds they built a temple of Flora next to that of Ceres, Liber and Libera, and set up

Figure 3.   Liber and Libera? Hypothetical reconstruction by Patricia S. Lulof
of one of the *acroterion* statue groups on the Mater Matuta temple
at Satricum in Latium, *c.* 490 BC.
(Courtesy of Thesis Publishers, Amsterdam.)

games in the goddess's honour. For more than sixty years the Senate refused to recognize the games of Flora as an annual public festival.[21] It is clear that Liber and his neighbours occupied a very particular place in the ideological spectrum of third-century Rome.

Liber's own games, according to one tradition, were the Romans' first stage-festival. His Athenian analogue Dionysus Eleuthereus was patron of the City Dionysia, most famous of all dramatic festivals, and some Latin authors emphasize the parallel by calling the Liberalia 'Dionysia'.[22] By the late third century, when the Roman games featured Greek plays in Latin form, one at least of the playwrights evidently tried to recreate the political freedom of the Athenian stage. Cn. Naevius was imprisoned 'for his constant abuse and insults against the leading men of the state, in the manner of the Greek playwrights'; he had to recant, and was then freed by the tribunes of the *plebs*.[23]

The historicity of this story, and with it the whole notion of Naevius as 'a figure of controversy, embroiled in politics', has been attacked by Erich Gruen in a characteristically incisive essay.[24] Much of his argument is based on St Augustine's quotations from the lost fourth book of Cicero's *De republica*, where Scipio, comparing Roman moral education with Greek, is made to deplore the political licence of the Athenian theatre and praise by contrast the discipline of the Roman stage.[25] But Cicero had his own political axe to grind: his idealised Republic depended on permanent moral supervision by the censors,[26] and it suited his case to make out that such control was traditional. If other evidence gives a different impression, it is not at all self-evident that Cicero must be right.

Elsewhere, Gruen well describes the political nature of the Roman stage-festivals: 'dramatic productions could provide a medium for public posturing, stir civic passions, or serve as forum for popular outbursts.' And nowhere more than at the games of Liber, as we know from a precious fragment of contemporary evidence, a line from Naevius himself:[27]

> Libera lingua loquimur ludis Liberalibus.
>
> At the Liberalia games we enjoy free speech.

II

It was a sign of the times that Naevius' free speech landed him in jail. The trauma of the war with Hannibal both sharpened popular anxieties and justified the exercise of senatorial authority. In 213 BC, for instance, two years after the battle of Cannae, the Senate became alarmed at the influence of 'prophets and sacrificers' in the Roman Forum and ordered the urban praetor to suppress them. The following year it was announced that among the confiscated literature had been found a prophecy that seemed authentic, instructing the Romans to institute games for Apollo in the Greek style, overseen by the urban praetor. If there were going to be innovations, the Senate and magistrates would control them.[28]

The prophecy was attributed to Cn. Marcius, a descendant of Marsyas the servant of Liber.[29] And yet Marsyas in the Greek story had been flayed alive by Apollo for his presumption in challenging him to a music contest.[30] The new games of Apollo evidently carried a message for the followers of Liber.

Apollo's games were introduced in order to bring victory in the war. In 208 they were made annual, but still victory did not come.[31] Then in 204, 'on the instructions of the prophets' (confirmed by the Sibylline books), the Great Mother of the Gods was brought from Phrygia; she was received in state, a splendid new temple on the Palatine was vowed to her, and in two years the war was over.[32] Apollo was involved to this extent, that his oracle at Delphi instructed the Romans to pick 'the best man'—necessarily an aristocrat—to receive the goddess. But the new cult must have been a blow to his prestige. After all, Marsyas was a Phrygian, and a devotee of the Great Mother.[33]

Livy offers three different dates for the inauguration of the Great Mother's games (*ludi Megalenses*); and there is a similar variety of versions about a controversial innovation that may have been introduced at the same time, the segregation of senatorial seats at theatre performances.[34] It was the curule aediles, not the aediles of the *plebs*, who were in charge of the *ludi Megalenses* and so enforced this divisive, and bitterly resented, statement of authority. We may doubt whether it applied at Liber's games. For Liber, however, there was something worse in store.

In 186 BC the Senate chose to take offence at another of those 'prophets and sacrificers' who had been dealt with in 213. This one had allegedly instituted a new and objectionable form of orgiastic Bacchic cult. The consuls were instructed to stamp it out, and they did so without mercy, imprisoning and executing large numbers of people throughout Italy.[35]

In all of Livy's long account of this affair (it takes up one-fifth of a whole book), as in the surviving text of the senatorial decree, the name of Liber does not appear. The guilty people were *Bacchae*, their rites *Bacchanalia*. But Bacchus was Dionysus, with whom Liber had long been identified, and the Grove of Stimula, centre of the banned cult and identified as the grove of Dionysus' mother Semele, was next to the ancient temple that Liber and Libera shared with Ceres.[36] The consul in Livy harangues the people on the need to defend the ancestral gods against 'depraved and alien rites'.[37] If the Bacchic cult was to be distinguished from the traditional worship of Liber, some creative reinterpretation was going to be necessary.

Two texts from later ages may show the result of it. In Cicero's dialogue on the nature of the gods, the Stoic spokesman Lucilius Balbus discusses deified mortals, and offers as examples Hercules, the Dioscuri, Aesculapius 'and even Liber':[38]

> Hunc dico Liberum Semela natum, non eum quem nostri maiores auguste sancteque Liberum cum Cerere et Libera consecrauerunt, quod quale sit ex mysteriis intellegi potest; sed quod ex nobis natos liberos appellamus, idcirco Cerere nati nominati sunt Liber et Libera, quod in Libera seruant, in Libero non item.

> I mean Liber the son of Semele, not the Liber whom our ancestors solemnly and devoutly consecrated with Ceres and Libera, the import of which joint consecration may be gathered from the mysteries; but Liber and Libera were so named as Ceres' offspring, that being the meaning of our Latin word *liberi*—a use which has survived in the case of Libera but not of Liber.

In this version the Roman Liber is not Dionysus, and Liber and Libera are derived not from *liber*, 'free', but from *liberi*, 'children'. The god who was always known as 'Father Liber' is now redefined as Ceres' son.[39] That idea evidently didn't stick, to judge by the final phrase in Cicero's explanation, but the identification of Libera as Persephone did. As we saw at the beginning of the chapter, Dionysius of Halicarnassus took it for granted, and his probable source (A. Postumius Albinus) was writing in the middle of the second century BC.[40]

The other text is in Ampelius' *Liber memorialis*, a check-list of useful knowledge compiled probably under Hadrian. One chapter lists variant versions of divine genealogies, including five different Libers:[41]

> Liberi quinque: primus ex Ioue et Proserpina: hic agricola et inuentor uini, cuius soror Ceres; secundus Liber ex Merone et Flora, cuius nomine fluuius est Granicus; tertius de Cabiro qui

regnauit in Asia; quartus ex Saturno et Semela ‹ . . .› dicunt; quintus Nisi et Hesionae filius.

There are five Libers. The first was born of Jupiter and Proserpina; he was an arable farmer and inventor of wine, whose sister was Ceres. The second Liber was born of Mero and Flora, from whose name is the river Granicus. The third was born of Cabirus who ruled in Asia. The fourth was born of Saturn and Semele; they say ‹. . .›. The fifth was the son of Nisus and Hesione.

Number four is a version of the familiar Greek myth, with Saturn (Kronos) replacing Zeus.[42] Numbers one and two may well be post-186 reinterpretations, to detach Liber from Semele and the Bacchae. The brother of Ceres and the son of Flora would both make good topographical sense in Rome, where Flora's temple was next to that of Ceres, Liber and Libera.[43]

Ampelius' second item is particularly revealing. When Zeus destroyed Semele by appearing to her in all his power, he rescued the unborn Dionysus and sewed him into his thigh. The Greek for thigh is *meros*, so 'son of Mero' looks like the rationalisation of an offensive myth.[44] As for Flora, her connection with the river Granicus, perhaps via a bilingual etymology,[45] associates her with the Great Mother, on whose mountain (Ida) the river rises. If we are right to date these versions to the aftermath of the Bacchanalia scandal, it seems that political pressure was bringing about some very creative mythography.

Where and how were such myths created? Surely at the dramatic festivals, by playwrights and producers sensitive to their audiences' needs. But what sort of plays were produced for the Liberalia after 186? Indeed, how long did the Liberalia survive as a dramatic festival? We know from Ovid that by the end of the first century BC Liber's games had been removed from the Liberalia on 17 March and amalgamated with those of Ceres in April. Numismatic evidence suggests that that was done before 78 BC.[46] But how long before?

It is clear that the ideological issues connected with the *ludi scaenici* that can be detected in the years 213–194 BC continued throughout the first half of the second century. In 179 the censors let contracts for an auditorium and proscenium in front of the temple of Apollo. Their successors in 174 contracted for a stage 'for the aediles and praetors', probably in the same place (since only Apollo's games were the praetor's responsibility). In 173, after crop failures attributed to the goddess's anger, the games of Flora were at last recognised as an annual dramatic festival.[47] In 154 the censors started the construction of a stone theatre at the Lupercal, on the slope of the Palatine below the Great Mother's new temple; soon afterwards it was demolished by order of the Senate as a danger to public morals.[48] It must have been at some point in those obscurely contested years that the god of freedom lost his theatre games.

III

Livy's long account of the Bacchanalia episode in 186 has attracted a great deal of scholarly attention.[49] His narrative falls naturally into two halves, the discovery of the 'conspiracy' (XXXIX 8.1–14.2) and the Senate and consuls' action to suppress it (14.3–19.7); the latter includes a lengthy speech to the people by the consul Sp. Postumius Albinus. Since the names of the ringleaders appear differently in the two halves, it is likely that they came from different sources.[50]

The first part, as the latest editor, P.G. Walsh, puts it, 'is unique in Livy's pages in its approximation to a dramatic performance'.[51] In his excellent translation (slightly abbreviated), it runs as follows:

> I   Publius Aebutius, whose father had served in the cavalry-elite issued with a horse by the state, had been left a ward, and subsequently on the death of his guardians he had been brought up under the protection of his mother Duronia and his stepfather Titus Sempronius Rutilus. The mother for her part was under the thumb of her husband; the stepfather's record as guardian was such that he could not render an account of his stewardship, and accordingly he was anxious that his ward be either disposed of or by some hold placed in his power.
>
> The Bacchanalia was the sole means of seducing him. His mother accosted the young man, saying that in view of his illness she had made a vow to initiate him into the Bacchic rites as soon as he recovered; through the gods' kindness, she added, she was forced to keep her vow, and was anxious to discharge it. He must observe continence for ten days, and on the tenth day after feasting and ceremonial purification with clean water she would escort him to the shrine.
>
> There was a freedwoman called Faecenia Hispala who was a prostitute of some note. That occupation to which she had grown accustomed as a mere maidservant did not correspond with her

worth, but even after gaining her freedom she maintained herself in the same profession. Between Aebutius and herself as neighbours an intimacy had grown in no way prejudicial to the young man's property or reputation; in fact she had loved and sought him out without his taking the initiative. When his relatives begrudged meeting all his expenses, he was supported by the generosity of the fond courtesan. Indeed, following the death of her patron she had gone so far in the delight of the relationship as to apply to the tribunes and the praetor for a legal guardian, for she was under no-one's legal control; she made a will, and appointed Aebutius her sole heir.

II Since these pledges of love existed between them, and they kept no secrets from each other, the young man jokingly told Hispala not to be surprised at his sleeping apart from her for several nights; for reasons of religious scruple he proposed to be initiated into the Bacchic rites, in order to be discharged from a vow made for his recovery from illness.

When the woman heard this, she was appalled, and cried 'Heaven help us!' Better, she said, that they both should die than that he should take that action, and that she called down threats and hazards on the heads of those who had suggested it.

The young man in astonishment at both her words and her vehement distress bade her temper her curses, for it was his mother who with the concurrence of his stepfather had enjoined this course on him.

'Well, then', she said, 'your stepfather—perhaps it would be impious to blame your mother—is hell-bent by this action on ruining your virtue, reputation, and prospects in life.'

At this he marvelled all the more, and asked her what the problem was.

She then begged the benevolence and pardon of gods and goddesses if her affection for him compelled her to disclose what should be kept secret. She said that when she was a maidservant, she had accompanied her mistress into that shrine, but that she had never frequented it after manumission. She knew that it was a training-school for every form of corruption, and that it was a fact that no-one older than twenty had been initiated there in the previous two years. Each person escorted there was entrusted as a sacrificial victim to the priests, who led the individual into an arena

44

resounding with shrieks and blasts of musical instruments and the beating of cymbals and drums, designed to prevent the cries of the protesting victim being heard as the violence of sexual rape was inflicted. She then prayed and begged him by any means in his power to break up these proceedings, and not to be thrown into a situation in which he must first endure and later inflict all manner of sacrilegious acts. She did not let him go until the young man promised that he would boycott that ritual.

III   On his arrival home, his mother informed him of the necessary steps to be taken, so far as the sacred ritual was concerned, on that day and successively on the remaining days, but he said that he would not perform any of them, and had no intention of being initiated. His stepfather was present at this conversation.

The woman at once cried out that he could not forgo sleeping with Hispala for the ten nights; he was so steeped in the poisonous consolations of that snake that he had no respect for his mother, his stepfather, or the gods. The mother on the one side, the stepfather on the other, heaped him with reproaches, and drove him out of the house with four slaves.

The young man made his way from there to his aunt Aebutia, and told her why his mother had thrown him out; on her strong recommendation he then reported the matter the following day with no witnesses present to the consul Postumius.

The consul told him to return in three days, and sent him away; he then asked his mother-in-law Sulpicia, a reliable woman, whether she knew some old lady from the Aventine called Aebutia. When Sulpicia replied that she knew her as an honest woman of the old school, the consul said that he had to meet her, and instructed her to send a messenger asking her to come to see her.

IV   On this summons Aebutia came to Sulpicia, and shortly afterwards the consul dropped in apparently by chance, and raised the subject of her brother's son Aebutius.

Tears rose to the woman's eyes, and she began to lament the young man's misfortune, saying that he had been stripped of his possessions by the very last people who should have done so; he had been cast out by his mother, and was now lodging with herself, because the reputable youth refused to be initiated in what people were saying were lewd rites. She prayed that the gods would spare her for using the phrase.

The consul thought that he had sufficiently established that Aebutius as a source was reliable enough, so having let Aebutia go, he asked his mother-in-law to summon to her presence Hispala, a freedwoman from that same district of the Aventine who was not unknown to the neighbourhood; there were questions which he wished to put to her as well.

V   When Hispala received this message, she was alarmed at being summoned by so prominent and august a lady for a reason of which she was unaware; and when she saw in the entrance the lictors, the consul's retinue and the consul himself, she almost fainted.

She was led into the inner confines of the house. There the consul, with his mother-in-law in train, told her that there was no need to be agitated if she could induce herself to speak the truth. She could accept assurances from a woman of such integrity as Sulpicia, or from himself; she must reveal to him what regularly happened in the grove of Stimula during the nightly ritual at the Bacchanalia.

On hearing this, such panic and trembling seized the woman in all her limbs that for some time she could not open her mouth; but finally she rallied, and said that as a mere girl in service she had been initiated with her mistress, but that for some years, ever since she had gained her freedom, she had no knowledge of what went on there.

At this juncture the consul praised the fact that she did not deny that she had been initiated, but said that she must with the same candour reveal the rest as well. When she stated that she knew nothing further, he told her that she would not obtain the same pardon or favour if she were confuted by another as if she herself confessed; the person who had heard the story from her had revealed everything to him.

The woman divined the truth, that Aebutius was undoubtedly the one who had revealed her secret. She fell at Sulpicia's feet, and at first began to beg her not to consent to have a freedwoman's gossip with her lover magnified into a declaration not merely significant but even punishable by death. She had spoken as she did to frighten him, not because she had any knowledge.

At this Postumius was fired with rage, saying that she believed even then that she was bantering with her lover Aebutius rather than conversing in the home of a most august woman, and with the consul. Sulpicia too played her part; she raised up the trembling woman, and simultaneously encouraged her and soothed the anger of her son-in-law.

Hispala finally took heart; after inveighing at length against the treachery of Aebutius for having repaid in this way one who had deserved so well of him, she said that she was greatly afraid of the gods whose secret initiation-rites she was to disclose, but much more of the men who with their own hands would tear her limb from limb for playing the informer. She accordingly begged Sulpicia and the consul to consign her to some place outside Italy, to spend the rest of her life there in safety.

The consul bade her be reassured, and said that it would be his charge to ensure that she would reside safely in Rome.

Then Hispala explained the origin of the ritual. [. . .] Having completed her disclosure, she again fell before their knees, and repeated the same entreaty, that the consul should deport her.

He asked his mother-in-law to vacate some area of her house so that Hispala could move in. She was assigned the attic above the residence; the staircase leading to the outside was blocked off, and entry to the attic was diverted into the house. All Faecenia's possessions were at one brought over, and her house-slaves summoned. Aebutius was ordered to move into the house of a dependant of the consul.

At this point Livy has Postumius give a detailed report of his investigations to the Senate. Some scholars have believed that Livy's narrative derives from this report, its dramatic form due to the consul himself.[52] Others have taken it as Livy's own work, the historian having chosen to cast his narrative in the form of a New Comedy plot.[53] Neither idea seems even remotely plausible. Much more promising is the suggestion that the leading role played by the consul Sp. Postumius Albinus is due to his relative the historian A. Postumius Albinus (consul 151).[54] Although Postumius (who wrote in Greek) was not used by Livy, a Postumian scenario could easily have been transmitted via one of Livy's late-republican sources.[55]

The hypothesis fits perfectly with what little we know about Postumius Albinus' history. Just as he celebrated his distant ancestor's exploits at Lake Regillus with an epic battle in the style of Homer, he may have done the same with Menandrian drama for a recent relative's moment of glory.[56] And the two episodes were evidently linked, since he seems to have made the victor of Lake Regillus found the cult of 'Demeter, Dionysus and Kore', the reinterpreted non-orgiastic Liber cult which the Bacchanals had supposedly perverted.[57]

But that still doesn't account for the plot of the drama. It is all very well to suppose that A. Postumius created a historical scenario glorifying his cousin, and it is true that Sp. Postumius plays a responsible and patriotic role; but the heroine of the drama is the freedwoman Faecenia Hispala. Why should the patrician historian have invented *her*? We need to look one stage further back.

The impact of the suppression of the Bacchanals on the theatre people of Rome must have been very substantial.[58] How could the playwrights and actors who worked for the Liberalia festival limit the damage? One might expect such a play as Livy's text implies—respectful to the powers that be, but with a heroic role for just the sort of woman from the Aventine who might be an object of suspicion. See how the Roman *plebs* are loyal and faithful . . .

I suggest that such a play was indeed produced at the Liberalia, and gratefully received as the *fable convenue* by a traumatized populace; and that a generation later a Hellenised historian, used to presenting the Roman past to a Greek audience in a literary idiom they would understand, transcribed it as the detailed narrative of another episode glorifying his famous family. From there it was taken over into the Latin historiographical tradition, and thus at last to the text of Livy.

IV

That may seem an uncomfortably long causal chain (though I think each stage can be accounted for). So let me offer another play for the Liberalia, this time taken straight from an author who we know used drama as a source.

'Bacchus, whose hair is bound with berried ivy, if her house is your own, direct my song!' So Ovid begins his aetiology of the Matralia, the Roman festival of Mater Matuta on 11 June. Still addressing the god, he tells the tale:[59]

> Semele had burned, by Jupiter's indulgence; considerate Ino received you, child, and nursed you with the utmost care. Juno raged that Ino should rescue and bring up the concubine's son, even though he was of her sister's blood. So Athamas was driven by

furies and a false vision, and you, little Learchus, fell by your father's hand. His grieving mother had entombed Learchus' shade and paid all due honours at the gloomy pyre when she too, just as she was, tearing her hair in mourning, sprang up and snatched you, Melicertes, from the cradle.

There is a land confined in brief extent; one land drives back two seas, is beaten by two waters. Hither she came, clutching her son in her crazy arms, and threw herself with him from the high cliff into the deep. Panope and her hundred sisters received them unharmed, and bore them gently gliding through their realms. Not yet Leucothea, her boy not yet Palaemon, they reached the mouth of Tiber, dense with whirlpools.

There was a grove—who knows whether it is called the Grove of Semele or of Stimula? They say that maenads of Ausonia lived there.

Ino inquired of them what race they were, and heard they were Arcadians, and that Evander was king of the place.

The daughter of Saturn, concealing her divinity, craftily goaded the Bacchae with false words. 'O women too credulous, wholly taken in! This stranger comes no friend to our dancing rites. Her aim is treachery; she schemes to learn the ritual of our cult. But she has a pledge by which she may be punished.'

Hardly had she finished when they filled the air with shrieking. Hair streaming on their necks, the Thyiads cast their hands on her and fought to drag the boy away.

Ino called on the gods she did not yet know. 'O gods and men of this land, bring help to a wretched mother!'

Her cry struck the neighbouring rocks of Aventine. The hero of Oeta had driven the Iberian herd to the river bank. He heard, and raced towards the voice. At Hercules' coming those who had been ready to use violence turned their cowardly backs and fled like women.

'Aunt of Bacchus,' he said, for he had recognized her, 'What are you seeking here? Does the deity who hounds me hound you too?'

She told him, in part; but part the presence of her son kept back, and shame that the furies had driven her to crime.

Rumour is swift, and flew on beating wings. Your name, Ino, was on everybody's lips. It is said that you entered as a guest the faithful home of Carmentis, and there broke your long fast. Cakes, hastened with her own hand, the Tegean priestess is said to have given you, baked on a sudden hearth. (Even to this day cakes are what she likes at the Matralia festival.) Rustic generosity was more welcome than sophistication.

'Now, prophetess,' she said, 'unseal the coming fates, so far as is permitted. I pray you, add this to the hospitality you have given me.'

After a brief pause, the prophetess took on the powers of heaven, and in all her breast she was filled by her god. Suddenly you would hardly recognise her, so much holier, so much greater was she than before.

'I will sing good news. Rejoice, Ino, you have done with your labours,' she said. 'And ever after come propitious to this people! You shall be a divinity of the sea; your son too shall belong to the ocean. In your own waters take another name. You shall be called by the Greeks Leucothea, by our people Matuta; all authority over ports will be your son's, whom we will call Portunus and his own tongue Palaemon. Go, I pray, and both be favourable to our land!'

Ino had bowed assent. Her faith was promised. They put aside their troubles and changed their names. He is a god, she is a goddess.

I have marked with a space the point where Ovid shifts from the allusive summary of a Greek myth to a Roman story told at length in dialogue. The Grove of Stimula, Juno's 'goad' and the flight of the murderous and deluded Bacchae place the origin of the story beyond doubt. Here too we are in the aftermath of 186 BC.[60] This is Liber's story,[61] but with the dangerous aspects of his worship mythologized away.

And here too, surely, we have a play. Ino's conversation with Hercules reveals it. On the stage, her story has to be told to explain who the strangers are. Ovid's readers have been told it already, but he still reports *her* telling it, and even specifies what she left out. Here, as elsewhere,[62] he must be summarising a play his readers know.

What sort of play? Perhaps it began, after a snarling soliloquy by the disguised Juno, with the Bacchic dancing to which she later refers. The struggle for Melicertes and the sudden arrival of Hercules could certainly be played as farce. And then, in the last scene, Carmentis' prophecy tells the audience what it all means for Rome. We have seen this mixture before.

As with the Nonae Caprotinae in chapter 1, the talisman shield and the birth of the Lares in chapter 2, the favour of Fortune in chapter 3, we have to infer a stage performance which combined comic, even erotic, entertainment with a serious patriotic message at the end.[63] If the grammarians offer us no definition of that dramatic genre, so much the worse for the grammarians. Ovid, the master story-teller, is a better guide.

5

The Tragedy of Gaius Gracchus

I

Plays on contemporary themes are attested from the very beginnings of literary drama at Rome, with Cn. Naevius' *Clastidium* (on M. Marcellus in 222 BC), Ennius' *Ambracia* (on M. Fulvius in 189 BC), and Pacuvius' *Paulus* (probably on the battle of Pydna, 168 BC).[1] It is often assumed that the genre fell into disuse,[2] but that is hard to believe in view of the close connection between the *ludi scaenici* and the political élite. Plays were regularly put on to celebrate triumphs; or at the dedication of temples, which were themselves often triumphal *monumenta*; or at funerals, where the *res gestae* of the defunct would naturally be celebrated. How better than with a *fabula praetexta*?[3]

It is not surprising that few titles and fragments survive. Since topical subjects soon go out of date, no doubt only a few such plays, by the greatest practitioners, survived into the canon. We happen to know, from a letter of Pollio's in Cicero's correspondence, that one of the plays put on at the provincial *ludi* in Cordoba in 43 BC was a *praetexta* by the quaestor L. Cornelius Balbus, on the subject of his own experiences in the civil war, which moved him to tears as he watched it.[4] When casual evidence like that reveals the genre still flourishing in the theatre, the paucity of references to library texts of classic plays need not be significant.

A century ago, scholars were much more open than they are now to the possibility of Roman plays on contemporary subjects, and prepared to infer their existence from the dramatic treatment of particular episodes in historical narratives. Karl Meiser, for instance, in an address

52

to the Bavarian Academy in November 1887, offered as examples the death of Sophoniba, the plot of Pacuvius Calavius of Capua, Perseus and Demetrius in 182, and the tragic end of Gaius Gracchus.[5] However, Henry Bardon would have none of that:[6]

> Bel effort d'imagination, louable désir de ressusciter des fantômes; mais de ces songes philologiques ne naissent que des ombres palpables. À ce compte, que de tragédies ne taillerait-on pas chez Tacite!

It is true enough that historians were quite capable of writing vivid and dramatic scenes on their own account.[7] Understandably, therefore, Bardon's scepticism has prevailed.

Understandably, but in my view wrongly. Bardon's own argument from Tacitus is a two-edged weapon, since the one *praetexta* that survives, the pseudo-Senecan *Octavia*, is precisely a tragedy on Tacitus' own subject-matter, and one with which he may well have been familiar.[8] The *ludi scaenici* of the Principate still dealt with topical themes; normally, of course, the performances were concerned with honouring or flattering the emperor,[9] but the *Octavia* shows that once it was safe to do so, playwrights could handle the domestic dramas of the house of Caesar just as their predecessors had handled those of the house of Atreus or the house of Tarquin.[10]

The *Octavia* is in fact a very interesting play from our point of view. It is unlike any surviving tragedy in having a chorus (of Roman citizens) which takes a direct part in the action, nothing less than an attack on the imperial palace itself. It is also a very symmetrical play, in that there are two empresses (Octavia and Poppaea), two nurses (one for each empress), and two choruses (the empresses' respective supporters). It was clearly written for a fully-developed Roman *scaenae frons* with three doors—Octavia's quarters on one side, Poppaea's on the other, and the 'royal door' (from which Nero and the Prefect emerge at line 437) in the middle.[11]

Bearing that in mind, let us try to visualize a scene from one of Meiser's hypothetical tragedies, *Gaius Gracchus*. The date is 121 BC. Opimius, the hawkish consul, has just ordered the Senate and *equites* to take up arms against C. Gracchus and his *popularis* ally M. Fulvius Flaccus. Imagine a stage set: the central door, let us suppose, is the temple of Diana; on one side, a house with a statue in front of it; on the other, a house hung with weapons and trophies from a triumph. Here is Plutarch's narrative,[12] in the Langhorne brothers' 1770 translation:

53

Gaius, as he returned from the Forum, stood a long time looking upon his father's statue, and after having given vent to his sorrow in some sighs and tears, retired without uttering a word. Many of the plebeians, who saw this, were moved with compassion; and declaring that they would be the most dastardly of beings if they abandoned such a man to his enemies, repaired to his house to guard him, and passed the night before his door.

This they did in a very different manner from the people who attended Fulvius on the same occasion. These passed their time in noise and riot, in carousing and empty threats, Fulvius himself being the first man that was intoxicated, and giving in to many expressions and actions unsuitable to his years. But those about Gaius were silent, as in a time of public calamity, and with a thoughtful regard to what was yet to come, they kept watch and took rest by turns.

Fulvius slept so sound after his wine that it was with difficulty that they awoke him at break of day. Then he and his company armed themselves with the Gallic spoils which he had brought off in his consulship, upon his conquering that people, and thus accoutred they sallied out, with loud menaces, to seize the Aventine hill. As for Gaius, he would not arm, but went out in his toga as if he had been going upon business in the Forum; only he had a small dagger under it.

At the door his wife threw herself at his feet, and taking hold of him with one hand and of her son with the other, she thus expressed herself:

'You do not now leave me, my dear Gaius, as formerly, to go to the Rostra in capacity of tribune or lawgiver, nor do I send you out to a glorious war where, if the common lot fell to your share, my distress might at least have the consolation of honour. You expose yourself to the murderers of Tiberius, unarmed, indeed as a man should go who had rather suffer than commit any violence; but it is throwing away your life without any advantage to the community. Faction reigns; outrage and the sword are the only measures of justice. Had your brother fallen before Numantia, the truce would have restored his body; but now perhaps I shall have to go a suppliant to some river or sea to be shown where your remains are to be found. For what confidence can we have either in the laws or in the gods after the assassination of Tiberius?'

When Licinia had poured out these lamentations, Gaius disengaged himself as quietly as he could from her arms, and walked on with his friends in deep silence. She caught at his toga, but in the attempt fell to the ground and lay a long time speechless. At last her servants, seeing her there in that condition, took her up and carried her to her brother Crassus.

Fulvius and his men try to fight it out; Fulvius is killed; Gaius, who has taken no part in the fighting, retires to the Diana temple.

There he would have despatched himself, but was hindered by Pomponius and Licinius, the most faithful of his friends, who took away his dagger and persuaded him to try the alternative of flight. On this occasion he is said to have knelt down and with uplifted hands to have prayed to the deity of that temple, that the people of Rome, for their ingratitude and base desertion of him, might be slaves for ever.

Exit, pursued by Opimius' men; perhaps his flight and eventual death were reported in a messenger's speech.

II

The two doors in Plutarch seem to me to be *prima facie* evidence for real drama as the ultimate source, rather than merely dramatic writing by a historian. In which case it follows that at some point a non-theatrical author—either the biographer himself or one of his sources—took a dramatist's scenario as true, or at least as 'true enough' for his own purposes.[13]

There is nothing improbable in that. Plutarch is explicit in accepting as historical the tragedians' story of Phaedra and Hippolytus, in the absence of any alternative version in a historian.[14] Similarly, both he and the elder Pliny, who was a historian himself, report as fact episodes that are known to have been invented in the rhetorical schools as exercises in declamation;[15] one of them was about the murder of Cicero, which shows that even recent events, in the full light of history, were subject to the creation of instant legend.

The great historians understood the process perfectly well. As Tacitus observed, it was particularly the deaths of the great that encouraged the conversion of truth into fiction. He took it for granted that historians would present *fabulae*, to astonish their readers.[16] Thucydides referred to alleged events 'winning over into the mythical', a phrase explained in a wonderful passage of Francis Cornford's chapter on 'mythistoria and drama':[17]

> It suggests the transformation which begins to steal over all events from the moment of their occurrence, unless they are arrested and pinned down in writing by an alert and trained observer ... The facts *work loose*; they are detached from their roots in time and space and shaped into a story. The story is moulded and remoulded by imagination, by passion and prejudice, by religious preconception or aesthetic instinct, by the delight in the marvellous, by the itch for a moral, by the love of a good story; and the thing becomes a legend.

The stage was certainly one of the ways by which passion and prejudice could effect that transformation.

In the very 'primal scene' of ancient historiography, the story of Gyges, Candaules and the queen of Lydia, Herodotus offers his audience a play in two acts, each consisting of a dialogue followed by a dramatic bedroom scene. He introduces it with Candaules' observation that the eyes are more reliable witnesses than the ears, inviting us in effect to watch it happen, as if on the stage. Since 1949 we have known that the story was indeed a play; and it is not impossible that Herodotus knew it.[18] So if, as I suggest, Plutarch's source transcribed as history what he had seen played at the *ludi scaenici*, he may have been doing no more than the Father of History himself had done, nearly four centuries before.

III

So Meiser's idea is not self-evidently absurd. But there is a weighty objection to it, put by a scholar who was otherwise very receptive to the idea of drama as a source for the Roman historical tradition.

What Wilhelm Soltau asked was this: would the Senate and the leaders of reaction have allowed the performance of such a drama? Would it not have stirred up anew the popular enthusiasm for revolution, and paved the way for a fresh outbreak?[19] It is a good question, particularly in view of the way the Gracchan drama was exploited at the time of the French Revolution: Marie-Joseph de Chénier's three-act tragedy *Caïus Gracchus* was performed at the

Théâtre de la République in Paris on 9 February 1792, and a year later the revolutionary François-Noël Babeuf, in a deliberately symbolic gesture, renounced his given names and took the name of Gracchus.[20]

Soltau's question takes it for granted that the Roman Republic was an all-powerful oligarchy. It is certainly true that the Senate, the magistrates and the *nobiles* were disproportionately influential; but the Republic was *SPQR*, the Senate and People of Rome, and its politics were typically polarised between the interests of *plebs* and *patres*.[21] Although the evidence is very uncertain, that polarity may be detected in the history of the dramatic festivals.

Among the earliest of the festivals were the *ludi plebeii*, held each November in honour of Jupiter. The very name 'Plebeian Games' implies an origin in the political struggles of the early Republic, and that is indeed what a Ciceronian scholiast tells us.[22] The plebeians' achievement of the consulship in the fourth century BC was marked by some major development in the provision of drama at the *ludi Romani*, the details of which are unfortunately obscure in Livy's narrative.[23] The *ludi Apollinares* were set up in 212 BC at a time of popular unrest, evidently as a concession by the Senate and praetors to avoid something less controllable.[24] The *ludi Florales* were funded by the plebeian aediles' fines on wealthy landowners; it seems that the Senate at first refused to recognise them, but eventually gave way in 173 BC.[25] As for the late Republic, Cicero's evidence vividly shows how lively the political atmosphere was at the theatrical festivals in his time.[26]

In our one surviving example of a *fabula praetexta*, the liberty of the Roman People is a strong and constant theme.[27] The *Octavia* was written in or after AD 68, but this emphasis can hardly be an innovation; much more probably it indicates a continuing tradition of the genre. To have the Roman People as the chorus before whom the protagonists play out their conflicts would be a very natural convention for 'drama in Roman dress'. Whether it *was* so, we cannot say—but Plutarch's narrative of the crisis of 121 BC certainly encourages the hypothesis.

Just before the night scene at the two houses, quoted above, Plutarch offers us this (in the Langhorne translation again):[28]

> When the day came on which Opimius was to get those laws repealed, both parties early in the morning posted themselves on the Capitol; and after the consul had sacrificed, Quintus Antyllius, one of his lictors, who was carrying out the entrails of the victims, said

to Fulvius and his friends 'Stand off, ye factious citizens, and make way for honest men'. Some add that, along with this scurrilous language, he stretched his naked arm towards them in a form that expressed the utmost contempt. They immediately killed Antyllius with long styluses, said to have been made for such a purpose.

The people were much chagrined at this act of violence. As for the two chiefs, they made very different reflections upon the event. Gaius was concerned at it, and reproached his partisans with having given their enemies the handle they long had wanted. Opimius rejoiced at the opportunity, and excited the people to revenge. But for the present they were parted by heavy rain.

At an early hour next day, the consul assembled the senate, and while he was addressing them within, others exposed the corpse of Antyllius naked on a bier without, and as it had been previously concerted, carried it through the Forum to the Senate-house, making loud acclamations all the way. Opimius knew the whole farce, but pretended to be much surprised. The senate went out, and planting themselves about the corpse, expressed their grief and indignation, as if some dreadful misfortune had befallen them. This scene, however, excited only hatred and detestation in the breasts of the people, who could not but remember that the nobility [oligarchikoi] had killed Tiberius Gracchus on the Capitol, though a tribune, and thrown his body into the river; and yet now, when Antyllius, a vile serjeant, who possibly did not deserve quite so severe a punishment, but by his impertinence had brought it upon himself—when such a hireling lay exposed in the Forum, the senate of Rome stood weeping about him; and then attended the wretch to his funeral; with no other view than to procure the death of the only remaining protector of the people.

Here we have two successive scenes—one on the Capitol in front of the temple of Jupiter, and one in the Forum in front of the Senate-house, from which Opimius and the senators emerge to perform their prepared charade. In each case the reaction of the People is central to the drama. And what is played out before them is the polarised opposition of *plebs* and *patres*.

Was it the drama of real politics, or politics presented as real drama?[29] If we think it was the latter, then Soltau's question demands an answer.

As Sallust observes, Opimius and the *nobilitas* exploited their victory with a vengeful brutality that turned out to be counter-productive.[30] In

111 BC the tribune C. Memmius began the popular counter-attack.[31] The following year C. Mamilius instituted the People's inquiry into aristocratic collusion with Jugurtha, as a result of which Opimius was banished.[32] In 108 Marius was elected to the consulship. This period, described by its historian as 'the first challenge to the arrogance of the *nobilitas*',[33] surely offers an intelligible context for a tragedy on Gaius Gracchus. Now he was avenged, and the first Plebeian Games after Opimius' exile would be the proper time to celebrate the fact.

6

Crossing the Rubicon

I

On 7 January 49 BC (pre-Julian calendar) the Senate passed its emergency decree, effectively introducing martial law, and forced the tribunes M. Antonius and Q. Cassius to leave Rome.

Caesar was at Ravenna when he heard the news. He had already sent for his main army from across the Alps, but at present he had with him just one legion (the thirteenth) and his bodyguard—five thousand infantry and three hundred horse. He acted immediately. A group of centurions and other picked men was sent secretly to cross the border into Italy, carrying swords but in civilian dress; their task was to enter Ariminum without being noticed, and secure the city in advance.

Caesar himself was conspicuously nonchalant, in public view all day watching gladiatorial exercises, and then dining with his usual numerous guests. At about sunset, however, he slipped away from the dinner, as if temporarily indisposed. In a carriage drawn by two mules hired from the bakery next door, Caesar and a few of his staff quietly left Ravenna. After first taking the wrong road, he turned south towards Ariminum, with his cavalry following.

When Caesar reached the bridge over the Rubicon, which formed the boundary between Cisalpine Gaul and Italy, he stopped, got out, and stood for a long time in silence, pondering the enormity of his enterprise. He talked to his intimates, arguing the pros and cons.

> 'We can still go back; but once over that little bridge everything will have to be done by force of arms. If we don't cross it, this is the beginning of disaster for me; if we do, it's the beginning of disaster for the world. But what a story we shall leave for posterity!'

At last, impatiently abandoning rational calculation as if rushing into the abyss, he cried 'Let the die be cast!', and hurried across the bridge like a man possessed. His forces followed, and by daybreak Ariminum was in his hands.

That is the story as we have it in Plutarch, Appian and (in part) Suetonius.[1] There has never been any serious doubt about where it comes from, since Plutarch names Asinius Pollio among those who were present.[2] Poet, orator and tragedian, Pollio was also a historian with a keen eye for the dramatic moment and the telling quotation.[3] Caesar himself, in the more businesslike genre of *commentarii*, passes directly from his speech to the soldiers at Ravenna to the meeting with the tribunes at Ariminum.[4] He had no motive to dwell on the crossing of the Rubicon, but *historia* proper demanded a scene worthy of the moment, and Pollio duly provided it.[5]

However, in Suetonius the Pollio version extends only as far as the dialogue at the bridge. Then follows a most remarkable passage (*Divus Iulius* 32):

> Cunctanti ostentum tale factum est. quidam eximia magnitudine et forma in proximo sedens repente apparuit harundine canens; ad quem audiendum cum praeter pastores plurimi etiam ex stationibus milites concurrissent interque eos et aeneatores, rapta ab uno tuba prosiluit ad flumen et ingenti spiritu classicum exorsus pertendit ad alteram ripam. tunc Caesar 'Eatur' inquit 'quo deorum ostenta et inimicorum iniquitas uocat. iacta alea est' inquit.

> As he was hesitating there occurred the following prodigy. A figure of extraordinary size and beauty suddenly appeared, sitting close by playing on a reed pipe. As well as shepherds, many of the soldiers too ran up from their posts to listen to him, including some buglers; whereupon he snatched a trumpet from one of them, sprang forward to the river, and starting with a mighty blast, went straight across to the other bank. Then Caesar spoke. 'Let us go,' he said, 'where the portents of the gods and the villainy of our enemies call. The die is cast.'

This scene is evidently *not* from Pollio. There is no sign of it in Appian or Plutarch, and its version of the famous phrase differs from theirs by being in the indicative: 'iacta alea *est*'.

It is not impossible that this tale of an apparition was invented by a historian; one thinks of the authors who earned Polybius' contempt by having 'gods and heroes' appear to Hannibal and guide him over the Alps.[6] But the 'stage-business' of shepherds and soldiers makes a dramatic source much more likely. As Livy remarks, 'the theatre delights in marvels'. Ovid says much the same, and both authors were evidently referring to plays on Roman historical subjects.[7]

One can even hazard a guess about the *type* of drama that may have been involved. A larger-than-life figure playing the pipe to shepherds must surely be Pan;[8] Pan belongs in the company of Dionysus and the satyrs; and there is clear evidence, notably in Vitruvius and Horace, that some form of satyr-play was current on the Roman stage in the first century BC.[9] Satyric drama had come a long way since the days of the Attic tragedians: already by the fourth century we find it being used for topical plots with contemporary characters.[10]

One of Caesar's most prominent partisans, very possibly present at the crossing of the Rubicon, was C. Vibius Pansa, whose *cognomen* alluded to a legendary descent from Pan. The coins struck by his father in 90 BC, and by Pansa himself in 48, prominently feature the head of Pan, portrayed as a mask.[11] Pansa may well have issued his coins as aedile,[12] in which case he would have been among those responsible for the *ludi scaenici* of the first year of Caesarian Rome. What better context for a play presenting Pan as Caesar's divine authority at the Rubicon? 'Let us go, where the portents of the gods and the villainy of our enemies call. The die is cast!'

II

The young Virgil was in Rome in 48 BC, newly arrived from Mantua via Milan. He if anyone would surely be at the *ludi scaenici*, if only to see which poet was the popular favourite that year.[13] So we may imagine him watching a pastoral idyll (Pan and the shepherds) set in the Italian countryside, juxtaposed with the realities of civil war. Seven or eight years later he would be offering the audience his own fantasia on that theme, which we know as the first *Eclogue*.[14]

'Tityre, tu . . .' The herdsman with the oaten pipe who personifies the pastoral mode is named after a kind of satyr.[15] Since *tityristai* were evidently satyric performers (we hear of them as mime-dancers in Roman pageants like the triumphal procession),[16] Virgil's choice of name may be, in part at least, a graceful tribute to a less sophisticated dramatic genre.

What matters is not the difference but the common factor. The theatre audience was the Roman People, eager for topical material but also familiar with the conventions of many types of stage performance. If Theocritean pastoral could handle the settlement of triumviral veterans, satyr-play could as easily cope with the crossing of the Rubicon.

7

The Poet, the *Plebs*,
and the Chorus Girls

I

With its material arranged by the days of the year, Ovid's *Fasti* is by its
nature episodic. But the length and treatment of the episodes varies
enormously, as one expects from so subtle and versatile a poet. Which
of the 'times distributed through the Latin year' (as he defines his
subject) does Ovid choose to treat at length?[1]

The first day, and Janus the primal god (226 lines); the festival of
Vesta, guardian of Rome's safety (220); the Lupercalia and Parilia, both
associated with the foundation story (186 and 142 respectively); the
Regifugium, celebrating freedom from Tarquin's tyranny (168); the
festivals of Ceres and Flora, goddesses of fruitful growth (228 and 196
respectively); and the Megalensia, in honour of the Great Mother of the
Gods (194).[2] In this august company, it is a surprise to find Anna
Perenna. Her day was the Ides of March, and Ovid gives her 174 lines,
followed, as an afterthought, by a mere fourteen lines on the
assassination of Caesar.[3]

Most of those 174 lines are taken up by 'the virtuoso miniature
Aeneid' of Dido's sister Anna and her metamorphosis as the nymph of
the river Numicius.[4] But that brilliantly witty narrative does not stand
alone. It is part of an integrated aetiological argument, which may be
summarised as follows:

1. On the Ides, the festival of Anna Perenna is held by the Tiber.
The common people (*plebs*) come and lie on the grass in couples,
drinking in the sunshine. Some pitch tents, some make shelters of

64

branches, some put up reeds like columns and stretch togas over them. They drink as many cups as the years they want to live; they sing songs learned in the theatres; and they dance, the men clumsily, their girl-friends gracefully with their hair down. Then they stagger back to town in procession, a spectacle for the crowd, who call them blessed. [523–42]

2. Who is Anna Perenna? There are many false stories, and Ovid will not conceal any of them [543–4]:
(i) She was Dido's sister Anna, shipwrecked in Latium, sheltered by Aeneas and Lavinia, warned by Dido in a dream of Lavinia's jealousy, concealed by the river-god Numicius and turned into a water-nymph. Because she hides in a perennial river (*amne perenne*), she is called Anna Perenna. [545–656]
(ii) She is Luna, the moon, whose months fill the year (*annus*). [657]
(iii) She is Themis, or Io. [658]
(iv) She is an Arcadian nymph, who fed the infant Jupiter. [659–60]
(v) But the truth is that she was an old woman from Bovillae, who provided hot cakes for the plebeians when they seceded to the Mons Sacer, and was honoured by them with a statue. [661–74]

3. Why do the girls gather to sing obscene songs? When old Anna had just been made a goddess, Mars asked her to procure Minerva for him as his bride. She promised, but kept putting him off. Eventually she told him it was all arranged, but when Mars came to the bridal chamber and lifted the bride's veil, he found it was Anna herself. Anna laughed, Venus laughed, and the god's deception became a theme for old jokes and indecent songs. [675–96].

Anna Perenna's festival took place at the first milestone on the Via Flaminia, where the riverside meadow evidently included a sacred grove (fig. 1).[5] Martial refers to the grove 'delighting in the blood of virgins', which may imply another aetiological story, evidently involving human sacrifice, to add to those listed by Ovid; whether the Sicilian cult of 'Anna and the Girls [*paides*, fem.]' had anything to do with that is not known.[6]
According to Macrobius, the festival involved a sacrifice and prayers for the successful completion of this year and all others, 'ut annare perannareque commode liceat'.[7] It is clear that Anna Perenna was once the goddess of the new year, as Ovid himself implies earlier in book III.[8]

The etymology *annus/Anna* is a very obvious one, and is duly alluded to in this passage (657). But it is striking that in all three sections of his account Ovid also uses the word *anus* ('old woman')[9]—emphatically and without obvious relevance in the description of the festival (542), and as an integral part of the aetiologies of Anna's identity (668) and the indecent songs (684). Two of the 'false versions' Ovid lists make Anna a nymph (653, 659); in the one he calls true, she is an old woman.

II

Ovid's summary list of identifications at lines 657–60 may be expanded a little. Luna, the moon goddess, governs the months, and is thus an appropriate identity for the goddess of the year; so too is Themis (658), who is the mother of the Seasons.[10] But why Io, 'the Inachian cow'? What relevance could she have?

For communities like Rome, peripheral to the Greek world, myths of geographical wanderings were particularly useful.[11] Wandering heroes came there, like Aeneas and Hercules; and wandering gods as well, like Saturn in flight from Jupiter's *coup d'état*, who hid in Latium (and thus named it)[12] and founded the *Saturnia regna* on the Capitol.[13] Io was a wanderer *par excellence*,[14] and creative mythographers could have brought her to Rome, just as they brought Orestes, who was buried in front of the temple of Saturn, and Ino, who became the Roman goddess Mater Matuta.[15]

According to the story as we have it, Io was transformed into a heifer by the jealous Hera, who set the myriad-eyed Argus to guard her; but Argus was killed by Hermes, whence the Homeric epithet Ἀργειφόντης.[16] There was a street at Rome called Argiletum, which should mean 'the killing of Argus'. When Virgil refers to it, as a grove pointed out by Evander to Aeneas, he puts the word at the end of the hexameter, in the position that Hermes' epithet always occupies in Homer.[17] It is natural to infer that Virgil was alluding to a version of the story in which Io's keeper is killed at Rome, where Hermes (Mercury) had a place in local myth as the father of the Lares.[18] It is true that neither Servius nor Servius *auctus* records such a version,[19] but I think their silence cannot be decisive against the combined effect of what Virgil and Ovid imply. Someone evidently set the Io story in Rome, to provide an aetiology for both Anna Perenna and the Argiletum.[20]

It may be relevant that for two days after Anna Perenna's festival, on 16 and 17 March, the ritual of the *Argei* took place.[21] Ovid calls Io

'Inachian', after Inachus the river-god, first king of Argos. Her story is specifically an Argive one, and the all-seeing Argus who guarded her was an eponym of the city.[22] Since the Roman *Argei* were supposedly Argives,[23] it is possible that the proximity of that ritual gave rise to the identification of Anna Perenna as the unfortunate princess of Argos.

Io as a cow was identified with the horned Moon.[24] As we have seen, the moon goddess and Themis are natural identities for Anna as a year-goddess; but they have something else in common. Both were born in Arcadia.[25]

Themis was an Arcadian prophetess, who came to Italy with her son Evander, chose the site of Rome for his colony, set up the cult of Pan at the Lupercal, and foretold the apotheosis of Hercules at the Ara Maxima.[26] Hence the next identity for Anna Perenna in Ovid's list, as an 'Azanian' nymph who fed the infant Jupiter: Azania was a district of Arcadia,[27] and the Arcadian story was that Zeus was first fed on Mount Lykaios by the nymphs Theisoa, Neda and Hagno.[28]

Rome's Arcadian legend goes at least as far back as Eratosthenes in the third century BC,[29] and I think it can be shown to pre-date the Romulus and Remus foundation story.[30] It is associated with the very ancient Lupercal cult, and with that of Victory on the Palatine, whose temple was dedicated in 294 BC.[31] The cult of the moon-goddess was supposedly founded by Servius Tullius, and that of Mercury, the Arcadian god who was believed to be Evander's father, dates back to the early Republic.[32] So the stories Ovid alludes to here may have quite a long history.

But he does nothing with them. Anna as the sister of Dido is what challenges his parodic skill, as Stephen Hinds has brilliantly shown; and yet even that *tour de force* is signalled as a false story, along with the others.[33] The truth, he claims, is that Anna was an old woman of Bovillae. And if we are to make sense of that, we must look at the whole extent of Ovid's treatment—not just the identifications (item 2 in the summary above), but the nature of the festival itself and the story of Anna and Mars (items 1 and 3).

III

Let us begin with a detail from Ovid's opening scene. The plebeian revellers pitch tents, make huts from boughs, or stretch togas over upright reeds. A similar custom applied at other festivals: certainly at the Neptunalia in July, when huts made from leafy boughs were called *umbrae*, and possibly at the Volcanalia in August, if we may trust the report of a fifth-century author that on that day 'the credulous mob hang up garments to the Sun'.[34] But July and August are one thing, mid-March is something quite different. The booths and tents of Anna Perenna's festival cannot have been put up just to provide shade.

Other parallels may be more helpful. The author of the *Pervigilium Veneris* begins his celebration of the festival of love with this promise:

> Cras amorum copulatrix inter umbras arborum
> implicat casas uirentes de flagello myrteo.

> Tomorrow in the shade of the trees the goddess who joins in love
> weaves green huts from branches of myrtle.

Those bowers or canopies, made from Venus' own myrtle-branches, were clearly meant to shelter lovers: 'amorum *copulatrix*' could hardly be more specific.[35]

Another example may be the *Nonae Caprotinae* festival on 5 July. On that day servant girls processed out of the city in their mistresses' clothes, to a place 'under the shade of fig-tree boughs', where they were served at a banquet.[36] The nature of that festival is revealed by the aetiological story that purported to explain it. The Latins, under Postumus Livius of Fidenae, taking advantage of Roman weakness after the Gallic sack, march on Rome, encamp outside the city and demand that the Romans hand over their wives and daughters. At the suggestion of a servant girl called Philotis (or Tutula), she and her fellow *ancillae* are dressed as free women and surrendered to the enemy. Livius distributes them throughout his camp, and that night, as the Latins lie drunk and exhausted, Philotis gives a prearranged signal to the Romans watching from the wall, who rush out and slaughter them.[37]

The story is explicitly erotic (even Philotis' name is significant),[38] and it must imply an erotic element in the festival. The natural inference is that bowers were set up like the tents of the Latin camp, and that after the slave-girls' banquet what happened in the story happened also at the festival. One detail may be helpful for our purposes: in the story, Philotis spreads a cloak or coverlet over the fig-tree to shield her signal from the enemy. That too must represent an element of the ritual, and so we may perhaps infer that the slave-girls in their mistresses' dresses later hung the dresses over the boughs to provide the necessary privacy for making love.[39]

That brings us back to the analogous description in Ovid of the shelters put up for Anna Perenna's festival. But one detail is at first sight puzzling (529f): 'Some have set up reeds like stiff columns, and stretched out togas over them.' But these are the *plebs*, and they are on holiday. The toga was notoriously city dress, not appropriate to holidays,[40] and especially not appropriate to plebeians.[41] It would be an absurdly inappropriate garment to wear on this occasion. Or at least, it would be for a *man*. Women wore togas too, and for them, in Ovid's time, it signified something quite different.

The toga was, in effect, a large semicircular wrap. Originally it had been worn by both sexes;[42] the *toga praetexta* remained the dress for girls, and the *toga pura* for brides,[43] but at least by the late Republic the dress of a married woman was the long *stola*—essentially a sleeved tunic extended to ankle length. The whole point about the toga was that it could be thrown open easily, as was done by candidates for election showing their battle-scars.[44] For a woman to wear it was to advertise her availability; by the late Republic it was the mark of the prostitute or adulteress, just as the *stola* symbolised the respectable matron.[45]

We must be clear about what was happening on Anna Perenna's day. It was not a general picnic for the whole working population of Rome. The grove and meadow at the first milestone of the Flaminia could hardly have catered for such numbers; besides, as Nicholas Horsfall acutely pointed out, on Anna Perenna's day in 44 BC there were large crowds elsewhere, watching the gladiators in Pompey's theatre or thronging the dictator's route to the Senate meeting.[46] Not everyone was lucky enough to take part in the festival; when the celebrants came reeling back in a drunken procession, the crowds lining the way called them the blessed ones.[47]

It is obvious enough that a certain investment of time and money was involved. No doubt you would want to prepare your love-nest in advance; you would certainly need plenty of wine, and food as well; and above all you would need a girl. Ovid is explicit that this was a festival for couples.[48]

Note too that he draws a clear distinction between the clumsy dancing of the men and the elegance of their girl-friends. The *culta amica* who danced with her hair down at line 538 had no doubt come to the festival smartly dressed in the toga which now hung on the reed frame of her partner's bower.[49] (If so, she was half undressed, in just her tunic: 'tunica velata recincta' is how Ovid describes the Anna of his *Aeneid* parody, as she climbs out of the bedroom window and runs towards the river.[50]) Since singing, dancing and smart clothes characterize the *puellae* for whom Ovid's *Ars amatoria* was written,[51] this *amica* could easily be one of those talented young women whose real existence we infer behind the literary constructions of New Comedy and Roman elegiac poetry.[52]

There, by the river bank, the revellers sing as well as dance; and the songs are 'whatever they have learned in the theatres' (535). But the last *ludi scaenici* were the Compitalia in early January,[53] and two and a half months is a long time for even the catchiest tune to stay in the audience's mind. It is surely the girls who have learned the songs, as professional performers; they sing, they dance, and their partners drunkenly join in. Two passages from other poets help us to identify them.

First Propertius, confessing his susceptibility:[54]

> Nulla meis frustra lustrantur compita plantis;
>   o nimis exitio nata theatra meo,
> siue aliqua in molli diducit candida gestu
>   bracchia, seu uarios incinit ore modos!
> interea nostri quaerunt sibi uulnus ocelli,
>   candida non tecto pectore si qua sedet . . .

> My feet pace no cross-roads in vain; oh, theatres are made for my total ruin, whether some girl spreads her white arms in a graceful gesture, or sings in a varied cadence! All the time my eyes are seeking their own hurt, if some beauty sits with her breast uncovered . . .

And then Statius, celebrating the after-dinner entertainment laid on by the emperor in the Colosseum:[55]

> Huc intrant faciles emi puellae,
> hic agnoscitur omne quod theatris
> aut forma placet aut probatur arte.
> hoc plaudunt grege ludiae tumentes,
> illo cymbala tinnulaeque Gades . . .

> Here come the girls who are easy to buy, here we recognise all the beauty that gives pleasure in the theatre, all the art that's applauded there. For one group buxom showgirls are clapping their hands, for another it's the castanets of tinkling Gades . . .

What we have to do with here is the common ground of show-business and prostitution.[56]

There is a famous story of Cato at the *ludi Florales* in 55 BC; his mere presence inhibited the audience from calling for the girls on stage to take their clothes off. (He went out, and the show went on.) Valerius Maximus calls the performers *mimae*, Seneca calls them *meretrices*.[57] In fact, they were both. Flora's games were famous for their erotic nature,[58] but the *mimae* sang and danced at other dramatic festivals too.[59] Here is Lucretius discussing dreams, and the effect of sitting day after day watching the games:[60]

> Per multos itaque illa dies eadem obuersantur
> ante oculos, etiam uigilantes ut uideantur
> cernere saltantis et mollia membra mouentis
> et citharae liquidum carmen chordasque loquentes
> auribus accipere . . .

> So for many days the same things pass before their eyes, with the result that even when they are awake they seem to see dancers with their soft limbs moving, and hear in their ears the liquid song of the lyre and its speaking strings . . .

Clearly Propertius was not uniquely impressionable.

Part of the problem in imagining this Roman *demi-monde* is the inadequacy of the English language to describe it. To think of these young women as 'whores', 'tarts' or 'hookers' is grossly misleading. And it is not just a question of modern idiom. Sir James Frazer, in his 1929 translation of the *Fasti* into what must even then have been very archaic English, calls the girls at Flora's games 'a crowd of drabs'.[61] But drab is just what they were not; what these girls had was *glamour*.

(I don't, of course, want to imply that prostitution itself is in any way glamorous. But a beautiful body and the ability to sing and dance have always provided young women—and young men too—with an escape route out of poverty.)

Our literary sources, with their emphasis on the élite, mention by name only the most successful women in this profession. Dionysia was a famous dancer in the seventies BC, whose 200,000 HS appearance fee at the games is referred to in Cicero's defence of Roscius the actor.[62] Otherwise we hear only of those who were the mistresses of prominent men—Nicopolis of Sulla,[63] Flora of the young Pompey,[64] Tertia of Verres,[65] Cytheris of Antony and Cornelius Gallus,[66] Quintilia of a senior senator in the time of Caligula.[67] Such stars would hardly be available for Anna Perenna's festival, but the girls who were—the *plebs scaenica*, as Statius calls them[68]—were surely artists in the same profession.

71

IV

Ovid takes pride in giving all the rival versions of the identity of Anna Perenna, and he marks out the last one as 'not unlike the truth'.[69] This is the tale that Anna was an old woman who fed the plebeians with hot cakes during their secession to the Mons Sacer.

An old woman providing hot cakes may well have been a feature of the festival, as we know she was two days later at the Liberalia.[70] So it is possible that the story of the hungry plebeians originated as an aetiology for the plebeian festival of Anna Perenna. If so, however, Ovid chooses not to make it explicit. At this point it is necessary to distinguish carefully between two different sorts of argument. It is one thing to make inferences—necessarily tentative and provisional—about earlier aetiologies *not* exploited by Ovid, for which nevertheless his text may provide some tenuous evidence; it is something else entirely to follow the sequence of thought in his text in order to see how *he* used the material. In this second category, what is interesting in Ovid's presentation is the way the story of the old lady is presupposed in his next section (item 3 in our summary).

Here his task is to explain why the girls sing indecent songs. I suggest that the songs are the ones 'learned in the theatre', and that the aetiological story of Mars and Minerva is the plot of a mime. Certainly the laughter at the end of it is reminiscent of other Ovidian stories which have been thought to derive from mime,[71] and for this particular plot we even have an author and title for the likely source. D. Laberius wrote a mime called *Anna Peranna*, of which the only surviving fragment (*conlabella osculum*, 'give me a kiss on the lips') would fit the unveiling scene very well.[72]

In this scenario, Anna is an old woman who has just been made a goddess.[73] That clearly identifies her as the old lady from Bovillae in the previous section—but here her business is not just with hot cakes. Mars comes to her as a besotted young man might come to a *lena*, to fix him up with the girl he wants. What exactly is a *lena*? John Barsby has a good note on the subject:[74]

> The word is difficult to translate into modern English (bawd, procuress, go-between, madam, brothel-keeper). It denotes a woman who for her own profit arranges introductions between girls and men, and covers a wide range of operations, from those of the professional brothel-keeper employing a large establishment to those of the old nurse arranging liaisons for a particular client.

She was a familiar type in comic drama, including mime,[75] from where she was taken over by the love-poets of Roman elegy.

Phryne in Tibullus, Acanthis in Propertius, Dipsas in Ovid's *Amores*,[76] all do what Anna does here, but from the point of view of the supposedly impoverished poet-lover they appear not as genial old ladies but as witches and drunken hags. Such a character appears also in the *Fasti* (in book II on the Feralia), an old woman with girls, drunk and engaged in magic.[77] Here, however, the *lena* is seen from a different angle; in this story Mars is a *dives amator*, just the sort of customer she likes best, the rival the love-poets hate and fear. Cheating him makes a comic happy ending, and provides, I think, an example of those 'tales unworthy of the gods' to which Varro objected in the theatre of his day.[78]

Let us return for a moment to the old lady from Bovillae. She wears a *mitra*, which was a head-dress associated with easterners,[79] and her hot cakes are described as *rustica* and *fumantia*. Those three words happen to appear in the opening passage of the pseudo-Virgilian poem *Copa*, where the Syrian dancing-girl advertises the pleasures of her tavern.[80] Both trades, tavern-keeping and erotic dancing, were associated with Syrians at Rome.[81] Now, Anna is an eastern name, Jewish or Phoenician (hence Dido's sister),[82] and a tavern might well be the source of the hot cakes. It might also be a source of partners for the blessed participants in Anna Perenna's festival. We know that jurists regarded tavern-keepers as potential *lenae*; as Ulpian observed, many such women kept girls for prostitution on the pretext that they were waitresses.[83] There is an inscription from the Samnite town of Aesernia giving the bill at a tavern: wine and bread, one *as*; supper, two *asses*; fodder for mule, two *asses*; girl, eight *asses* (the customer comments, 'that mule will be the ruin of me').[84]

I suggest, then, that Ovid wants us to see Anna as Laberius had portrayed her in his mime—a cheerful old lady whose establishment provided pleasures of more than one sort. My guess is that Laberius' *Anna Peranna* was a two-act play—first the secession, the cakes and the deification of Anna, then the Mars and Minerva comedy—with the *archimima* in the role of a landlady plying the different parts of her trade for men and gods respectively.[85]

But why does she come from Bovillae? It seems a totally gratuitous detail, and one which makes no topographical sense. Anna Perenna's festival took place at the first milestone on the Via Flaminia; the Mons Sacer, scene of the aetiological cake distribution, was just beyond the third milestone on the Via Nomentana.[86] Both those roads ran north-wards out of Rome, but Bovillae was thirteen miles *south*, on the Via Appia.

Here we must remember Io. As Ovid tells us (658), some earlier mythographer had identified Anna Perenna as the 'Inachian cow'. If Laberius—or anyone—was now presenting her in a realistic human story, the supernatural element had to be rationalised away. It was a familiar technique; as the philosopher Dicaearchus observed, 'by eliminating the excessively fabulous one reduces it, by reasoning, to a natural meaning'.[87] Did Theseus really kill the monstrous Minotaur? No, said the Athenian historians Philochorus and Demon: he defeated king *Minos* and his general *Tauros*. Was Cyrus of Persia really suckled by a bitch? No, says Herodotus, but by a woman called *Kyno*. Were Romulus and Remus really suckled by a she-wolf? No, said Licinius Macer, but by a woman called *Lykaina*.[88] Was Anna Perenna really bovine? No, said Laberius (or whoever): she came from Bovillae.[89]

Ovid's text has led us into the complexities of several overlapping milieux—ritual, prostitution, dramaturgy, mythography—with which his Roman readers were no doubt much more familiar than we are. My final suggestion may seem far-fetched, but perhaps it would not have been so for them.

We recall that the *mimae* at Flora's games, and no doubt elsewhere, were *meretrices*. When the aedile hired them, did he negotiate with a *lena*, or an *archimima*? I think the two categories must have overlapped. A successful *meretrix* might graduate in middle age to the business-woman status of a *lena*; when she got a good booking for her girls at the *ludi scaenici*, why shouldn't there be a part in it for her? It is quite possible to imagine her as still a star, but now taking on comic roles rather than just doing the glamour. If we are right to think of Laberius writing a play about a *lena* who was also a landlady, perhaps he cast it for a *lena* who was also a leading lady.

Whatever the likelihood of that, I think we can at least be sure that the same girls could be hired for Anna Perenna's festival, and that part of what they provided there was songs and dances from their repertoire. It is quite possible that the aetiological myth Ovid insists on as 'true' had been created for the mimic stage only two generations earlier. Why not? For the 'blessed ones' with their chorus girls under the spread togas, it made a lot more sense than Io or Themis.

8

Valerius Antias and the Palimpsest of History

I

Historiography began at Rome about 200 BC, with the *Roman Histories* ('Ρωμαϊκά) of Q. Fabius Pictor and L. Cincius Alimentus.[1] During the following two centuries, the history of Rome from the foundation (or even earlier) was successively recounted by C. Acilius, A. Postumius Albinus, M. Porcius Cato, L. Cassius Hemina, L. Calpurnius Piso Frugi, C. Sempronius Tuditanus, Cn. Gellius, C. Licinius Macer, T. Pomponius Atticus, Valerius Antias, Q. Aelius Tubero, T. Livius of Patavium and Dionysius of Halicarnassus; and there may well have been others.

As Polybius pointed out,[2] a historian whose subject had been thoroughly dealt with by earlier writers

> must either commit the disreputable act of claiming as his own what is really the work of others, or else must clearly be wasting his labour, since there is no denying the fact that the material which is the object of his research and composition has already been adequately recorded and handed down to posterity by his predecessors.

Livy, however, took a different line: even on hackneyed subjects there are always new writers, who hope to provide either more accurate information or at least a more elegant style of narrative.[3] Presumably each of the authors in the Roman historiographical tradition claimed to be offering something new, or at least different, in their respective versions of *ab urbe condita*. For some authors (Tuditanus and Atticus,

75

for instance), the new element might be just chronological accuracy, with no more than a skeleton narrative. For others, it was a huge expansion of the narrative itself.

Looking back over the whole tradition, Dionysius observed that the pioneers Fabius and Cincius had written in detail about the foundation story, and about what was for them recent history, but only 'summarily' about 'early history after the foundation'.[4] The pseudo-historical details he himself narrates, like those of Livy in the first decade, must have been progressively created by their predecessors, the succession of historians and annalists in the second and first centuries BC.[5]

It is important to remember what the 'expansive' historians were doing. Each had his own interpretation of the events, and to create plausible details in order to support that interpretation was just what he and his educated readers had been trained to do, in their *controuersia* exercises at the rhetorical school. His predecessors' material, whether authentic or not, was the equivalent of the *thesis* set by the *rhetor*: his job was to reinterpret that material, freely elaborating the 'facts' where necessary, in order to convince his readers of his own version of the events.[6] The Roman past was never a neutral, value-free area for the exercise of objective research; the historians' creative reinterpretations were for the sake of exploiting a 'usable past' for their own times.[7] And the result, as we see it in Livy and Dionysius, is a composite narrative inheriting the interpretations and reinterpretations of six or seven generations of creative historiography—a sort of palimpsest of accumulated tendentiousness.

It is too easy to ignore that creative accumulation, especially when exciting archaeological discoveries seem to confirm the historicity of the Roman tradition. The remains of an eighth-century wall have been found below the north slope of the Palatine;[8] but that does not mean that the story of Romulus and Remus is true. Similarly, although the late sixth-century dedication by 'Poplios Valesios' and his *suodales* at Satricum reveals Publius Valerius as a historical character, it does not validate as authentic the acts attributed to P. Valerius 'Publicola' in our literary sources.[9] I believe that, on the contrary, the alleged *res gestae* of Publicola are a particularly fine example of historical creativity; but before exploring the historiography of the patrician Valerii, we should briefly consider the more general question of Roman family traditions and their effect on Roman history.

One index of the Romans' perception of themselves and their past is provided by their coinage. Progressively through the second and first centuries BC—that is, at the same time as the development of the Roman historiographical tradition—a marked change occurs in the design of Roman coins. More and more the standard symbols of the Roman community were replaced by 'private' types, referring in particular to the family of the moneyer responsible for the design.[10] Tonio Hölscher sums up the development in a striking formulation:[11]

> La 'Storia' appare qui non più come patrimonio comune della collettività, ma viene frammentata in 'storie', che per interessi e conoscenza particolari erano ritagliate su singole famiglie della *nobilitas*.

It had evidently become important for Roman aristocrats to familiarise the Roman people (who voted magistrates into office) with the glorious history of their own *gentes*.[12]

The coinage was one medium for doing that; the stage, and particularly the *fabula praetexta*, was probably another.[13] A third, I think, was historiography—for there was evidently a mass audience for at least some types of history.[14] At any rate, whatever their audience, there certainly were historians who wrote to gratify noble families: Plutarch tells us so in his account of the sons of Numa, supposedly ancestors of the Calpurnii, Pinarii, Pomponii and Marcii,[15] and I think we may also infer a historian who systematically defended the patrician Claudii against the equally systematic denigration of them by one of his predecessors.[16] Historians who were themselves of noble family were naturally tempted to exaggerate the glory of their own ancestors; Livy remarks that Licinius Macer was prone to that fault.[17]

The historical traditions of the patrician Valerii were the subject of Friedrich Münzer's inaugural dissertation for the University of Berlin. Defending his thesis on 26 June 1891, the young Münzer came to a firm conclusion:[18]

> Valeria igitur gens de re publica Romana optime merita erat omnibusque temporibus domi atque foris excellebat. Attamen permulta exstant mendacia in rebus eorum, quae e singulis fabulis narrationibusque orta ab uno uiro diligenter collecta, exculta, historiae inserta sunt. [. . .] Fabularum pars de sacris gentiliciis, de caerimoniis funebribus, de aedibus, de statuis, de cognominibus, aliis rebus originem ducebant, falsi honores ac triumphi iam in stemmate et elogiis legebantur, res gestae in laudationibus augebantur. Sed is, qui has res omnes congessit, turpiores gloriosiores reddebat,

nouas addebat, eas quae de aliis tradebantur ad Valerios referebat, uetustiores scriptores eo consilio emendabat, Valeriorum erga plebem fauorem laudibus efferebat, certus quidam auctor est, Valerius Antias.

So the *gens Valeria* had deserved very well of the Roman Republic, and was prominent at all periods in both internal and external affairs. And yet there are many conspicuous falsehoods among their deeds, which grew out of particular stories and narratives and were carefully collected, developed and planted in the historical record by a single man. [. . .] Some of the stories originated in family rituals, funeral ceremonies, temples, statues, *cognomina*, etc; spurious magistracies and triumphs could already be found in family trees and epitaphs; achievements were magnified in eulogies. But the man who collected all these items, glorified the shameful, added new ones, attributed other people's traditions to the Valerii, deliberately 'corrected' the older authorities, praised to the skies the favour shown by the Valerii to the *plebs*—he is one particular author, Valerius Antias.

Following in Münzer's footsteps a century later (and as a tribute to that now unfashionable historian), I shall analyse the Valerian element in twelve well-known episodes of early Roman history, in the hope of identifying part of Valerius Antias' contribution to the palimpsest.

II

1. *The treaty of Romulus and T. Tatius.* When the Sabines under T. Tatius made war on Rome to recover their kidnapped daughters, the final battle took place in what was later the Forum—the valley between the Capitol and the Palatine.[19] Neither side was able to get the upper hand, and the issue was finally decided by the intervention of the young women themselves, now no longer Sabine *virgines* but Roman *matronae*. In Livy's dramatic scene (immortalized by Jacques-Louis David), the women rush into the battle itself, 'among the flying weapons'; in Ovid, Plutarch and Dio, with more regard for probability, they come out with their children between the battle lines before the engagement can begin;[20] Dionysius of Halicarnassus, whose source here is probably Cn. Gellius, keeps them out of the battle altogether and presents their plea as a formal embassy to Tatius.[21]

78

Dionysius' detailed narrative continues with allusions to the treaty at the Comitium and the purification at the shrine of Cloacina.[22] He then reports that after the treaty, Tatius and three noble Sabines remained in Rome with their friends, followers and clients. One of the three was Volusus Valerius, later referred to by Dionysius as an ancestor of P. Valerius Publicola.[23]

Now, it is clear from all the surviving accounts of these events that it was the pleas of the women themselves, either *en masse* or through their spokeswoman Hersilia,[24] that brought about the treaty and the 'mingling' of the two peoples.[25] Plutarch, however, in his life of Publicola, refers to a different version:[26]

> Publicola was evidently descended from a Valerius of old who had been most responsible for the Sabines and Romans becoming one people instead of enemies; for it was he in particular who persuaded the kings to come together to the same place and make peace.

The reference to the treaty at the Comitium is unmistakable,[27] but in this scenario what matters is not the women's appeal but a *suasoria* speech from Volusus Valerius. Not surprisingly, all the surviving historians of the reign of Romulus, including Plutarch himself, prefer the more dramatic story. But the author from whom Plutarch took most of his material on Publicola evidently thought it worth while to play down the bared breasts and the pathetic babies in order to glorify the Valerii.

2. The calling of Numa. After the disappearance of Romulus and the subsequent interregnum, the Romans resolved to offer the kingship to Numa Pompilius of Cures.[28] An embassy of leading senators, representing both the Roman and the Sabine factions of the community, was sent to ask Numa to accept the responsibility.[29] He was reluctant, but yielded in the end to the advice of his father Pompon, seconded either by his brothers (in Dionysius) or by his kinsman Marcius (in Plutarch).[30]

It seems therefore that there were at least two different versions of the embassy scene, with its opportunity for deliberative speeches. In the version followed by Plutarch, two of the Roman ambassadors are named. One of them was Proculus—that is, presumably the Julius Proculus who had brought the message from the deified Romulus—and the other was 'Velesus' of the Sabine faction.[31] Once again, therefore, a Valerius is inserted into the story to persuade the protagonist to carry out his destined role for the good of Rome.[32]

79

3. *The avenging of Lucretia.* The tragedy of Lucretia requires her to have a father and a husband, to hear her speech and witness her suicide. The heroic tale of Brutus requires a moment when his feigned stupidity is thrown off and the liberator leads the rising against the tyrants. Perhaps the two stories were originally independent, but if so they were soon merged into one; in the dramatic scene our sources offer, Brutus has a necessary place. Lucretia's audience, therefore, must consist of Sp. Lucretius Tricipitinus, L. Tarquinius Collatinus and L. Iunius Brutus. So what is P. Valerius doing in this company?

In Livy, Lucretia sends for her father to come from Rome, and for her husband to come from the camp at Ardea. Collatinus happens to be on his way to Rome with Brutus when they meet Lucretia's messenger; Brutus therefore comes with him to Collatia.[33] Lucretia's father comes with P. Valerius (son of Volesus), but no explanation of the latter's presence is offered.[34] In Dionysius, Lucretia goes to Rome herself, to her father's house where 'some kinsmen happened to be present'. She then asks him to send for all the friends and kinsmen he can find, and thus tells her story to a gathering of 'the most distinguished men'. One of them is P. Valerius, who is sent to the camp to summon Collatinus; he meets Collatinus with Brutus on their way to Rome (as in Livy), and all three repair to Lucretius' house. Brutus reveals his true self and leads the company in the oath to free Rome from the tyrants. Valerius asks who will summon the assembly of the people (answer, Brutus as *tribunus celerum*).[35] It is obvious enough that in both the Livian and the Dionysian versions Valerius' presence is deliberately contrived, and not an integral part of the drama.[36]

Again, Plutarch's life of Publicola shows what has happened. His Valerius is Brutus' right-hand man in driving out the kings, and Brutus wants him as his consular colleague (when Collatinus is elected, Valerius withdraws from public life).[37] Naturally, he has to have a role in the Lucretia story, and his presence at the catalytic moment of her suicide gives him the opportunity for a speech contributing to the foundation of the Republic. Part of it, no doubt, was the constitutional query in Dionysius.

4. *The conspiracy.* Tarquin's ambassadors come to the infant Republic to demand the tyrant's property. They make contact with a group of young nobles dissatisfied with the new regime: the Vitellii, brothers of Brutus' wife, who involve Brutus' own sons in the plot, and the Aquillii, sons of Collatinus' sister.[38]

As Fausto Zevi has convincingly argued, the wealth of the Tarquins and the question of its ownership are probably authentic sixth-century issues, preserved perhaps by the author of the 'Cumaean chronicle'.[39] The conspiracy, however, is transparently a late element in the tradition. The earliest known Vitellius, son of a freedman cobbler, was alleged to have got rich as an informer and by trafficking in confiscated estates. If that was in the Sullan proscriptions, one can imagine a late annalist using the unpopular name for the first traitors of the Republic.[40]

The story as told by Dionysius and Plutarch runs as follows. Brutus is against releasing the Tarquins' treasure, but Collatinus speaks in favour and narrowly prevails. The envoys pretend to be making arrangements, but are secretly plotting with the Aquillii and Vitellii to bring back the tyrants.[41] The conspirators meet at the house of the Aquillii and swear a great and dreadful oath on bowls of human blood, just as the Catilinarians were alleged to have done at the house of Laeca.[42] They vow to kill the consuls, and write to Tarquin to keep him informed. But all has been overheard by a slave, Vindicius; rather than report to the consuls (for the guilty men are Brutus' sons and brothers-in-law and Collatinus' nephews), he goes to P. Valerius, who is known to be kindly and approachable.[43]

Valerius, like Cicero in 63, realises that written evidence is needed to incriminate the plotters. Leaving his wife to guard Vindicius, he sends his brother Marcus to surround the royal residence, and goes himself, with a band of friends and clients, to the house of the Aquillii. The letters are seized, and the conspirators forcibly dragged before the consuls.[44]

There follows Brutus' condemnation and execution of his own sons, a great scene which must surely predate the invention of the Catilinarian scenario.[45] Collatinus, unable to match Brutus' self-control, wants to spare his nephews. Valerius protects Vindicius, whom the Aquillii are claiming back, and complains to Brutus of Collatinus' weakness. Brutus demands his colleague's abdication. Collatinus, aware of the people's hostility, resigns his consulship and goes into exile. Valerius is immediately elected in his place.[46]

This version of Collatinus' abdication is not what we find elsewhere. In Cicero, Collatinus is an innocent man unjustly forced into exile merely because of his name; that version goes back at least as far as L. Piso in the late second century.[47] Livy combines the traditional innocence of Collatinus with the new Catilinarian plot: in his version Brutus and Valerius are already consuls, and Vindicius takes his information directly to them.[48] Livy thus avoids the element of the conspiracy story which is prominent in Dionysius and (especially) Plutarch, namely the heroic role of P. Valerius as a private citizen.

The story is entirely coherent without him, and better focused on the tragedy of Brutus. Thus Virgil:[49]

> Vis et Tarquinios reges animamque superbam
> ultoris Bruti, fascisque uidere receptos?
> consulis imperium hic primus saeuasque securis
> accipiet, natosque pater noua bella mouentis
> ad poenam pulchra pro libertate uocabit,
> infelix, utcumque ferent ea facta minores:
> uincet amor patriae laudumque immensa cupido.

> Do you want to see also the Tarquin kings, and the haughty soul of Brutus the avenger and the *fasces* regained? He will be the first to receive the authority of a consul and the cruel axes, and when his sons stir up a new war he will summon them to their punishment for the sake of glorious freedom—unhappy man, however posterity relates the deed! What will prevail is love of one's country and a boundless appetite for praise.

The story of the captured letters is trivial by comparison. It must have been written later than December 63 BC, with the evident intention of giving Valerius the protagonist's role.

5. *Tarquin's field.* After the exposure of the conspiracy, the Romans reverse their decision about Tarquin's property and give it to the people to plunder. However, the land 'between the city and the Tiber' is dedicated to Mars, and the grain from it thrown into the river.[50] Tarquin's field becomes the Campus Martius.

But even this fundamental aetiology did not go unchallenged. Zosimus, narrating the history of the Secular Games, refers to a Greek dedicatory inscription on the altar of Dis at the bend of the Tiber (fig. 1):[51] 'I, Publius Valerius Publicola, dedicated the corn-bearing plain to Hades and Persephone; and I led the festival in honour of Hades and Persephone for the freedom of the Romans.' Censorinus, who had certainly read Valerius Antias, attributes the first Secular Games to Publicola in the first year of the Republic (see Appendix B below); and Valerius Maximus says the same, even calling Publicola the first consul.[52]

Zosimus and Valerius Maximus link this item with the story of the miraculous discovery of the altar of Dis by Valesius the Sabine, who became the first Manius Valerius (named after the *Manes*).[53] Valerius Maximus, who (to judge by his name) probably belonged to the patrician *gens*, mentions that Valesius had a villa at Eretum, by the Tiber eighteen miles north of Rome; the Valerii of the late Republic certainly had a villa there, as we know from a poem by Messalla Corvinus' niece Sulpicia.[54] The context of all this material is probably not the Augustan Secular Games of 17 BC, but rather the period when the *saeculum* was actually due to end, in the forties BC.[55] The Valerii Messallae, with consuls in 61, 53, 32, 31 and 29, were particularly influential about that time.

6. *Horatius Cocles*. Tarquin gains the alliance of Porsenna, whose assault on Rome comes in the second or third year of the Republic, and the second or third consulship of P. Valerius Publicola.[56] Porsenna's army takes the Janiculum, leaving Rome defenceless while the bridge still stands. So at any rate Livy and Dionysius say: their narratives seem to presuppose a defensive circuit that included the Janiculum, ignoring the wall parallel to the river.[57] In Plutarch, on the other hand, the Romans fight Porsenna 'in front of the gate, by the river', in a topographically unintelligible engagement which *precedes* the heroic holding of the bridge by Horatius Cocles.[58]

These difficulties are probably the result of late annalists incorporating a hitherto unattached episode into their historical narratives. Like 'Cincinnatus at the plough', so 'Cocles at the bridge' was evidently an exemplary scene, of which the precise historical context was less important than its power as a paradigm of virtue. That at least is how it appears in our earliest sources, Polybius and Cicero.[59]

It was a famous story,[60] too famous to be simply appropriated by the Valerii. But the Valerian annalist had other techniques to hand. In Dionysius and Plutarch, Publicola commands the Romans in a pitched battle with Porsenna's forces, but is gravely wounded and carried out of the battle; that saves him from comparison with Cocles when the bridge has to be held, but he is back in action immediately afterwards, killing five thousand Etruscans in battle.[61] Not only that, but Cocles himself is subtly denigrated. In Dionysius and Plutarch, still evidently following the same source, he gets wounded in the buttocks by an Etruscan spear-thrust.[62] The traditional hero loses his dignity so as not to outshine Valerius Publicola.

83

7. *Cloelia.* After Cocles and Mucius 'Scaevola', the third tale of Roman bravery attached to Porsenna's siege is that of Cloelia.[63] At the top of the Sacra Via, opposite the temple of Jupiter Stator, was a bronze statue of a girl on horseback.[64] It was explained as the statue of Cloelia, one of the group of girls and boys sent as hostages to Porsenna, erected in her honour after she had escaped back across the Tiber.

One version of her story was that she had got hold of a horse and thus been able to ford the river.[65] Others said she swam across; but Porsenna was so impressed by her bravery that when she was returned to him, he not only freed her but presented her with a war-horse, a suitable gift for a girl with the courage of a man.[66] An alternative to that version, equally explicit in its exemplary message, was that Porsenna wrote to the Romans asking them to give her a 'masculine' reward, and they put up the equestrian statue.[67] (However, the story could also be told as a paradigm of female decorum. According to Livy, Porsenna allowed Cloelia to take some of the hostages with her to freedom; she chose the youngest, as being the most vulnerable to abuse.[68])

Here too, as with Cocles, Dionysius and Plutarch have a more complex narrative, and one which involves P. Valerius Publicola. The consul has asked Porsenna to arbitrate between Rome and the Tarquins on the question of their property. Porsenna agrees, and sits in judgement with his son Arruns. This young man, 'wise beyond his years', has already advised his father to seek the Romans' friendship.[69] The news of Cloelia's escape, with the other girl hostages, comes as the hearing is in session. Publicola, whose own daughter is one of the fugitives, assures Porsenna that they will be returned, and goes to bring them back. But Tarquin, with his Latin son-in-law Octavius Mamilius, treacherously attacks them as they return. Publicola's daughter escapes from the *mêlée*, and Arruns Porsenna comes with his cavalry to the rescue.[70] The king gives his verdict to the Romans and banishes Tarquin and Mamilius from his camp.

Although Plutarch does not say so, his source must have made Valeria's escape from the ambush more than just an act of self-preservation. Presumably it was she who raised the alarm and thus enabled Arruns to save the day. Her role in the story *must* be that of a heroine, to justify the revisionist claim that the equestrian statue was not of Cloelia at all, but of Valeria.[71]

8. *The coming of the Claudii.* The story of Attus Clausus' arrival at Rome with his family and followers is generally regarded nowadays as

an essentially authentic memory of archaic conditions.[72] One version of it, perhaps Augustan, dated the event to the time of Romulus and Tatius,[73] but Livy, Dionysius and Plutarch agree in assigning it to Publicola's fourth and last consulship (504 BC by the Varronian reckoning).[74]

The context is a war with the Sabines, in which Publicola's brother Marcus, as consul the previous year, was supposed to have killed thirteen thousand of the enemy without a single Roman casualty.[75] According to Plutarch, though Livy and Dionysius are silent on the matter, Publicola took the initiative in urging Clausus to come to Rome, and welcomed him 'with eager goodwill' when he did so.[76] Once again, a familiar story has been given a new, and Valerian, emphasis.

9. The first dictator. The office of *magister populi*, or dictator, was instituted in the consulship of T. Larcius (i.e. either 501 or 498 BC), and the first to hold the office was Larcius himself.[77] That at least was the predominant tradition, but there was a late variant, preserved in Festus and known to Livy (but rejected by him), which named the first *magister populi* as M'. Valerius M.f. Volesi n.—that is, Publicola's nephew Manius, son of Marcus Valerius the consul of 505.[78]

Why was Valerius' name substituted? Livy tells us: according to this version, the dictatorship became necessary because the consuls were untrustworthy, suspected of being supporters of Tarquin. With that scenario, it was of course impossible that one of the consuls should himself be appointed dictator.[79] Livy objects that Valerius was not a *consularis*; and if the Romans had wanted a Valerius, why did they not choose his father Marcus, whose improbably spectacular victory in the Sabine war surely qualified him?[80]

To the latter objection, at least, there was an answer: M. Valerius was at the grove of Ferentina at Aricia, on an embassy to the Latin cities who were being stirred up by Mamilius, on Tarquin's behalf, to make war on Rome. Like the Athenians at Sparta in 432 BC, he asked leave to speak to the assembly of the enemy alliance.[81] The revisionist version offered the Valerii, father and son, as simultaneous champions of Rome, against external foes and treachery within. Ogilvie is surely right to describe the dictatorship variant as 'a clear case of the *gens Valeria* claiming precedence under the inspired hand of Valerius Antias'.[82]

10. The battle of Lake Regillus. The next time we meet Marcus Valerius, his role is not Thucydidean but Homeric.

85

Even Livy noticed, and tried to explain, the anachronistic nature of the tradition on the battle of Lake Regillus, which presented the leaders of both sides engaged in single combat like the heroes of the *Iliad*.[83] The Romans were commanded by the dictator A. Postumius Albus and his *magister equitum* T. Aebutius Helva, the Latins by Octavius Mamilius, accompanied by his father-in-law, the aged Tarquin, and one or more of Tarquin's sons.[84] T. Herminius, who had stood with Cocles at the bridge, was serving as *legatus*.[85] The duels take place: Postumius against Tarquin (Tarquin wounded), Aebutius against Mamilius (both wounded), Herminius against Mamilius (both killed).[86]

M. Valerius is paired with young Tarquin, but his duel is significantly different. In the first place, it is closely modelled on that of Menelaus and Paris in *Iliad* III. The great hero, brother of a greater, is infuriated at the sight of the king's son vaunting himself; he attacks, and the boastful prince shrinks back among his men to save his life.[87] Secondly, the duel never takes place. As Valerius gallops furiously into the fray, he is hit from the side by an anonymous spear; unlike Pandarus' arrow, which stopped Menelaus in the *Iliad* scene, Valerius' wound is mortal. He falls, and there follows a heroic defence of his body by the two sons of Publicola, who then charge into the Tarquins' lines and die together, outnumbered but defiant.[88]

The tradition on the battle of Lake Regillus is a good example of the 'palimpsest' of history. Its most famous episode was the appearance of the Dioscuri, both in the battle and at Rome, watering their horses at the Lacus Iuturnae.[89] Postumius the dictator vowed a temple to Castor; his son dedicated it, and the day of the dedication was the day of the later *transuectio equitum*, the parade of the knights from the temple of Mars on the Via Appia to the temple of Castor in the Forum.[90] The *transuectio* was instituted in 304 BC, and it is possible that the legend dates from that period.[91]

A similar epiphany of the Dioscuri was supposed to have occurred at the time of the battle of Pydna in 168 BC.[92] One of the praetors of 168 was called Aebutius Helva; and the young officer who took the defeated king of Macedon into custody after the battle was called A. Postumius, probably the A. Postumius Albinus who was later consul in 151. That Albinus was a well-known historian, and a coin-type of one of his kinsmen two generations later shows the Dioscuri watering their horses, as in both versions of the legend.[93] It is natural to suppose that Postumius Albinus' history was the first to elaborate the heroic deeds of Postumius the dictator and his deputy Aebutius Helva at the battle of

Lake Regillus. Albinus wrote in Greek, and may well have found it natural to use a Homeric format for his epic battle.[94]

But do the gallant deaths of Marcus Valerius and his nephews belong to that stratum of the tradition? It seems to me more likely that the episode was added by the Valerian annalist, outdoing his predecessors in Iliadic pastiche. When M. Valerius sees the young Tarquin, his headlong attack is for the family honour, that the Valerii, who expelled the kings, should have the glory also of killing them.[95] It was of course Brutus who expelled the kings—but the Valerian annalist had already inserted Publicola into the liberation story. Brutus killed Tarquin's son Arruns at the battle of the Arsian Wood, and died himself as he did so;[96] M. Valerius' furious charge gives that episode too a Valerian rival. Brutus lost his two sons, but they were traitors; now we are shown Publicola's two sons dying in glorious battle. The parallels are too rhetorically convenient to be accidental.

11. The secession. The news of Tarquin's death marked a turning point in the history of the early Republic. Sallust and Livy both note the moment as the end of internal harmony and the beginning of the 'struggle of the orders'.[97] So the next great story in the tradition is that of the secession of the plebeians to the Sacred Mount. It was a tale many times told and re-told, as the variants show,[98] and here too there is a Valerian stratum in the palimpsest.

The political crisis in 494 BC led to the appointment as dictator of Manius Valerius, another brother of Publicola, previously unheard of.[99] Despite his advanced age, he leads a successful campaign against the Sabines, celebrates a triumph, and then resigns in protest at the Senate's refusal to give relief to the debtors. The secession follows. The plebeians are eventually persuaded to return by wise old Menenius Agrippa, who tells them the fable of the Belly and the Limbs.[100] That must be an old story, but by 46 BC there was a newer one, replacing Menenius.

In his *Brutus*, published that year, Cicero includes Manius Valerius the dictator among his examples of ancient eloquence; for it was he who by his speech put an end to the discord between the orders, and was given the honorary *cognomen* 'Maximus' for that very reason.[101] That was also how it appeared in the inscription under Valerius' statue in the Forum of Augustus: 'Plebem de sacro monte deduxit, gratiam cum patribus reconciliauit.'[102]

12. Coriolanus. My final example concerns a lady who had a mystical experience at the Capitoline temple. The year was 488 BC;

Marcius Coriolanus and his Volscian army were just five miles from the city. Invincible and implacable, he had dismissed with contempt three consecutive embassies from Rome, and it seemed that nothing could stop him from taking vengeance on his ungrateful country. The lady was Valeria—either Publicola's daughter, some twenty years after her adventure as one of Porsenna's hostages, or else his sister, 'a woman of mature years and prudent judgement'.[103]

Valeria is among the women thronging the temple as suppliants when she is suddenly seized by a divine inspiration. (Plutarch, who was interested in this phenomenon, says it was like those Homeric situations when one of the gods puts an idea in the hero's mind.[104]) Taking her stand at the top of the temple steps, she calls the women together and urges them to act:[105]

> 'Wearing this squalid and shabby garb and taking with us the rest of the women and our children, let us go to the house of Veturia, the mother of Marcius; and placing the children at her knees, let us entreat her with tears to have compassion both upon us, who have given her no cause for grief, and upon our country, now in the direst peril, and beg of her to go to the enemy's camp, taking along her grandchildren and their mother and all of us—for we must attend her with our children—and becoming the suppliant of her son, to ask and implore him not to inflict any irreparable mischief on his country. For while she is lamenting and entreating, a feeling of compassion and tender reasonableness will come over the man. His heart is not so hard and invulnerable that he can hold out against a mother who grovels at his knees.'

The women go to Veturia, the mother of Coriolanus. Valeria delivers a speech. Veturia is reluctant. Valeria renews her pleas. Veturia yields. After the women's embassy to Coriolanus has succeeded in its aim, a temple is set up to Fortuna Muliebris, with Valeria chosen as its first priestess.[106]

It is perfectly clear that Valeria is not integral to the story. What turns Coriolanus back has to be the pleading of his mother and his wife.[107] Why should they need someone else to suggest it to them? Valeria's role here is like that of the Valerius in our first example, who suggested making peace to the two kings after the intervention of the Sabine women.[108]

III

We have seen how twelve famous stories of early Roman history were adjusted, or rewritten, in such a way as to provide a starring role in each of them for a member of the patrician Valerii. It seems to me beyond serious doubt that all of them are the work of one author, a historian whose purpose was systematically to enhance the glory of the Valerian name.

Some of his characteristics stand out very clearly. His work was highly rhetorical, taking every opportunity to insert significant speeches (items 1, 2, 3, 8, 9, 11, 12). It is noticeable that neither Numa (2) nor the mother of Coriolanus (12) yields to persuasion at the first speech;[109] a second is needed, offering the author the chance to demonstrate his rhetorical versatility. The content of the speeches was resolutely patriotic, whether in putting the justice of Rome's case to her enemies (8) or urging harmony on warring factions within the citizen body (11).

But the author could also compose scenes of dramatic action (4, 7, 10), recycling Homer for the battle of Lake Regillus and contemporary events for the conspiracy of the Vitellii. Perhaps 'melodramatic' would be a better description, in the light of young Valeria's desperate escape from Tarquin's treacherous attack. The action, like the speeches, was clearly designed as exemplary, setting up the Valerii as models of courage, wisdom and piety. And if the process involved subtly devaluing some old-established reputations, like those of Brutus or Cocles (3, 6), or even displacing them entirely, like Menenius Agrippa or Larcius the first dictator (11, 9), no doubt that was a small price to pay for the coherence and immediacy of the narrative.

It was written between the exposure of the Catilinarians in December 63 (4) and Cicero's writing of the *Brutus* in 46 (11). In an important but inconspicuous article, Duncan Cloud long ago demonstrated that the *terminus post quem* of 63 BC applies also to Livy's account of the trial of Horatius for killing his sister, and that Livy's source for that episode was probably Valerius Antias.[111] As it happens, none of our twelve items features in the surviving fragments of Antias, though two of them come very close.[112] But who else could the Valerian annalist have been? Münzer was surely right to assume that it was Valerius Antias who contributed this particular element to the palimpsest of history.

9

The Minucii and their Monument

I

The Minucii were a family of some importance in republican Rome. Public *monumenta* of various sorts perpetuated their name. The Via Minucia, for instance, provided the most direct route to Brundisium, across the uplands of Apulia.[1] The Pons Minucius was one of the main bridges on the Via Flaminia.[2] A celebrated Porticus Minucia in the Campus Martius was built by M. Minucius Rufus (*cos.* 110 BC) from the spoils of his long campaign against the Thracian Scordisci.[3] The early-imperial Porticus Minucia *frumentaria* extended the family's name to the third century AD, with the *curatores aquarum et Minuciae*.[4] (One or other of these porticoes was the great colonnade to the north of Via delle Botteghe Oscure, marked conspicuously as 'MINI[CIA]' on the Severan marble plan.[5])

Roads, bridges and porticoes are one thing; a city gate at Rome is quite another. The Porta Minucia is unique as an example of a gate with the name of a Roman family.[6] It was twice annotated in Festus' etymological dictionary; Festus' full text is lost, but in Paulus' epitome the items are as follows:[7]

> Minucia porta Romae dicta est ab ara Minuci, quem deum putabant.
> Minucia porta appellata est eo, quod proxima esset sacello Minucii.

> The Porta Minucia at Rome was called after the altar of Minucius, who they thought was a god.
> The Porta Minucia was so called for this reason, that it was next to the shrine of Minucius.

90

What exactly was the altar or shrine of Minucius?

Since 'quem deum putabant' is evidently a comment by Paulus, it is not absolutely certain that Minucius was the object of worship at the shrine: the analogy of phrases like *aedes Catuli* or *delubrum Cn. Domitii* makes it formally possible that the genitive proper name referred to the man who built it.[8] However, I know of no example with either *ara* or *sacellum*,[9] and it is surely preferable to suppose that Festus did indeed refer to a *deus Minucius* and a shrine that was sacred to him. Stefan Weinstock accepted that, and was prepared to believe in a 'god of the Gens Minucia' even though all the known Roman 'family divinities' are female.[10]

II

At this point, it may be helpful to look at two denarius issues of about 135–4 BC, that of 'C. Aug.'—i.e. C. Minucius Augurinus—and that of Ti. Minucius C.f. Augurinus, no doubt his brother (fig. 4). I reproduce the descriptions in Michael Crawford's catalogue:[11]

> Spiral column with Aeolic capital, decorated with two bells at the top and two lions' foreparts at the base; standing on column, togate statue holding staff in r. hand; behind each of the lions, corn-ear; on l., togate figure holding loaves (?) in both hands and placing l. foot on modius; on r., togate figure holding *lituus* in r. hand; above, C.AVG. Border of dots.

> Spiral column; standing on column, statue holding staff in r. hand; at base of column, two corn-ears; on l., togate figure holding loaves (?) in both hands and placing l. foot on modius; on r., togate figure holding *lituus* in r. hand; above, ROMA; on l., TI. MINVCI.C.F. upwards; on r., AVGVRINI downwards. Border of dots.

What makes it tempting to associate this scene with the 'altar of Minucius' in Festus is the possibly analogous juxtaposition of altar and column-statue in the *lapis niger* complex, probably of the fourth century BC (fig. 5).[12] Filippo Coarelli argues convincingly that that complex was a shrine (the Volcanal); but some ancient sources identified it as a tomb (of Romulus, Faustulus, or Hostus Hostilius),[13] and others, though recognising it as the Volcanal or *area Volcani*, evidently thought that the column carried an honorific statue to Horatius Cocles.[14]

91

Figure 4.   Coins showing the Minucian monument: denarii by
C. (Minucius) Aug(urinus) and Ti. Minucius C.f. Augurinus, *c.* 135–4 BC.
(Courtesy of the British Museum.)

Figure 5.   Column-statue and altar at the Volcanal.
(From F. Coarelli, *Il foro romano: periodo arcaico* [Rome 1983] 175 fig. 47,
courtesy of Edizioni Quasar.)

We have to allow for the fact that archaic monuments were interpreted, or misinterpreted, in various ways by later generations. It seems to me likely that the same variety of interpretation—shrine, tomb, honorific statue—applied to the Minucian monument as it evidently did to the Volcanal complex.

According to Pliny, the custom of setting up honorific statues on columns was a comparatively ancient one. The examples he gives are the statue of C. Maenius (338 BC), that of C. Duillius (260 BC)—and 'that of Lucius Minucius the *praefectus annonae* outside the Porta Trigemina, paid for by a collection of penny contributions (probably the first time this honour was conferred by the people, as previously by the Senate).'[15] The story of L. Minucius the *praefectus annonae* is told by Livy and Dionysius under the years 440–39 BC, though they report the honorific statue as granted by the Senate, not the people.[16]

Now, the statue on the column in the scene depicted on the coins can hardly be that of the *praefectus annonae*. He should be the togate figure to the left, if Crawford is right to see that figure as carrying loaves, with his foot on a *modius*.[17] The figure to the right, with the *lituus*, must be M. Minucius Faesus, a member of the first college of plebeian augurs.[18] That is, the two most prominent 'historical' Minucii, present at a family monument portraying—whom?

As Tonio Hölscher has well observed, outside the city gate one would expect a tomb, not an honorific statue; and what the coins show may well have been a fifth-century grave monument.[19] The moneyers evidently thought so too, since they give the statue on the column a staff, not a sceptre.[20] If that makes him a man, not a god, then the scene shows a family tomb, no doubt that of the founder of the *gens*.[21]

My suggestion, then, is that we have one archaic monument interpreted three different ways: as a tomb, by the Minucii Augurini moneyers; as an honorific monument, by Pliny's source; and as the altar and shrine of a god Minucius, by the source of Festus. It might seem natural to privilege the first interpretation, on the principle that the Minucii themselves should have known the facts. But if there *was* an altar there, as at the *lapis niger*, then the third interpretation should not be dismissed out of hand.

III

Before we try to analyse the various traditions about the Minucii, there is a topographical question to attend to. If the monument was outside the Porta Trigemina, how could it give its name to the Porta Minucia? What, and where, *was* the 'Minucian Gate'?

Mario Torelli avoids the problem by identifying the Porta Minucia with the Porta Trigemina, the latter replacing the former in a hypothetical rebuilding programme after the sack of the city by the Gauls.[22] But in that case, why would the name 'Porta Minucia' be remembered at all, and need explanation? And if it was remembered,

94

would Festus not have mentioned that it was the old name for the Porta Trigemina? True, we only have Paulus' excerpts; but Paulus on the Porta Scelerata includes in his précis the identification with the Porta Carmentalis, as he does on the other name for the Porta Collina (Agonensis), on which the original Festus text is lost.[23] It is asking too much to suppose that on two separate occasions he chose to omit this sort of information from the items on the Porta Minucia.

It is easier to suppose that there were two gates, so close together that the same monument could be described in relation to either. The approximate site of the Porta Trigemina is established in the vicinity of S. Maria in Cosmedin.[24] According to Coarelli, it was a gate in the wall running north to south parallel to the river, and through it passed a road running east to west, from the valley of the Circus Maximus to the Pons Sublicius.[25] I have argued elsewhere that this view is unlikely to be right, and that the Porta Trigemina was more probably the gate made necessary by the construction of a cross wall perpendicular to the river.[26] It is enough for our purpose here to point out that the Porticus Aemilia, south-west of the Aventine, is twice described by Livy as *extra portam Trigeminam*, which shows that the Trigemina was the gate by which one left to go down the road between the river and the Aventine slope.[27]

The Porticus Aemilia was a good 700 m. away from the site of the gate; but *extra portam* references cover a wide range of distances from the gate concerned, from 1200 m. or more (the Scipionic tombs *extra portam Capenam*) to a close proximity which could equally well be described as *ad portam*.[28]

Lanciani reports Roman paving, presumably imperial, on the line of the modern Clivo di Rocca Savella, which leads from S. Sabina directly down the Aventine hillside to a point about 150 m. south of S. Maria in Cosmedin (fig. 6).[29] This descent, steeper but shorter than the Clivus Publicius, was evidently found useful under the empire, as it has been in medieval and modern times; there is no reason to suppose it was not in use under the Republic as well. Steps down the side of the hill would have saved a long walk round. It is worth remembering the long flight of steps down from the Capitol at the equivalent position outside the Porta Carmentalis;[30] even without the attested paving, it would be reasonable to infer a similar stair or ramp down from the Aventine. If so, there must have been a gate through the 'Servian' wall—but not an important gate, since the exit it commanded was a secondary one.[31] The Porta Minucia would fit very well.

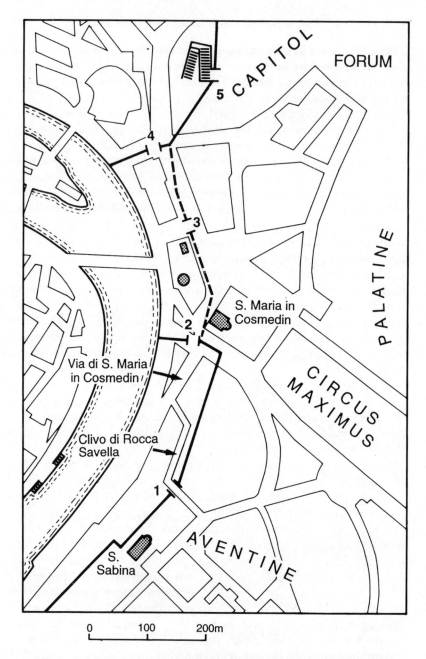

Figure 6.   Western section of the Rome city wall under the Republic;
the dotted line represents the section made obsolete by the two 'cross-walls'
to the river. Gates: 1. Porta Minucia? 2. Porta Trigemina. 3. Porta Flumentana.
4. Porta Carmentalis. 5. Porta Catularia?

At the bottom of this route—in modern terms, roughly where the Clivo di Rocca Savella joins the Via di S. Maria in Cosmedin—is the one place where the Minucian monument could have been, outside one gate and giving its name to another.

IV

In investigating a senatorial family, the historian's first recourse is to the index of T.R.S. Broughton's *Magistrates of the Roman Republic*. Rearranged and numbered in chronological order down to the middle of the second century BC, Broughton's list of Minucii is as follows:

1. M. Minucius Augurinus: q. 509, cos. 497, cos. II 491, leg. envoy 488.
2. P. Minucius Augurinus: cos. 492.
3. L. Minucius P.f.M.n. Esquilinus Augurinus: cos. (Livy) or cos. suff. (Fasti Cap.) 458, Xvir cos. imp. leg. scrib. 450–49, praef. annonae 440–39; tr. pl.?? 439.
4. Q. Minucius P.f.M.n. Esquilinus: cos. 457.
5. Sp. Minucius: pont. max.? 420.
6. M. Minucius: tr. pl. 401.
7. Minucia: Vest. virg. ?-337.
8. Ti. Minucius Augurinus: cos. 305.
9. M. Minucius Faesus: augur 300– .
10. M. Minucius C.f.C.n. Rufus: cos. 221, mag. eq. 217, dict. 217.
11. M. Minucius: tr. pl. 216.
12. Q. Minucius C.f.C.n. Rufus: leg. lieut. 211, aed. pl. 201, pr. 200, propr. 199, cos. 197, leg. amb. 189–8, 183, 174?
13. Q. Minucius Q.f.L.n. Thermus: tr. mil. 202, tr. pl. 201, aed. cur. 198, IIIvir col. deduc. 197–4, pr. 196, promag. 195, cos. 193, procos. 192–0, leg. amb. 189–8.
14. P. Minucius: tr. mil. 193.
15. Q. Minucius: tr. mil. 193, leg. amb. 174, pr. 164?
16. C. Minucius Augurinus: tr. pl. 184? (or 187?)
17. Ti. Minucius Molliculus: pr. peregr. 180.
18. L. Minucius Thermus: leg. lieut. 182–1, 180, 178, leg. envoy 177, leg. amb. 154, 145–4.
19. T. Minucius Rufus: leg. lieut.? (or prefect) 171.

One anomaly is immediately apparent. Nos. 1, 2, 3 and 8 appear in the Augustan *fasti* with the *cognomen* 'Augurinus', which surely derived from the Minucius who was among the first plebeian augurs; as Mommsen pointed out long ago, that fact casts doubt on the authenticity of the 'patrician' Minucii and their fifth-century consulships.[32]

In the preface to his great work, Broughton gave a brief statement of his position on the question of the early *fasti*:[33]

> I am inclined to accept almost the entire list of eponymous magistrates, excepting only a few possible interpolations and the 'Dictator' years . . . [T]he tendency of Roman families to glorify their beginnings led to some falsification of the tradition, as Cicero says (*Brut.* 62; cf. Livy VIII 40.4), but that same emphasis upon ancestral achievements may have assisted in preserving a fuller record of official careers among the great noble families.

I should like to focus on what is conceded here, rather than what is asserted. In the *Brutus* passage to which Broughton refers, Cicero complained about the funerary eulogies preserved by noble families:

> Multa enim scripta sunt in eis quae facta non sunt, falsi triumphi, plures consulatus, genera etiam falsa et ad plebem transitiones, cum homines in alienum eiusdem nominis infunderentur genus.

> Many things are written in them which did not happen—spurious triumphs, multiplied consulships, even false genealogies and transitions to the *plebs*, with people being smuggled into a different family of the same name.

The Minucii offer some fine examples.

Falsi triumphi: the triumph of Ti. Minucius Augurinus (no. 8), though reported in Livy, was not accepted by the compilers of the *fasti triumphales*.[34] *Plures consulatus*: the uncertainty in our sources about the consulships of L. Minucius Augurinus and his supposed brother Q. Minucius Augurinus (nos. 3 and 4) may reflect conflicting traditions in which the Minucii were successful in ejecting rival claimants.[35] *Ad plebem transitiones*: as we have seen, the use of the *cognomen* Augurinus for fifth- and fourth-century consuls implies a claim to patrician descent comparable to that of the Marcii.[36]

Livy too objected to the fictions of the funerary *laudationes*, and added another tainted source, the *tituli* on the *imagines* that noble families kept in their *atria*.[37] Here too the Minucii were guilty: they had on display an *imago* of L. Minucius (no. 3) with an inscription to the effect that he had 'crossed over' to the *plebs* and been co-opted as an

98

eleventh tribune. Livy found this in one of his sources and rightly rejected it; Pliny accepted it at one point (possibly from Piso, whom he used in book XVIII), but elsewhere followed the rival version that Minucius was *praefectus annonae*.[38]

I think it is clear that the Minucii of the early Republic are less a historical than a historiographical phenomenon. Let us therefore look more closely at the various versions of the story of L. Minucius (no. 3).[39]

V

The earliest identifiable version of the story is that given by L. Cincius Alimentus about 200 BC.[40] The Senate received information from Minucius that a certain Sp. Maelius was aiming at kingship; a senior senator proposed that Maelius should be put to death without trial; this was agreed, and the Senate instructed a young patrician called Servilius to carry out the execution. Maelius was just coming out of the Forum when Servilius, a short sword concealed under his arm, approached him and asked to speak to him in private.[41] Maelius told his bodyguards to move away; Servilius drew the sword and stabbed him in the throat. A furious crowd pursued Servilius as he ran back to the Senate-house with his bloodstained weapon, but when he shouted at them that he had killed a tyrant at the Senate's command, they let him go. Thereafter, Servilius was called Ahala, from *ala*, an armpit (where he had kept his sword). The Senate voted that Maelius' house be razed to the ground (hence the open space called 'Aequimaelium'), and that the informant Minucius be honoured with a statue.

Cincius wrote in Greek, and it is clear from Dionysius' report of his narrative that he played on the name Μηνύκιος as implying μήνυσις, information.[42] Minucius was 'the informer', but Dionysius' account of Cincius' version does not reveal the source of his information.

Cicero, who quite frequently cites the Maelius-Servilius story as an example of justifiable killing by a private citizen,[43] comments at one point that Maelius had made himself popular not only by squandering his private fortune but also by relieving a corn shortage.[44] If the Minucian moneyers' coin design is rightly interpreted, that is what, in the 130s BC, their ancestor Minucius was believed to have done.[45] So perhaps we can read back into the second century BC (even as far back as Cincius?) the version in which Minucius and Maelius were rival providers of corn in a famine, the former in an official capacity, the latter a private benefactor.[46]

VI

The version that made Minucius an anachronistic *praefectus annonae* was very probably that of Licinius Macer in the 70s BC. Livy cites, as the source for the title, the 'linen books' which Macer discovered in the temple of Moneta.[47] But a great deal of creative historiography had been written between Cincius and Macer, and among the political issues that inspired it were the polarised ideologies of the Gracchan period, which prominently included both grain for the people and alleged aspirations to *regnum*.[48] It is inconceivable that the story was not exploited for political effect—especially as the tribune who in 121 BC took the lead in attacking C. Gracchus' legislation was himself a Minucius.[49]

The main shift in the story, however, is probably the result of Sulla's dictatorship. In Livy and in Dionysius' main narrative, Cincinnatus as dictator orders Maelius' arrest, and Servilius as *magister equitum* carries it out: when Maelius resists he is killed.[50] And even in this developed version, two separate ideological treatments are detectable. The famine at the start of it all is attributed *either* to natural causes *or* to the pleasure of political meetings which kept the citizens away from agriculture. 'Both versions are attested,' Livy observes, and in his own characteristic way combines them as complaints by the *patres* of plebeian idleness and complaints by the tribunes of negligence and fraud on the part of the consuls. As Ogilvie rightly points out, 'the alternative explanations reflect the pro- and anti-plebeian standpoints of L.'s two chief authorities.'[51]

So too in the story of Maelius' arrest. Servilius appears with an escort of young patricians, all carrying concealed weapons, and demands that Maelius appear before the dictator. Maelius appeals to the *plebs* for protection, dashes to the *tabernae plebeiae* and seizes a butcher's knife to defend himself, but is overwhelmed by sheer numbers and cut to pieces 'like an animal'.[52] Dionysius reports in particular that his arm was cut off—evidently an alternative explanation for the name Servilius Ahala.[53] One wonders whether, in this scenario, Maelius' head was then exposed at the Lacus *Seruilius* on the other side of the Forum: that was what happened to the victims of Sulla's executioners.[54]

It is natural to think of Licinius Macer, the anti-Sullan tribune of 73 BC, as the author of this version. As Emilio Gabba has convincingly argued, Macer was interested in the early dictatorship precisely because of Sulla.[55] But Cincinnatus, even as dictator, was easier to portray as a man of *prisca uirtus* than as a bloodthirsty tyrant. Cicero in 44 BC refers to a version which must have been wholly favourable:[56]

100

In agris erant tum senatores, id est senes, siquidem aranti Lucio
Quinctio Cincinnato nuntiatum est eum dictatorem fuisse factum;
cuius dictatoris iussu magister equitum Gaius Servilius Ahala
Spurium Maelium regnum occupantem interemit.

In those days senators (i.e. 'elders') lived on their farms—if it is true
that L. Quinctius Cincinnatus was ploughing when it was
announced to him that he had been made dictator. It was at his
order as dictator that C. Servilius Ahala, the Master of Horse, killed
Sp. Maelius as he was establishing a tyranny.

Cicero's phraseology (*siquidem*), and the way he spells out the details,
implies that this was not a well-known story to be casually alluded to
(as he alludes elsewhere to the earlier version of Ahala's act); and the
exemplary scene of 'Cincinnatus at the plough' was usually associated
with a dictatorship nineteen years earlier.[57] I suspect that this passage
reveals the recent appearance of an anti-Licinian version of the story,
which accepted the dictatorship and gave Ahala an official position, but
interpreted the events in a manner favourable to the law-and-order
party.[58]

Not surprisingly, Livy's attempt to achieve a coherent narrative from
this complex and contradictory tradition is not a complete success. The
speech of Cincinnatus, for example, 'who with a fine mixture of rhetoric
and blunt speaking provides the deed with its historical significance and
moral justification',[59] seems to be based on a version of the events not
wholly consistent with the narrative.[60]

Livy's touch is equally unsure when he deals with L. Minucius. Was
he an honest and efficient provider of grain, or a useless bosses' stooge?
He was appointed by the people, but *haud adversante senatu*, and he
was honoured by the Senate, but *ne plebe quidem inuita*: that is, Livy
does not want to contradict any of his 'authorities'.[61] As for the
question of Minucius' reappointment, Livy throws up his hands: 'there
is no agreement.'[62]

VII

These late-republican readings are of interest in their own right,
particularly as Dagmar Gutberlet did not include the Sp. Maelius
episode in her discussion of Gracchan and Sullan material in Livy's first
decade.[63] For the story of the Minucii, however, whose monument was

ROMAN DRAMA AND ROMAN HISTORY

evidently of the fifth or fourth century BC,[64] the early strata are more significant. Broughton states the essential point with admirable clarity: 'Dion. Hal. found Minucius in the early tradition of Cincius and Piso simply as an informer.'[65] The Μηνύκιος-μηνυτής etymology, which survives in the later versions,[66] evidently went back, through Cincius, to at least the third century BC. It raises an interesting question about 'speaking names' in the Roman republican élite.

L. Cincius the historian had been praetor in 210. One of his near-contemporaries was C. Atilius Serranus (pr. 218), whose cognomen derived from an Atilius who had been called to the consulship while sowing his fields: Serranus a serendo.[67] (It would be good to know whether 'Cincinnatus from the plough' was a patrician counterblast to Atilius, or vice versa.) Serranus the exemplary plebeian was probably C. Atilius 'Bubulcus', as the Livian tradition calls him, consul in 245 and 235 and censor in 234.[68]

Even more famous in the annals of ancient virtue—indeed an essential feature of every moralizing list on the subject—was C. Fabricius Luscinus, consul in 282 and 278 and censor in 275.[69] He was normally known by his gentilicium, not his cognomen. What mattered was not his one eye, but the fact that he worked with his hands: Fabricius a fabre.[70] A faber uses a hammer, malleolus; the third-century Publicii took that as a cognomen, and their first-century descendants allude to it with pride.[71] But here too the gentilicium is more important. In the third century it was spelt 'Populicius',[72] and the bearers of it evidently thought of themselves as 'the people's men': Populicius a populo.[73]

These are all self-consciously plebeian etymologies. But there are patrician examples too. One of them may lurk behind the story of the cow's horns on the temple of Diana. A Sabine farmer has a wonderful cow, about which a prophecy is made: sacrifice it at the Diana temple on the Aventine at Rome, and your city will become the ruler of all Italy. He goes there, but is tricked by Cornelius the priest, who tells him to bathe in the Tiber first, and sacrifices the cow himself.[74] The context is evidently the late fourth or early third century BC (Rome as the caput Italiae), and we now know there was a pontifex maximus called P. Cornelius Scapula at about that time.[75] Cornelius a cornibus?

More directly relevant to the Minucii is a cluster of Greek etymologies that seem to have originated in this same period. As Munro pointed out in 1864, the fact that the Scipiones are constantly described as fulmina probably implies an etymology from σκηπτός, a

102

thunderbolt;[76] the first to use the *cognomen* was evidently the dictator of 306 BC.[77] The Pinarii were responsible for the cult of Hercules at the Ara Maxima; their name derived (Pinarius ἀπὸ τοῦ πεινᾶν) from the story that they arrived late at the hero's dedication sacrifice and had to go hungry. The context of the aetiology was probably 312 BC, when the cult was transferred to state control and the Pinarii deprived of their privileges.[78] That was also a time when the Romans were interested in Pythagoras,[79] after whose graceful son (Aemilius δι' αἱμυλίαν) the patrician Aemilii were named;[80] since *lepidus* is a calque on αἱμύλος, the first Aemilius Lepidus (*cos.* 285) provides the *terminus ante quem*.

The notion that Latin was a dialect of Greek is probably to be associated with the tradition of Evander introducing the alphabet to Rome.[81] Evander in Rome was a story known already to Eratosthenes, whose contemporary Callimachus included Rome in the concept of *pan-Hellas*.[82] And why not, when consuls from the new plebeian élite were calling themselves Philo and Sophus?[83]

With a little ingenuity, even the most intractable items could be made sense of in Greek. *Flamines*, for instance, evidently became *pilamenes*, from the felt cap (πῖλος) which was part of their insignia, and the native fertility god Inuus (from *inire*) was transliterated as ᾿Εννοῦς, son of Enyo the war-goddess.[84] The Roman Enyo was Bellona, whose temple was vowed by Ap. Claudius Caecus in 296 and dedicated a few years later.[85] As for the *flamines* etymology, that occurs in the context of the Flamen Quirinalis, supposedly introduced by the 'Pythagorean' Numa: the temple of Quirinus was dedicated in 293.[86]

In the light of these indications, obscure and hard to interpret as they are, I think it is reasonable to put the origin of the Μηνύκιος-μηνυτής etymology at some time not too far from 300 BC.

VIII

Precisely in 300 BC, the *lex Ogulnia* opened the colleges of augurs and *pontifices* to plebeian membership. The first plebeian augurs are named by Livy as C. Genucius, P. Aelius Paetus, M. Minucius Faesus, C. Marcius, and a 'T. Publius' whose *gentilicium* must have been either Publilius or Publicius.[87]

The Marcii—to judge by their later coins—claimed descent from Marsyas, whose envoys taught Italy the science of augury.[88] Augury was part of prophecy, and Cn. Marcius, a famous (and no doubt legendary) prophet, was a member of the noble house.[89] Cicero, who tells us this, also mentions a prophet called Publicius.[90] It looks as if two of the first plebeian augurs, C. Marcius and T. 'Publius', laid claim to inherited skill in the art of divination. Two of the others, C. Genucius and M. Minucius Faesus, belonged to families which attributed to their supposedly patrician forebears the *cognomen* Augurinus,[91] implying distant prophetic ancestors of the same sort.

I suggest that the bilingual pun on the name Minucius originally referred to μήνυσις in the sense of 'revelation', disclosure of the gods' will, and of future events, by divination or inspired prophecy. In that case, we must infer a proto-Minucius, like the prophets Marcius and Publicius, on whom M. Minucius Faesus based his claim to a place in the first mixed college of augurs. And that, in turn, provides at last an explanation of the Minucian monument illustrated by the Minucian moneyers in the 130s BC. The two men on ground level can be L. Minucius the grain-provider and M. Minucius Faesus the augur; the staff-bearing figure on the column must be the ancestral Minucius, whether thought of as a mortal or a god.

IX

Now let us draw together the threads, and attempt a chronological view of the Minucii.

The starting point must be the monument—evidently situated at the most direct descent from the Aventine to the river harbour, and so firmly associated with the Minucii that when the city wall was built, about 380 BC, the gate was called the Porta Minucia. We cannot tell what sort of people the fifth-century Minucii were, but the monument itself implies they were prominent. Perhaps L. Minucius was a merchant? One ship-load of imported grain, brought to a starving community in a famine year, might be enough to account for the consistent association of his name with the corn supply.

After the power-sharing compromise of 367 BC (or whenever it was), the plebeian Minucii could hope for high office; they achieved it with the consulship of 305. The late fourth century was a period of great creative energy, not least (I think) in the elaboration of distinguished ancestries for members of the new plebeian élite.[92] If the Minucii were indeed presenting themselves as hereditary experts in the arts of revelation, their reward was a place on the first joint augural college, in 300 BC.

The next consular Minucius was M. Minucius Rufus (221), whose reputation has suffered through the Fabian tradition on the events of 217, when he was the unsuccessful *magister equitum* of Q. Fabius 'Cunctator'.[93] Fabius represented senatorial authority, a theme emphasised in his contemporary L. Cincius' account of the Sp. Maelius affair, in which Minucian 'revelation' was reduced to mere crime-reporting.

Minucii Thermi and Rufi were consuls in 197, 193 and 110; all three won triumphs, and the last of them built the Porticus Minucia from his Thracian spoils. By then the historiographical tradition was developing the Sp. Maelius story, and L. Minucius with it, in terms appropriate to the politics of the post-Gracchan age. Sulla added a further dimension, duly exploited by Licinius Macer, who claimed to have found a reference in the *libri lintei* to L. Minucius as *praefectus annonae*. Livy and Dionysius wove the various tendentious versions into their own narratives, from which modern scholars do their best to disentangle them.

The Minucius Thermus who was thought a certainty for the consulship of 64 failed to get it (or if he did get it, it was under a different name).[94] There were no more Minucian consuls. By the Augustan age, the family was a spent force. But the name still carried its double significance: corn, symbolized by the Porticus Minucia *frumentaria* (and the imperial *curatores Minuciae*), and revelation, as reflected in Dionysius' continued play on the μηνυτής etymology. Precisely those two elements were alluded to on the Minucian coin-scene, of two representative Minucii at their family monument, with loaves and an augur's staff respectively.

I hope this investigation of the history and pseudo-history of one family may serve to illustrate the complex processes that created the historical tradition on republican Rome. And if, in consequence, we come to doubt whether the early names in Broughton's great catalogue are as authentic as he thought they were, we must also remember with gratitude that without *The Magistrates of the Roman Republic* such enquiries could never be undertaken at all.

10

Rome and the Resplendent Aemilii

I

In 1987, about 2030 years after its destruction, the Basilica Aemilia was rediscovered. Margareta Steinby's characteristically unassuming article demonstrated the existence of a substantial middle-republican building immediately to the east of (and aligned with) the temple of Castor.[1] The foundations suggest a *stoa*-like building, just like the Basilica Aemilia as illustrated on M. Lepidus' coin of 61 BC (fig. 7).

Steinby's identification is clearly preferable to the *communis opinio*, universally accepted since 1899, that the Aemilia was the great basilica on the north side of the Forum, excavated by Boni in that year. That basilica was an aisled hall fronted by shops, nothing like the building on the coin, and the ancient sources consistently refer to it as 'Basilica Paulli'.[2] It was originally built by M. Fulvius Nobilior as censor in 179, along with the food market (*macellum*) immediately behind it, and then rebuilt and renamed by L. Aemilius Paullus in the fifties BC.[3]

But L. Paullus' building presents us with a problem. Cicero refers to it in July 54 (*Ad Att.* IV 16.8):

> Paullus in medio foro basilicam iam paene texerat isdem antiquis columnis. illam autem quam locauit facit magnificentissimam. quid quaeris? nihil gratius illo monumento, nihil gloriosius.

> Paullus has now almost finished his basilica in the middle of the Forum, using the original columns. The one he put out to contract he is doing in really magnificent style. In fact nothing could be more popular than that building, nothing more glorious.

106

Figure 7.   Coin showing the Basilica Aemilia: denarius by
M. (Aemilius) Lepidus, *c.* 61 BC. (Courtesy of the British Museum.)

Paullus is busy with two basilicas: (a) one *in medio foro* which he is
rebuilding, using the old columns, and (b) another, site not indicated,
for which he has let the contract and which is going to be particularly
magnificent. There are clearly two different buildings involved, so (b)
cannot be the replacement of (a), as Shackleton Bailey supposed.
Steinby thinks her discovery has solved the problem: (a) must be the
newly-identified Basilica Aemilia, (b) the Basilica Paulli, which was
indeed magnificent. But there is an unsurmountable difficulty.

As Steinby observes in other contexts, and as the very title of her
article shows, the Basilica Aemilia which she has so convincingly

107

identified was at the eastern limit of the Forum.[4] It was adjacent to the
Regia, and could perhaps even be thought of as an extension of it; and
the Regia is explicitly described as at the edge of the Forum.[5] So it
cannot be the 'basilica in medio foro'.

The Basilica Paulli, however, *can* be. The Forum was not just the
piazza we know so well. It also included the *macellum*, sometimes
referred to as *forum piscatorium* or *forum cuppedinis*. As we have
seen, this food market with its surrounding shops was created, along
with the basilica, by M. Fulvius Nobilior in 179 BC (Varro's etymology
of the various names was based on an aetiological story involving both
Fulvius and his colleague M. Lepidus);[6] it was destroyed by the fire of
AD 64, and the site was used by Vespasian for the garden of his temple
of Peace. We know from a fragment of Varro's *Menippean Satires*,
probably written in the seventies BC, that the butchers' shops of the
macellum could be described as *in foro*; and the house of Valerius
Publicola, notoriously looming over the Forum, was on the height of
the Velia above the *macellum* (a hill partly destroyed to build
Maxentius' Basilica, and wholly destroyed to build Mussolini's Via
dell'Impero).[7]

Our conception of the Basilica Paulli as forming the northern limit of
the Forum is quite mistaken, based on the fallacious premise that the
Forum was coterminous with the excavated piazza with which we are
so familiar. The Basilica Paulli was in fact concealed from the Forum
piazza by the line of shops (and later by Augustus' portico); but we
know that it was open on the other side, towards the *macellum* which
was created as part of the same programme.[8] 'In medio foro' is precisely
the phrase to describe its position (fig. 8).

But where does that leave the Cicero passage? The newly-identified
Basilica Aemilia, plausibly attributed to L. Paullus in his censorship
(164 BC), restored by M. Lepidus the consul of 78 and decorated with
the shields visible on his son's coin design,[9] clearly cannot be the
basilica magnificentissima for which the contract had been let in 54 BC.
Neither can the Basilica Paulli, which must be the first of the two
basilicas mentioned by Cicero. So where, and what, was the second?

It is important to remember the context of Cicero's letter. Caesar had
completed the conquest of Gaul and was about to invade Britain. The
outcome of that campaign was eagerly awaited, as was Caesar's return,
which was expected to help C. Memmius' consular candidature if the
elections could be postponed long enough.[10] It is clear that Caesar was
expected back in Rome the following winter (54–53). Nobody knew

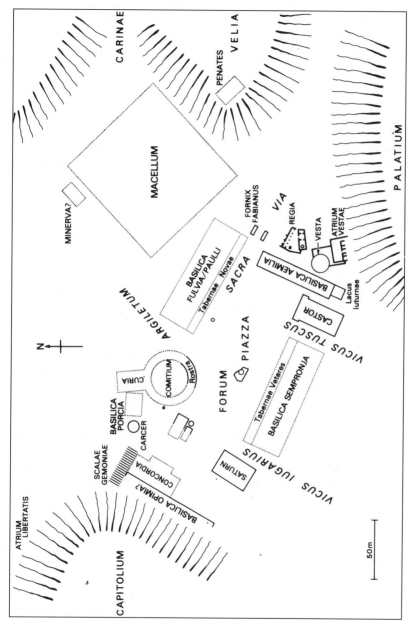

Figure 8.   Sketch-map of the Roman Forum, c. 54 BC.

what Ambiorix and the Eburones (not to mention Vercingetorix) had in store for the *unicus imperator*.

Caesar's friends—including Cicero, as he tells Atticus somewhat defiantly—were therefore preparing the huge building programme with which Caesar was going to rival Pompey's theatre and portico as *monumenta* of triumphal conquest. It is in that context that Cicero refers to Paullus' basilicas—as a rival display of *gloria* and conspicuous expenditure which Caesar must outbid. The Caesarian projects he mentions are the extension of the Forum (i.e. the Forum Iulium), and the Saepta Iulia in the Campus Martius. Why does he not mention the Basilica Iulia on the south side of the Forum piazza? That was certainly a great Caesarian *monumentum*, and one which must have directly challenged Paullus' efforts. The impression one gets from Cicero's phraseology is that Paullus' activity had forced Caesar to build outside the piazza, as if there were no room left within it.

The solution must be that the *basilica magnificentissima* for which Paullus had let the contract in 54 BC was the magnificent basilica which was eventually completed as the Basilica Iulia. We know that Paullus was able to finish his basilica *in medio foro* (the Basilica Paulli) only with the help of a 1500–talent subvention from Caesar.[11] It is an easy guess that the deal involved the transfer of Paullus' other planned basilica to the victorious proconsul of Gaul.

If that is indeed the explanation of the Cicero passage, then we must attribute to L. Paullus, who in 54 BC was not yet even a praetor, a plan of staggering grandeur: to build two great basilicas on the two long sides of the Forum piazza, and thus (with the existing Basilica Aemilia on the short eastern side) effectively to surround the whole open space with *monumenta* of his family—to do, in fact, precisely what Augustus did a generation later. But Paullus, though he made it to the consulship (50 BC), was no Augustus. Is it conceivable that such an apparently minor character could have had such grandiose ambitions? The answer, I think, is yes.

II

The exposition begins in the *mythistoria* of early Rome.

The patrician Aemilii, like their equals the Fabii and Cornelii, gave their name to one of the primordial rural tribes. The *tribus Aemilia* is not firmly located, but the most likely hypothesis is that it was in the *ager Laurens* near Lavinium. According to one author known to

Plutarch, Aemilia was the daughter of Aeneas and Lavinia, and the mother of Romulus.[12]

This version of the foundation story predates (or at least ignores) the invention of the Alban king-list, which was already in Fabius Pictor, and of the name Ilia for the Vestal who bore the twins to Mars, as in both Fabius and Ennius. We may compare the early second-century Pergamene version, which called the mother of the twins Servilia; clearly the great patrician families did their best to insert their own eponyms as the story took shape.[13] The Aemilii had another Vestal story to tell, in one of those pious miracle stories of the Roman tradition which could not quite justify a place in serious history: Aemilia, the *uirgo maxima*, had entrusted the sacred fire to a novice, who let it go out; with a prayer to Vesta, Aemilia placed some fine linen from her own dress on the cold ashes, which immediately burst into flame.[14]

Another version of the origin of the *gens Aemilia* derives it from Amulius. That is attested only in Silius Italicus, but it is likely to have originated before the saga of Amulius the wicked uncle (already in Fabius Pictor) became canonical. Yet another aetiology makes Aimylos the son of Ascanius and brother of Iulus—a version that may perhaps have originated in the first century BC, when it mattered particularly to be equal to the patrician Iulii.[15]

The first Aemilius in the consular *fasti* is L. Aemilius Mamerci f. Mamercus (*cos.* 484, 478, 473), and Mamercus or Mamercinus as a *cognomen* frequently appears in fifth- and fourth-century Aemilian consuls. But from the consul of 285 onwards, the Aemilii start using the *cognomen* Lepidus ('graceful').[16] That gives the context for a story Plutarch uses to prove Numa's acquaintance with Pythagoras:

> Another proof is that one of the four sons born to Numa was called Mamercus after the son of Pythagoras. From him they say is named the house of the Aemilii, which is mixed with the patricians [ἀναμιχθέντα τοῖς πατρικίοις]; for that was what the king called the grace and αἱμυλία of his speech.

It is clear that *Lepidus* is a calque on αἱμύλος.[17]

Elsewhere, Plutarch's account of Numa's sons seems to confuse the Aemilii (Mamerci) with the Marcii:[18]

> From Pompon they say the Pomponii are descended, from Pinus the Pinarii, from Calpus the Calpurnii, and from Mamercus the Mamercii, who for this reason also have the *cognomen* Reges, i.e. Kings.

The Aemilii did not, in fact, use Rex as a *cognomen*. But they did use Regillus,[19] and they associated themselves with kings in so many other ways that Plutarch's mistake is a venial one.

They claimed, for instance, that the Senate had sent M. Lepidus to Egypt in 200 BC to act as guardian to the young king Ptolemy V Epiphanes. Polybius and Livy know nothing of it, but a recent and authoritative discussion allows that the tradition may be genuine.[20] If so, it was the first, and very precocious, appearance in history of one of the two Aemilii whose parallel careers form the high-water mark of the family's fortunes. M. Lepidus and L. Paullus held the aedileship together in 193 BC:

> Aedilitas insignis eo anno fuit M. Aemilii Lepidi et L. Aemilii Paulli; multos pecuarios damnarunt; ex ea pecunia clupea inaurata in fastigio Iouis aedis posuerunt, porticum unum extra portam Trigeminam, emporio ad Tiberim adiecto, alteram ab porta Fontinali ad Martis aram qua in campum iter esset perduxerunt.

> That year was notable for the aedileship of M. Aemilius Lepidus and L. Aemilius Paullus. They found many cattle-breeders guilty [of grazing on public land], and used the fines to set up gilded shields on the pediment of the temple of Jupiter, and to build two long porticos: one outside the Porta Trigemina, with an adjacent commercial centre by the Tiber, another from the Porta Fontinalis to the altar of Mars, to make a route into the Campus Martius.

The first of these porticos was the huge market hall and warehouse south-west of the Aventine; rebuilt in 174, in its final form (as attested on the Severan marble plan) it was 487m long by 60m wide; with its *emporium adiectum* it represented the creation of Rome's new commercial quarter.[21] The second was equally conspicuous in a different way, providing a colonnade along the street that led from the gate closest to the Forum to the great new road to the north, the Via Flaminia. And both constructions evidently gave rise to the toponym *Aemiliana*, surviving in both places even in the imperial period.[22]

Lepidus and Paullus were praetors together in 191, but then Paullus suffered a setback in Spain and fell behind. Meanwhile, L. Aemilius Regillus, praetor in 190, defeated the fleet of king Antiochus in a battle off Samos and held a spectacular triumph for it.[23]

Lepidus was consul in 187, and built the great road from Ariminum to Placentia.[24] On his Via Aemilia Lepidus founded a settlement, just as the builders of the Viae Appia, Clodia, Aurelia and Flaminia had done on their roads; but where they had called their foundations Forum Appi, Forum Clodi, Forum Aurelii and Forum Flaminii, Lepidus uniquely named his *Regium* Lepidum.[25]

In 179, Lepidus was censor with M. Fulvius Nobilior. Fulvius, we may recall, built the basilica and adjacent *macellum* in the Forum. He also built, among many other things, the piles for a new stone bridge across the Tiber. But the bridge was always known as the Pons Aemilius—and one late source even calls it the Pons Lepidi. According to Plutarch, it was originally built by an Aemilius who was quaestor; Coarelli convincingly dates it to the mid-third century and assumes that it was destroyed in the great flood of 192 BC. Fulvius was thus responsible for the first stage of its reconstruction, which was completed by the censors of 142, L. Mummius and P. Scipio Aemilianus.[26]

Among Lepidus' own acts as censor was the dedication in the Campus Martius of the temple his kinsman Regillus had vowed to the Lares Permarini in the battle against Antiochus' fleet. The inscription made great play with the notion of a king's defeat: the words *rex* and *regnum* conspicuously recur.[27]

By now Lepidus was *princeps senatus* and *pontifex maximus*; in 175 he was consul for the second time. But in the end L. Paullus outshone even him. Paullus was consul in 182, and then again in 168, when he was given command against king Perseus of Macedon. The victory of Pydna, the surrender of Perseus and the abolition of his throne provided the climax and the justification of the Aemilian obsession with kings. This staggering shift in the balance of world power—unprecedented in history, as it appeared to Polybius—was symbolised by the heir of Alexander the Great walking as a captive in a Roman triumph.[28]

Once again, it was Margareta Steinby who pointed out that the Lacus Iuturnae complex, with its statue group of the Dioscuri, must be a triumphal monument of L. Paullus; on the day of the battle, the twin gods were seen there with their white horses, washing off the blood and dust. The newly-identified Basilica Aemilia adjoined the *lacus*, and Steinby's attribution of it to Paullus—no doubt as censor in 164—is entirely convincing. Interestingly, it was not a basilica in the sense of an aisled hall, but more like the Athenian *Stoa Basileios*; moreover, it adjoined, and was evidently designed as an extension of, the *Regia*.[29]

If the king's conqueror was acting too much like a king himself, Nemesis was certainly swift: two of Paullus' four sons died at the time of the triumph. The survivors had already been adopted into the Fabii

Maximi and Cornelii Scipiones, and the three *gentes* kept up their close relationship for at least five more generations (see fig. 9). The glory of conquest was immediately renewed with the triumphs of P. Scipio Aemilianus over Carthage and Numantia and of Q. Fabius Aemiliani f. Maximus over the Allobroges in Gaul (146, 132 and 120 BC). The triumphal arch of Fabius Allobrogicus was—as we now know— adjacent to the Basilica Aemilia.

The temple of Hercules Victor in the Forum Bovarium is described by Festus as 'aedes Aemiliana' (Scaliger's emendation of *familiana*), and may well have been a triumphal or censorial monument either of L. Paullus or just possibly, as Coarelli argues, of Scipio Aemilianus.[30] Another Aemilian triumph and censorship (M. Scaurus, 115 and 109 BC) produced two temples in Rome and a second Via Aemilia, extending the Aurelia up the Ligurian coast.[31]

By the end of the second century, therefore, there were in Italy two *uiae Aemiliae*, one of which gave the family name to an entire region,[32] while the city of Rome could boast a *pons Aemilius*, two *porticus Aemiliae*, two corresponding districts called *Aemiliana*, a *basilica Aemilia*, an *aedes Aemiliana*, and perhaps already also a *ludus Aemilianus*.[33] With all that and Regium Lepidum too, the family's record of self-advertisement amply justifies the phrase Sir Ronald Syme found to describe them—'the resplendent Aemilii'.[34]

III

Once Sulla had done the unthinkable, by turning his army on Rome and giving himself autocratic power, the first man to emulate him was, not surprisingly, a patrician Aemilius. M. Lepidus (*cos.* 78) failed in his attempt and died in exile, but what is striking is how little effect his failure had on the fortunes of the family.

Lepidus was not like Catiline, a maverick with no resources except his own force of character. On the contrary, he represented a great tradition of glory and achievement. He had restored the Basilica Aemilia, from which shield portraits of the great Aemilii stared down on the Forum. He called one of his sons L. Aemilius Paullus; another, killed in the fighting in 77, was by adoption a Scipio.[35] The family name itself was eloquent, as Sallust shows in the speech he gave Lepidus in 78:

> Mihi quamquam per hoc summum imperium satis quaesitum erat
> nomini maiorum, dignitati atque etiam praesidio, tamen non fuit

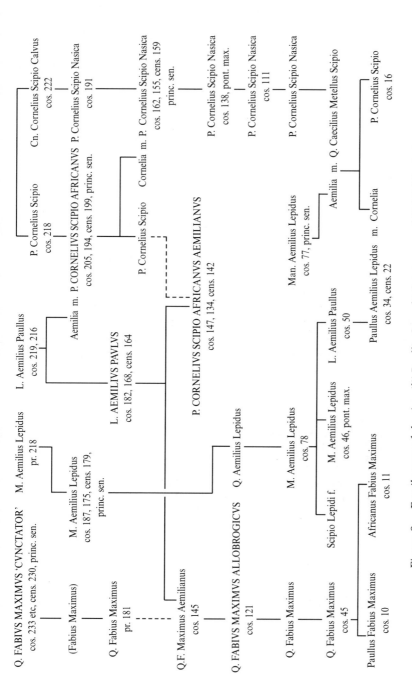

Figure 9. Family tree of the Aemilii Paulli, Cornelii Scipiones and Fabii Maximi.

115

consilium priuatas opes facere, potiorque uisa est periculosa libertas
quieto seruitio. quae si probastis, adeste, Quirites, et bene
iuuantibus diuis M. Aemilium consulem ducem et auctorem
sequimini ad recipiendam libertatem.

'As for me, even though by reaching this supreme command I had
done enough to satisfy my ancestral name, my dignity and even my
security, it was still not my plan to enjoy personal power, and I
preferred a dangerous freedom to peaceful slavery. If you have
taken the same choice, citizens, then come! With the gods on your
side, follow Marcus Aemilius the consul as your leader and
champion to win back liberty!'

As Sallust makes Philippus observe in 77, even after Lepidus took up
arms against the Republic there were many who defended him by
recalling the great deeds of the Aemilian house ('gentis Aemiliae bene
facta').[36]

The achievements continued, despite Lepidus' debacle; Mamercus
Lepidus (*cos.* 77) was named as *princeps senatus* by the censors of
70–69.[37] But the sixties presented a new and unexpected challenge—the
victories and conquests of Pompeius Magnus, the Roman Alexander.
Even the heirs of the great Paullus might feel themselves overshadowed
by a man who presented himself as the conqueror of the world.[38]

Pompey returned to Rome in 62 BC, and held his spectacular two-day
triumph in 61. Precisely in those years L. Paullus and M. Lepidus, sons
of the rebellious consul of 78, were responsible for coin issues
celebrating the achievements of the Aemilii.[39] Paullus' reference to his
great namesake included the legend *TER*: the family evidently claimed
that L. Paullus, like Pompey, had triumphed three times.[40] Lepidus
presented a wide selection of Aemilian worthies: the miraculous Vestal,
a precocious Lepidus who killed an enemy in battle at fifteen years of
age, the tutor to king Ptolemy in Alexandria, and his own father who
restored the Basilica Aemilia (fig. 7, *AIMILIA REF.*).

It was no doubt in this context that Atticus undertook his
genealogical study of the Fabii and the Aemilii, 'at the request of
Cornelius Scipio and Fabius Maximus'.[41] The latter must be Q. Fabius
(later consul in 45 BC), who as aedile in 57 restored the Fornix Fabianus
built by his grandfather. Allobrogicus' arch was next to Paullus' Basilica
Aemilia, and Allobrogicus himself was a grandson of Paullus and
nephew of Scipio Aemilianus; so it is not surprising to find Cicero
praising the aedile for restoring the *gloria* of all three families:[42]

Nihil Maximus fecit alienum aut sua uirtute aut illis uiris
clarissimis, Paullis Maximis Africanis, quorum gloriam huius
uirtute renouatam non modo speramus uerum etiam uidemus.

Maximus has done nothing unworthy either of his own excellence
or of those most distinguished gentlemen the [Aemilii] Paulli, the
[Fabii] Maximi and the [Scipiones] Africani. Through his courage
we not only hope but see that their glory has been renewed.

The arch was adorned with statues, from which three *tituli* survive,
including that of its restorer:[43]

Q. FABIVS Q.F. MAXSVMVS
AED. CVR.

L. AEMILIVS L.F. PAVLLVS
COS. II CENS. AVGVR
TRIVMPHAVIT TER

P. CORNELIVS PAVLLI F. SCIPIO
AFRICANVS COS. II CENS.
AVGVR. TRIVMPHAVIT II

'Paulli Maximi Africani.' The descendants of Rome's old heroes were
renewing their glory in the face of the achievements of Rome's new
hero. *Gloria* was made visible and permanent in buildings constructed
ex manubiis: the greater the conquest, the greater the booty, the greater
the building programme. Pompey's victories produced three temples
(Hercules, Minerva, Venus Victrix) and a theatre and portico in the
Campus Martius that were the wonder of the age.

The Hercules temple was by the *carceres* of the Circus Maximus,
close to the Forum Bovarium, where Hercules Pompeianus was now a
direct challenge to Hercules Aemilianus. The Venus Victrix temple—
which a contemporary called 'aedes Victoriae'—was incorporated into
Pompey's theatre (fig. 1), in an architectural complex which included not
only the great portico, with a Senate-house attached, but also Pompey's
own house in the Campus.[44]

As for the Minerva temple, the goddess of work and crafts would be
best housed among the *tabernae* of the Argiletum and the Macellum
(fig. 8), which were close to Pompey's town-house in the Carinae; that
was where Domitian's Minerva temple was, and it is an attractive
hypothesis that Pompey's had been on the same site and destroyed in AD
64.[45] Building the temple there would be a very proper acknowledgment

to the *tabernarii* who had voted Pompey his great commands in 67 and 66 BC.[46] If that hypothesis is correct, it helps us to see what was in young Paullus' mind when he planned his own building programme as curule aedile in 56 BC.[47]

Facing the putative Minerva Pompeiana across the *tabernae* was the old basilica built by M. Fulvius Nobilior in 179. On the other side (it was, we recall, *in medio foro*), the Fulvian basilica reached as far as the Fornix Fabianus, which effectively linked it to the Basilica Aemilia; the work of M. Lepidus and Q. Fabius had already turned both arch and basilica into commemorative *monumenta* of the Aemilii and their relatives. Since there were no Fulvii left to object, Paullus could now rebuild their basilica as a further extension of the complex, which would at the same time outface Pompey's Minerva.

On the other side of the piazza, behind the old shops (which were still extant in Catullus' time), was the Basilica Sempronia, built by Ti. Sempronius Gracchus as censor in 170 BC.[48] The Sempronii too were all but extinct, for the same reason as the Fulvii (the bloodshed of 121 BC), so that site too was potentially available for redevelopment. If the interpretation suggested above for Cicero *Ad Atticum* IV 16.8 is correct, by July 54 Paullus had got permission to do it, and had already let the contracts for a *basilica magnificentissima*. But how could such a grandiose project be entrusted to a mere ex-aedile? And how could he hope to find the money for it?

The first question can be answered in one word: Caesar. Gaul had apparently been conquered by 56 BC; spectacular campaigns in Germany and Britain could be expected, after which Caesar would return in triumph. His building programme, like Pompey's, would certainly be spectacular, and if his opponents wanted to minimise its impact they would have to put some of the prime sites beyond his grasp. Paullus was a good sound optimate, 'a citizen of singular courage, a man born to save the Republic'.[49] As for his father (and in a better cause), for him too the 'great deeds of the Aemilian house' guaranteed senatorial favour. If he was prepared to turn practically the whole Forum piazza into a splendid monument to the heroes of the old Republic, the majority in the Senate were hardly likely to object.

As for the money, like all grandiose projects it was a gamble. Paullus could count on getting his consulship *suo anno* (as he duly did, in 50), after which he would need a great command. With his background, creditors would surely consider him a good risk. By the year 52, with his praetorship safely behind him, Paullus must have felt confident that such a command would be available.[50] Crassus' dreams of Babylon and India had collapsed in the disaster at Carrhae. Caesar's German and British projects had been abandoned in the face of Gallic rebellions, and he was now in imminent danger of defeat and death at the hands of Vercingetorix.[51] The Caesarian building programme of which Cicero had boasted in 54 must now have been suspended.

Even in 54, as we noticed above, Caesar had to find new space for his Forum project. Paullus had claimed the main part of the piazza. Between Paullus' sites and the Capitol there were: the Curia, rebuilt by Sulla and bearing his name; the Basilica Porcia, Cato's family *monumentum*; the temple of Concord and the Basilica Opimia, monuments to the oligarchic reaction of 121 BC; and the old temple of Saturn, the treasury of the Republic.[52] With the exception of the Saturn temple, all these were ideologically unsympathetic to Caesar, and it is no surprise to hear that he planned a great theatre in the Forum which would have swept most of them away.[53] That never happened, but the fact that plan was public knowledge gives an idea of what was at stake.

In the end, Caesar overcame Vercingetorix. He made a deal with Paullus (now consul), who must have given up one of his basilicas in return for 1500 talents to pay for the other. The main part of his project was still intact—two basilicas, and a joining arch over the Sacra Via, which gave the Aemilii and their descendants a monopoly of the Forum piazza between the Curia (now being rebuilt by Faustus Sulla) and the temple of Castor.[54]

But once Caesar crossed the Rubicon, all these plans came to nothing. Paullus' younger brother, M. Lepidus, now steps into the limelight. As praetor in 49 he was left in charge of Rome by Caesar, and it was he who carried the legislation making Caesar dictator. Then he looked after Spain for two years, and held a triumph before entering on his consulship in 46.[55] He was now Caesar's deputy—*magister equitum* in 46, 45 and 44—and it was in that capacity that he made his own contribution to the building programme in the Forum. The old Curia, which Faustus had been rebuilding, was replaced by a temple of Felicitas; it must have given Lepidus some satisfaction to have taken over in his own name the attribute his father had sneered at in 78.[56] Thus the Aemilian and Caesarian building programmes were effectively combined, since the new Curia Iulia, attached to the new Forum Iulium, was flanked on one side by Lepidus' temple and on the other by Paullus' basilica.

After the Ides of March, Lepidus became Pontifex Maximus; eighteen months later he was Triumvir, with Antony and the young Caesar. (The first name on the proscription list was that of his brother Paullus.) He had taken over one of Caesar's more spectacular building projects, the Saepta porticos in the Campus Martius, but an old Aemilian monument was now lost. Caesar's funeral pyre had been right in front of the Basilica Aemilia, and may well have damaged it. It was never repaired. Instead, it was demolished to make space for the temple of Divus Iulius, authorized in 42, which henceforth would dominate the east end of the Forum.[57]

Paullus' ambitious scheme for three basilicas had shrunk to one. But it was a splendid one. Paullus' son dedicated it as consul in 34 BC; it was rebuilt after fire damage in 14, and again in AD 22 (by Paullus' grandson). Tacitus describes it as 'Aemilia monimenta', and so it was. To keep even that, in a piazza which by then had become almost wholly a showpiece for the Julian family, was a very substantial achievement.[58]

IV

The rest of the story of the patrician Aemilii can be read in Syme.[59] As always, they aimed high—often beyond their capacities—and the quasi-monarchy of the principate even offered the chance to turn their ancient obsession with regal status into a reality.

M. Lepidus the Triumvir, who already had supreme power, was stripped of it in 36 BC; his son was executed after an abortive plot six years later.[60] The other branch of the family, however, did spectacularly well under the restored Republic of Augustus. Paullus' son, consul in 34, was censor in 23; one of his grandsons (L. Paullus *cos.* AD 1) married Augustus' grand-daughter Julia, and the other (M. Lepidus *cos.* AD 6) was judged by the *princeps* to be 'capable of ruling' (*capax imperii*); Paullus' great-grandson married Germanicus' daughter Drusilla and was named by Gaius as his heir, to inherit the principate itself.[61]

But proximity to absolute power was fatal in the end. Both Julia's husband and Drusilla's were executed for treason.[62] The death of Gaius' heir marked the extinction of the patrician Aemilii. But though their day was over, their monument remained. The Basilica Paulli was cited by the elder Pliny as equal in magnificence to the Forum Augustum and Vespasian's temple of Peace. And his contemporary Statius describes it in a line which must have consoled the resentful *manes* of the Aemilii:

illinc belligeri sublimis *regia* Paulli

On that side, the lofty *palace* of Paullus the warrior.

The association of ideas was still irresistible.[63]

11

E.S. Beesly and the Roman Revolution

I

The name of Edward Spencer Beesly (1831–1915) is best known to historians of the Labour movement.[1] He was an energetic supporter of the early trades' unions, both helping them with practical advice and forcefully stating the justice of their case for middle-class readers in the mainstream journals.[2] He arranged and presided over the inaugural meeting of the International Working Men's Association in 1864 (the 'First International'), and thereafter was in regular contact with Karl Marx, though his own Comtean Positivism was not to Marx's taste. As Beesly himself somewhat wryly put it, 'Dr Marx and I were always good friends; to the end of his life I had a great esteem and regard for him: and I am sure that he considered me to be a well-meaning person—which was more than he was willing to allow with regard to most people who differed with him.'[3]

But Beesly was also an academic historian. His first job after graduating in *Literae Humaniores* at Oxford (1853) was as assistant master in history at Marlborough College; in 1859 the political influence of John Bright, and the prolonged industrial dispute in the London building trades, brought him to the capital; the following year he was appointed to the Professorship of History at University College, and that of Latin at Bedford College, posts which he held until 1893 and 1889 respectively. His combined professorial income was £300 a year, representing something like £15,000 by today's values.[4] But the duties were not demanding: at University College he had to give lectures only once or twice a week, and he sometimes took the opportunity to abandon the University of London syllabus and lecture 'on wide fields and long periods of history, a practice, in my opinion, much more appropriate to the Chair, and more useful educationally'.[5]

For a follower of Auguste Comte's 'secular religion', history had to be understood according to the Positivist creed of progress, as humanity evolved from theological to abstract (or metaphysical) interpretations of experience, and from there to positive scientific understanding.[6] One can imagine the college authorities having a different view of what the history curriculum required.

It so happened that in the very year of Beesly's appointment the Professor of Modern History at the University of Cambridge published his inaugural lecture. This was the Rev. Charles Kingsley, author of *Alton Locke*, *Hypatia* and *Westward Ho!*, Chaplain in Ordinary to the Queen, and Rector of Eversley, Hampshire; the title of the lecture was *The Limits of Exact Science as Applied to History*. Beesly gave it a withering 32–page review:[7]

> We know what it is that goeth before destruction, or we should be amazed that, not content with uttering this stuff before a select audience, Mr Kingsley should have surrendered it irrevocably to the handsome type and substantial binding of Messrs Macmillan . . . The lecture is a bad one, from the title-page to the conclusion—bad in conception and in execution, in argument, in style, and even in grammar.

Beesly insisted, against the novelist's idea of history as 'the history of men and women, and nothing else', that there are indeed laws which the course of civilisation has followed and will continue to follow:[8]

> The most important laws that govern human progress are few, simple, and beyond our interference. The heat of a southern summer, the cold of a northern winter, are influences which we cannot alter. Englishmen *must* consume more nutritious food than Neapolitans, they *must* be better housed and clothed, they *must* use more fuel. The labour necessary for procuring all these comforts *must* have a certain effect upon their character. Again, such statical laws as the preponderance of the affective faculties in the individual over the intellectual, of the personal instincts over the social, are facts in our nature which we must accept. Comte's great dynamical law of the three stages through which the various branches of human knowledge have passed is, in our opinion, no less universally true.

122

An acquaintance with these and such like general uniformities in the course of nature is the first requisite for useful speculation on social questions. Taken by themselves, indeed, they would be but poor guides of action. We could not construct from them a complete deductive science of society, as geometry is, based upon a few axioms and postulates. But when we compare them with the observed facts of history, we can distinguish, with more or less exactness, certain derivative laws, and these again, by the aid of such specific observation as the nature of the case may admit, will give us rules for action in the present and expectation as to the future; not, indeed, *exact* rules, but such as we can have no hesitation in accepting as the only rational basis of all efforts for the amelioration of our condition.

That final phrase sums up his position. History, as properly understood, is useful for the present. It is a 'guide of action'.

In the latter part of his review, Beesly addressed the 'great men' conception of history. Kingsley had argued that their will alone was sufficient to determine events. The Positivists had a subtler view: 'men of genius, whether speculative or active, influence their age precisely in proportion as they comprehend and identify themselves with its spirit.'[9] Let Julius Caesar illustrate the point:[10]

Never before or since has human being exhibited in so high a degree all the qualities, noble as well as useful, of a born ruler of men. Never had a great man a grander *rôle* to play. To preside over the most important crisis in the history of the most important branch of the human race—this was a task which could not but fall to a great man. It fell to the greatest. Here then, if anywhere, we shall see destiny shaped and bent by human genius. For once the future of a nation, or rather of the world, is bound up in the life of an individual.

But Caesar was assassinated. His old enemies of the aristocracy destroyed him. 'The game is played over again, with hardly a variation in the moves; and at Philippi the reactionists are at length made to comprehend that they are beaten. How far was the history of Rome altered by the murder of Julius?' Caesar's great design was simply carried out by Augustus, 'a man every way his inferior'.

And what was that design, the achievement of which Beesly identifies as the most important crisis in the history of the most important branch of the human race?[11]

From early manhood, nay, almost from boyhood, has the great plan been maturing in the splendid calm of that self-contained, self-counselling mind. For nearly half a century he has marked the signs of the political horizon. No word has he breathed of his inner purpose . . . [T]he Empire—the combination of the dictatorial and tribunitian powers, to be wielded in the interest, not of Rome nor of Italy, but of the world—that is an idea which one brain alone has grasped.

Beesly was a convinced republican, an admirer of Mazzini and of Abraham Lincoln; he saw the Union victory in the American Civil War as giving 'a vast impetus' to republican sentiments which would shake 'the tottering edifice of English society'.[12] Why should he exult in the coming of the Roman Empire?

II

In March 1865 a new journal was launched, with the purpose 'of aiding Progress in all directions'. Its editor, G.H. Lewes, invited Beesly and his friend Frederic Harrison to contribute to the first issue, on any topic 'short of direct attacks on Christianity'.[13] Beesly's offering was an article on Catiline as a party leader. Marx read it, and was quite impressed:[14]

> Professor Beesly hat vor einigen Wochen in der '*Fortnightly Review*' einen Artikel über Catilina, worin dieser als Revolutionsmann vindiziert wird. Es ist allerlei Unkritisches darin (wie von einem Engländer zu erwarten, z.B. Falsches über die stellung Cäsars zur damaligen Zeit), aber die intensive Wut über die Oligarchie und die 'Respektabeln' ist hübsch. Auch die Hiebe auf den professionellen englischen 'dull littérateur'.

> Professor Beesly has an article on Catiline in the *Fortnightly Review* a few weeks ago, justifying him as a revolutionary. There's all sorts of uncritical stuff in it (as you'd expect from an Englishman, e.g. he's wrong on Caesar's position at that time), but the intense rage at the oligarchy and the 'respectable' is nice. Also his digs against the professional English 'dull littérateur'.

It was followed by 'Cicero and Clodius' in 1866 and 'The Emperor Tiberius' in 1867–8, a trilogy later published in book form.[15] Read against his political preoccupations at the time, these polemical essays give a vivid picture of Beesly's qualities as a historian. They may also cast some light on the origin of the title of Sir Ronald Syme's masterpiece—an incomparably greater work, but one which similarly grew out of contemporary political realities.[16]

In telling the story of Catiline 'calmly and consistently with common sense,' writes Beesly,[17]

> I protest, by anticipation, against the supposition that I am amusing myself by maintaining a paradox. My sole desire is to do something towards the elucidation of a much misunderstood period of Roman history. I care nothing about the memory of Catiline, except so far as he was the representative, for a time, of the revolution which it is sought to blacken through him, just as the French revolution is blackened by calumniating Danton and Robespierre.

In itself, the idea of a Roman revolution was not new. The Abbé de Vertot's history of the revolutions of the Roman Republic was one of the most widely read historical works of the eighteenth century. For him, however, the revolution *par excellence* was the achievement of Roman freedom in the early Republic;[18] the word was used, quite casually, in the same context by Nathaniel Hooke in his *Roman History* of 1738, while the translator Thomas Gordon even attributed it to Sallust in his excursus on the establishment of the Republic.[19]

Hooke's use of the word is particularly relevant, since his *History* was consciously 'byass'd to the popular side' in order to counter the influence of Vertot, who was 'devoted to the aristocratical faction'.[20] His work is cited with approval by one of Beesly's radical predecessors, John Thelwall (1764–1834), in his *Rights of Nature, Against the Usurpations of Establishments*.[21] Hooke and Thelwall were agreed that 'after the *Gracchi*, there never arose a tribune, or any other magistrate, honest and generous enough to espouse the true interests of the people . . . till at length *Sylla*, having seized the dictatorship, changed the very form of the Republick, almost annihilated the tribunitian power, and reduced the government to an aristocracy'.[22]

For Beesly, on the other hand, the Gracchi were the *beginning* of the revolution.[23] His introduction continues with an explanation of the phrase:[24]

> Let us first endeavour to get some true conception of what the Roman revolution was, and what its course had been before Catiline became a prominent actor in it. It did not, like the French

revolution, owe its birth to the growth of ideas and the progress of speculation. It was purely a revolt against intolerable practical evils. No government has been such a scourge to the governed, as was that of the Roman oligarchy during the last century of its existence.

There follows a lengthy analysis of the nexus of political corruption and provincial extortion in the age of Verres. It was an

infamous system of government maintained by the nobility for the most selfish and sordid ends. This was the system round which the respectable friends of order (*optimates*) rallied, the Catos, the Ciceros, and the Catuli. This was the system which the irreverent advocates of reform (*populares*), the Gracchi, the Catilines, the Caesars, strove to beat down. The reformers were not all pure-minded patriots, not all men of stainless lives. But if we would deal them even-handed justice, let us never forget what that thing was that they were labouring to destroy and their opponents to keep alive.

It was 'the systematic, the methodical torture inflicted by the Roman oligarchy on the Roman world'.

Note, the *world*. In his Kingsley review Beesly had welcomed the Empire because the emperor's powers were to be wielded 'in the interest, not of Rome nor of Italy, but of the world'. As a young man he had harangued the Oxford Union on the motion 'that our foreign policy as dictated by the governing classes is selfish, shortsighted, and unworthy of a free people'; as a professor of history, he wrote that England's maritime power was marked by 'flagrant violation of the simplest principles of morality, by contemptuous disregard of the rights of the weak and by an assumption of superiority intolerably wounding to the legitimate dignity of our neighbours'; as a petitioner to Parliament, he would soon be deploring the atrocities committed by the British army in Ireland, India and the West Indies.[25] Beesly had no objection to imperial rule as such, but it had to rest 'on the only true basis for any government, the welfare of the community, and the consent of the large majority of the governed'—and that is what he believed the Roman revolution brought about.[26]

That may help to explain his otherwise baffling description of Gaius Gracchus:[27]

The first really great man that Rome in six centuries had produced, imperial in his aims, fearless in his choice of means, he gathered up the whole force of the revolution in his single arm and smote the oligarchy with a mortal blow . . . [His policy] was in effect to incorporate the Italians with Rome, and to substitute a single ruler responsible directly to the people for the sham Republic.

No evidence or argument is offered for this extraordinary idea. But if the revolution was the pursuit of a single aim, its result must necessarily have been intended from the beginning.

Much more convincing is Beesly's running theme of the symmetry of political violence. The revolution was begun by Tiberius Gracchus; 'the nobles beat his brains out in the street.' Saturninus resorted to violence; 'but how could he do otherwise when the nobility were ever ready to meet constitutional action by the bludgeon and the dagger?' Livius Drusus, an honest aristocrat, tried to shame the oligarchy into reform; 'he was assassinated. He had fully expected it.' Next came Sulpicius; 'the conservatives [were] eternally prating about order and the laws, while they knocked on the head every man who attempted reform by constitutional means. They had appealed to the sword, and so would he.'[28]

The same applied to Catiline. He, Beesly insists, was the popular leader in Rome in the absence of Pompey:[29]

Sallust tells us so in so many words, 'Cuncta plebes Catilinae incepta probabat.' Let us once understand this clearly, and Catiline's position becomes perfectly simple. He was the successor in direct order of the Gracchi, of Saturninus, of Drusus, of Sulpicius, and of Cinna, and was recognised as such both by friends and enemies. The popular cause, it must be owned, might have been in better hands; but . . . [i]t is fit and proper that when a Gracchus or a Drusus is murdered, the murderers should have to deal with a Catiline.

Beesly constantly, and rightly, stresses the unreliability of Cicero's rhetorical allegations about Catiline.[30] But he does not dispute the charge of attempted murder:[31]

That Catiline may at this time have laid plans against the life of Cicero is probable enough. He was not a man whom we could expect to rise superior to the manners of his class. The nobility had never shrunk from assassination where it served their purpose; and Cicero, though he disliked it as applied to himself, could applaud it loudly where a Gracchus or a Caesar was the victim. Assassination is a form of crime which has always been especially characteristic of oligarchic manners.

Catiline was, of course, a patrician: 'his ancestors had been consuls and decemvirs when the Metelli and the Domitii were clapping their chopped hands and throwing up their sweaty nightcaps on the Aventine or Mons Sacer.'[32] So Beesly can have his cake and eat it: in so far as Catiline *was* a villain, it was because he was an aristocrat!

The real point, however, is not obscured by this sleight of hand. Catiline 'did not mean to be knocked on the head like the Gracchi or Saturninus, whose cases Cicero was always quoting as wholesome precedents',[33] and he knew that that was a real possibility. So do we, if we read our sources carefully enough. When Catiline walked out of the Senate on 20 October 63 BC, 'Cicero . . . had hoped that he would be murdered on the spot';[34] 'Cicero distinctly states that he would have had it done if he had thought that his single death would have broken up the revolutionary party';[35] and when Catiline asks Catulus to protect his wife and daughter, 'even while he writes he learns that the assassins are on his track'.[36]

That sort of insight, achieved by reading the sources 'against the grain', seems to me the mark of a serious historian. It is clear enough, I think, that what made Beesly sensitive to Catiline's situation was his own experience of radical politics. Two generations earlier, he might easily have found himself (as Thelwall did in 1794) in the Tower of London on a charge of high treason. Even in mid-Victorian England the risks were serious. His close friend Frederic Harrison warned him about his outspokenness: 'I take it that if you were ever drawn into a notorious religious or political fracas (and what is to prevent it?) it would avail you little in the world being a scholar and a gentleman.'[37]

Beesly very soon was drawn into just such a 'political fracas', and it was one which directly involved his two themes of imperial misgovernment and the violence of authority.

III

On 11 October 1865 there was a riot at Morant Bay, Jamaica, in which eighteen people were killed and 31 wounded. It gave rise to a rebellion, and on 13 October Governor Edward Eyre declared martial law. The rebellion was contained, but during the thirty days of martial law 439 people were shot or hanged, over six hundred were flogged, and about a thousand houses and cottages were burned down. The most conspicuous victim was G.W. Gordon, a member of the colony's legislature.

He was arrested on 17 October, tried for high treason on the 21st, and executed two days later.[38]

News of the affair quickly reached England. Indignation at Eyre's actions was focused in the creation in December 1865 of the 'Jamaica Committee', with the aim of having him recalled to face trial for murder. John Bright, J.S. Mill and Charles Darwin were its leading lights; Beesly was one of the junior members. In January 1866 a Royal Commission of Enquiry was appointed. Its report, published in June, found that Gordon's guilt was not proved, and that Eyre had acted with 'unnecessary rigour'. The Governor was replaced, and left Kingston in July amid great demonstrations of support. As he sailed home, a rival committee was formed, to give him a hero's welcome and raise funds for his defence. Prominent among its members were Tennyson, Carlyle, Ruskin, Dickens, and Beesly's *bête noire* the novelist-professor Charles Kingsley.[39]

Beesly's attitude to the Eyre controversy is seen most clearly in a letter he wrote to a left-wing weekly protesting at the middle-class bias of magistrates:[40]

> It has at last come to this, that when a quiet and unoffending man is half-killed by a policeman and makes his complaint to justice, the magistrate coolly refuses to administer the law, and tells the injured man that he should have kept out of the way. Perhaps the London workmen can now begin to understand what took place in Jamaica . . .
>
> Let those who have made themselves conspicuous recently on the popular side look out for themselves. Some day it will be their turn. Nay, unless an example is made of Mr Eyre, I fully expect that Mr Bright himself may one day be treated with no more ceremony than Mr Gordon . . .
>
> If a serious riot should take place in Lancashire a few years hence, and martial law be proclaimed—a very conceivable supposition—I have not the smallest doubt that the country gentlemen and officers of the army would take the opportunity to get rid of Mr Bright, though he might have neither said or done anything stronger than he has at the present time. No doubt the Tory Minister of the day would deplore it as a most unfortunate occurrence, and admit that the evidence had been quite insufficient to justify a conviction. Perhaps even a magistrate might be dismissed, and a colonel cashiered. But the deed would have been done, and Lord W.G. Osborne would go round with the hat.

Presumably Osborne was one of the fund-raisers of the Eyre Defence Committee.

The return of Eyre seems to have made Beesly reflect on the exile and return of Cicero. In July 1866 the *Fortnightly Review* carried his article on 'Cicero and Clodius'.[41] Once again, he insists that the conventional interpretation has got it all wrong:[42]

> We are asked to believe that, stained with the blood of the popular leaders, Cicero was respected and beloved by the vast majority of Roman citizens, and that the troubles which subsequently befell him were simply the result of a personal quarrel with Clodius. To maintain this paradox—for paradox it must appear to any one accustomed to reflect on political phenomena—the *ex parte* statements of the least trustworthy of ancient writers have been adopted by modern historians as sober truth; his carefully cooked narratives have been cooked over again till the basis of fact has entirely disappeared . . .

How has this come about? Partly because of 'the credulous unphilosophical spirit, the ignorance of practical politics, the conservative tone of mind, and the literary *esprit de corps* too common among historians'. But it is also because Cicero satisfies the modern writer's longing for 'a full and vivid representation of events, with ample details as to the actors, and warm, sensational colouring for his scenes'. And that is the fault of people like Charles Kingsley.

Beesly repeats Kingsley's dictum that 'history is the history of men and women, and of nothing else', and contemptuously dismisses it:[43]

> We might be well content . . . to leave the trivial details about 'men and women' to scholars, gossips and antiquaries, if they could indulge their taste without a serious perversion of such important passages in history as the Roman Revolution. There we must resist them, and establish the truth, even though in doing so we have to shock an amiable spirit of hero-worship.

(Note that the revolution has now attained the dignity of capital letters.[44]) Literary historians' sympathy for Cicero had already attracted Beesly's irony in a splendid passage at the end of his Catiline essay:[45]

> The little army of Catiline died round their leader like the Spartan Three Hundred round Leonidas at Thermopylae . . . The world has generally a generous word for the memory of a brave man dying for

his cause, be that cause what it will. But for Catiline none. The execrations of nineteen centuries lie piled on the grave of the successor of the Gracchi and the forerunner of Caesar. It is not good to make a literary man your enemy . . .

An unequal struggle. The man of letters has had the ear of the world ever since, and has told his story without contradiction. More than that, the literary men have stood by one another, as they always do—like game-preservers or Whitechapel thieves.

It was surely a sign of the sharpening of the topical issues—all those literary giants lining up behind Eyre—that Beesly now directed his polemic at 'Professor Kingsley' by name.

Once again, his mastery of the source material enables him to see behind the Ciceronian facade. 'I have no doubt that the father of his country was universally hooted by the mob'; and the evidence is there, in the letter where Cicero tells Atticus about the time it didn't happen.[46] Of course Cicero was hated by the people, and his exile was the proper punishment for what he had done in 63; but 'if there is a childish way of explaining a political movement, a literary man will generally adopt it'.[47] His return from exile was voted by the wealthy in the *comitia centuriata*, and even there the custody of the ballot-boxes was entrusted to members of the Senate: 'If this was merely the statement of a Clodian partisan, I should not ask any one to believe it. But it rests on the authority of Cicero himself, who mentions it twice.'[48]

The most elegant of Beesly's demolitions comes at the critical point, where Clodius proposes the bill restating exile as the punishment for putting Roman citizens to death without trial:[49]

Now [Cicero] might be seen in a squalid dress, followed by a train of crest-fallen aristocrats, and pelted with mud and stones while he strove to excite the compassion of his fellow-citizens. He tells us that 'twenty thousand men' (senatus hominumque viginti milia) went into mourning with him. Sanguine as he was of obtaining the applause of posterity, he perhaps hardly expected that the historians would solemnly one after the other repeat his wild exaggeration, as a reliable statistical fact.

Plutarch specified 'twenty thousand young men'; Conyers Middleton in 1741 made that 'the young nobility to the number of twenty thousand'; Cicero's latest biographer, William Forsyth QC, was now writing of 'twenty thousand of the noblest youths of Rome'. Beesly comments drily in a footnote: 'London is nearly ten times as large as Rome in the time of Cicero; but "twenty thousand noble youths" would be rather difficult to get together even in the height of the season.'[50]

The enemy of the people, the man who committed murder under the guise of martial law, suffered 'a most just retribution'.[51] Would that happen to Eyre? Perhaps not. After all, the Senate reversed Cicero's exile by bringing in the country gentlemen:[52]

> [L]arge numbers of Italians were collected in Rome on an appointed day, and under cover of these bands the Senate passed a resolution that any tribune exercising his constitutional right to impede the bill for the recall of Cicero, should be treated as a public enemy—in other words, knocked on the head.

It was just a month after the essay was published, and a week after Eyre had landed at Southampton, that Beesly wrote his letter about the danger to John Bright, and others 'conspicuous recently on the popular side'.[53]

IV

In March 1867 Eyre was prosecuted as an accessory to murder, and the Shropshire magistrates dismissed the case. In the same month a Royal Commission began the investigation of trades' unions. On 27 March Beesly lectured in Bradford on the emperor Tiberius.

He began by explaining to his working-class audience what sort of regime had been overthrown by Caesar and Augustus:[54]

> Now I must first ask you to dismiss from your minds all those prepossessions in favour of the Republican Government which are derived from its name. It was no Republic. It was that worst of all governments, the monopoly of power by a privileged class. You know what that means. A single man ruling with despotic power must take some thought for the well-being of his subjects, or his reign will not last long. But a privileged class with immense landed property ... can perform with security feats of injustice and oppression from which a despot would recoil with dismay.

Then he told them what had happened to this 'convenient instrument for aristocratic misrule':[55]

> The people carried Julius Caesar to power, in order that he might crush privilege and establish something like equality. That was the

132

leading idea of the Imperial system as carried out by Julius, Augustus, and Tiberius, its three great founders. They were, in fact, tribunes and champions of the people against the nobility, and of the provinces against Rome. Only, instead of relying upon oratory, and agitation, and street demonstrations, and monster meetings, they carried a sharp sword. So, at length, the aristocracy was tamed.

The sub-text comes across loud and clear. Later that year, in Bradford again, Beesly would be drafting proposals for an independent political movement, the embryo of a Labour party.[56]

Most of the lecture was a defence of Tiberius' character, against Tacitus and 'the *servum pecus* of modern writers'.[57] But he focused in particular on the political trials:[58]

> The fact is that the state trials of Tiberius afford the clearest indication of the basis on which his power rested. He crushed a lawless nobility, and dragged to justice governors who had been guilty of oppression and outrage in the provinces, and who found sympathy among their own class as similar criminals do now.

That was the result of the Roman revolution. One day, perhaps, it might happen in England too.

In June that year William Broadhead, secretary of the Sheffield Sawgrinders' Society, admitted to the Royal Commission that he and his fellow-members had organized assaults on non-union workers, some of which had been fatal. A mass meeting of trade unionists was held in Exeter Hall on 2 July to dissociate the movement from these crimes. Beesly was horrified at the revelations,[59] but in his speech at the rally he urged the unions not to be defensive. 'Murder by trade unionists is no better and no worse than any other murder.' What about Eyre, the darling of the middle class, whose hands were red with the blood of more than four hundred men? 'This man committed his crimes in the interests of his employers as Broadhead committed his in the interest of the workmen of Sheffield.'[60]

There was a howl of venomous indignation in the press, and the President of the Senate of University College urged the dismissal of Beesly as being unfit to instruct students. When that attempt narrowly failed (thanks to George Grote), Beesly wrote to Marx: 'The combat is only adjourned. In some shape it must sooner or later be renewed, for when duty calls I hope I shall never be silent.'[61]

A brave man and an honest man, Beesly continued to speak out when he thought he could do some good,[62] but he had no more to say in public about Roman history. Even so, his trilogy of essays on the Roman revolution is a document of some importance. From one point of view, it illustrates the dangers to a historian of having an *a priori* pattern to substantiate. What but the Comtean dogma could have brought this enthusiastic republican to praise 'the splendid calm of two centuries, unparalleled hitherto in the history of the world, which followed the battle of Actium'?[63] On the other hand, his experience of the reality and the dangers of radical politics enabled him to read the Ciceronian evidence with a sensitivity to *popularis* thinking unparalleled in any historian before or since.

12

Late Syme: a Study in Historiography

I

'"Late Syme", as in "late Henry James"? One can see a resemblance . . .'

That comment, by one of Sir Ronald Syme's few equals in the art and science of history,[1] alluded to the notorious difficulty, even obscurity, of the work of Syme's later years. Oblique, elliptical, and often sibylline in expression, it makes demands of the reader which not everyone is prepared to tolerate.

Typical of the unease with which Syme's admirers approach this phenomenon is Glen Bowersock's description of *The Augustan Aristocracy*, 'a huge book of 504 pages (plus seventeen genealogical stemmata)', published 'to the amazement of everyone' in 1986:[2]

> The new book was, even for Syme, unusually dense and allusive, and few are likely to have read it through consecutively from beginning to end. But all marvelled at the energy and erudition of its octogenarian author.

How different from his other great work on that theme, *The Roman Revolution* of nearly fifty years earlier, of which a reviewer wrote: 'If the art of history is to instruct delightfully in what is permanent, Mr S. has achieved it'!?[3]

Part of the problem is inherent in the nature of history. Finding and presenting the evidence, and making sense of it by argument, inference and conjecture, is a very different exercise from telling the story of what happened. But telling the story is what history is about, and sorting out the evidence, however complex and time-consuming it may be, is but a means to that end. 'I shall have to confess,' wrote Syme in 1962, 'where my sympathies lie. They lie with the narrative historians Gibbon and Macaulay . . .'[4] To his readers of twenty or thirty years later, that declaration would be simply baffling.

For the historian, the artistic dilemma is always the same: how to combine, in the same text, argument about the legitimacy of inference from inadequate information with a historical narrative that is chronologically coherent and intelligible. Syme's mastery of the detailed literary and epigraphic evidence was unparalleled, as was his finesse of judgement in making inferences from it. But his method of combining such technical argument with the necessary narrative underwent a detectable change, which I think one can date to the late sixties.

II

In *The Roman Revolution* (1939), the competing claims of narrative and analysis are kept brilliantly in balance. The structure is made clear in the opening sentences:[5]

> The subject of this book is the transformation of state and society at Rome between 60 BC and AD 14. It is composed round a central narrative that records the rise to power of Augustus and the establishment of his rule, embracing the years 44–23 BC (chapters vii-xxiii).

That is, six chapters of analysis, on the late Republic and the dictatorship of Caesar; seventeen of narrative, from the Ides of March to 23 BC, as defined in the preface; and ten more of analysis, on the nature of the Augustan principate.

In *Tacitus* (1958) there is only an implied narrative, that of the *Annals* and *Histories* from AD 14 to 96, extended to cover Tacitus' own career under Nerva and Trajan (and possibly Hadrian). The subject matter of the book is immensely complex. Tacitus, 'the political historian', cannot be understood in isolation:[6]

> The events must be known, his coevals registered in their careers and activities. The theme demands a broad canvas and a mass of detail. Much of the material has never been put together, let alone properly interpreted.

But Syme is still careful to make it all clearly intelligible to his readers. The forty-five chapters are divided into nine sections, each with its own title: 'The Political Setting', 'Tacitus and Pliny', 'The *Historiae*', and so on. And the analytical material is hived off into appendices—95 of them, taking up 182 pages. Here, still, was the great literary artist of *The Roman Revolution*, as was recognized by the (not uncritical) reviewer in the *Journal of Roman Studies*:[7]

> The Camden Professor has written a tremendous book, fantastically fertile in ideas and constructions, at times outrageously provocative, always with immense learning shrewdly and economically applied. It is also a contribution to literature rare in the writing of professional history.

That shrewdness and economy of application is also visible in Syme's Sather Lectures volume, *Sallust* (1964). Though on a smaller scale than *Tacitus* (only two appendices), here as well the investigation of a historian was through his social and political background,[8] and by reading his subject-matter against the events of his own time:

> It is expedient to provide the social and historical setting of [Sallust's] life and works in some detail. Of the writings, most space goes to the *Bellum Catilinae* . . .

Syme had recast his six lectures into 'a different mode of exposition',[9] fifteen chapters long: the first introductory, then four on background, four on the *Catiline*, four on the *Jugurtha* and the *Histories*, and two to conclude on style and influence.

That structure is straightforward enough, but it is worth noticing that the guidance in the preface is a good deal less explicit than it had been in *The Roman Revolution*. Indeed, in retrospect the opening paragraph of the preface to *Sallust* looks a bit ominous:

> It was the rule among the classic historians of China to keep their personal statement for the end. They preferred the facts to speak. Nor need a preface be long, unless the author has been abnormally incompetent or expects dull readers.

From now on, Syme was evidently expecting very bright readers indeed.

During the next twenty years there appeared *Ammianus and the Historia Augusta* (1968), *Ten Studies in Tacitus* (1970), *Danubian Papers* (1971), *Emperors and Biography* (1971), *History in Ovid* (1978), *Some Arval Brethren* (1980), and *Historia Augusta Papers* (1983). Some of these were collections of previously published articles,

137

and those that were not looked as if they were. Characteristic of 'late Syme' is a comment in the preface to *Emperors and Biography*:

> A number of these essays were written separately, before a design began to emerge. It was the intention that each should be self-contained and intelligible without recourse to the others.

Similarly in *History in Ovid*:

> Each of the twelve chapters was composed to be read and understood by itself. Coherence and structure has been accorded proper attention, so I trust. The time and order of composition may (or may not) engage the curious and the erudite.

Over to you; sort it out for yourself.

As it happens, *Emperors and Biography* and *History in Ovid* are the two books in this sequence in which the contents-list is used to indicate structure: the chapters are arranged in groups, of five and four respectively. But in neither case do the groups have titles (as they had in *Tacitus*), and no explanation is offered of the reason for the grouping. The same applies to *The Augustan Aristocracy* (1986). Here the grouping of chapters in the contents-list is almost imperceptible, the significant (or presumably significant) gaps between chapter titles being just one millimetre greater than the others.[10] Syme's treatment of his readers was becoming increasingly cavalier.

The characteristics of 'late Syme' are equally clear in the two posthumous books, *Pliny and Italia Transpadana* (which appeared as *Roman Papers* VII)[11] and *Anatolica: Studies in Strabo*. The latter is particularly interesting, in that the surviving chapters, written in 1944–45, were left unpublished because the book was not complete; there were only 28 chapters out of a planned total of forty or more. Among the unwritten chapters were four or five that were evidently intended as a historical and chronological nucleus, the fifth of eight parts, entitled 'Caesar, Antonius, and Augustus'.[12] Early Syme had grouped his chapters and given each group a title, to make the sequence intelligible; what he had in mind was evidently a complex but coherent single argument, on the lines of *Tacitus*. Late Syme, whose standards had shifted in the meantime, commented of the surviving chapters that 'these Strabonian items could (and perhaps should) have issued in a volume'.[13]

The books after *Sallust* are like Syme's later articles, on a larger scale. The articles are always divided into sections—sometimes numbered, sometimes not—and the direction of argument, often oblique, is rarely explicit. 'As always,' he wrote in 1982,[14] 'material determines treatment.' Problematic evidence has to be sorted out, and as its implications and inter-connections are pursued in various directions, the argument ramifies. It seems to be largely fortuitous where the process stops: at one level, with an article-sized text; at another, with a collection of essays 'when a design begins to emerge'.[15] That, I think, is a technique quite different from the ruthless control of the material and focus on a single argument that is so conspicuous in *The Roman Revolution*, *Tacitus*, and *Sallust*.

III

At first sight, *The Augustan Aristocracy* is like the other 'late Syme' books, only longer. As the author says in the preface,

> A subject of this kind defies continuous exposition. The present volume comprises a sequence of studies (arranged not without care for coherence), each composed so as to be intelligible in itself and by itself.

Similarly at the end of the introductory chapter (14):

> The subject deters an annalistic narration—which could not without effort be kept separate from the actions and policy of Caesar Augustus, whereas biographies of emperors are a menace and an impediment to the understanding of history in its structure and processes. A different approach is worth trying: a sequence of interlocking essays.

Syme's life-long antipathy to imperial biography is well known. To make sure we don't forget it, he adds a footnote to a passage in chapter 25 where Augustus' *Res Gestae* are briefly mentioned (358 n. 94): 'By conception and structure, the present volume does not comport discussion of either the *Res Gestae* or the Autobiography.' But it is possible to write narrative that isn't imperial biography, as in *The Roman Revolution*; and in part, *The Augustan Aristocracy* does just that.

The key statement is not in the text at all, but on the cover: '*The Augustan Aristocracy* may be taken as supplement no less than sequel to *The Roman Revolution* (1939) and *Tacitus* (1958).' Its relationship with *The Roman Revolution* is clear from the items common to both books—the appendix showing the consuls of 80 BC-AD 14, and the stemmata beginning with 'The Metelli', 'The Kinsmen of Cato' and 'The Family of Augustus'. Its relationship with *Tacitus* is subtler but still unmistakable, in the constant reference to common themes: Tacitus' realization of the importance of the late-Augustan period at *Annals* III 24.3; the *capax imperii* idea introduced at *Annals* I 13.2; and the ubiquity of *adulatio*.

The subject-matter of the book ranges over the periods covered in both the previous works. Its chronology is defined as follows (13f):

> To comprehend the aristocracy entails what preceded and what followed: not only the period of the Triumvirs but the reign of Tiberius Caesar, for so much of the documentation derives from Cornelius Tacitus. Eighty years therefore, or even a century and a half. Men and families look backward to Sulla and forward to the fall of the dynasty.

That is, eighty years from 43 BC to AD 37; or 150 years, from 82 BC to AD 68. (It is characteristic of late Syme that the reader has to work out the dates.)

On the other hand (14):

> Restriction is enjoined, and concentration . . . An economical recourse offers, namely the aristocratic consuls who adorn the single decade (16 to 7) that is of central value for estimating favourably the achievement of the reign.

That refers to chapter 4, 'Sixteen Aristocratic Consuls'. The family connections of the consuls concerned are worked out in chapters 8–28. Five of them have chapters to themselves: ch. 21 on Cn. Lentulus the Augur (*cos.* 14), ch. 23 on P. Quinctilius Varus (*cos.* 13), ch. 24 on L. Piso the Pontifex (*cos.* 15), ch. 26 on Cn. Piso (*cos.* 7), ch. 28 on Paullus Fabius Maximus (*cos.* 11).

So far, so good. But the main structural principle of *The Augustan Aristocracy* is nowhere spelt out; it has to be detected by close reading. It is, in fact, similar to that of *The Roman Revolution*: analytical chapters, followed by narrative, followed by more analytical chapters. The proportions of the three parts are quite different, but the principle is the same as in 1939. Then, however, there was a clear announcement in the preface; this time, the reader must do all the work without assistance.

Chapter 1 is introductory, on *nobilitas*, and it begins with the years 29–27 BC.

Chapter 2, 'The Hazards of Life', is summed up as 'mortality and marriages, warfare, disease, and the plague' (31). A mere line-break at p. 25 tacitly introduces a chronological account, of the fluctuating numbers of consulars active in the years 82, 71 (followed by a digression on women, not signalled as such), 49, 44, 42, 33 and 28, thus returning to the point at which chapter 1 began.

Chapter 3, 'Nobiles in Eclipse', deals with the years 27–17, in which Augustus was frequently absent from Rome. Discussion of the *ludi saeculares* of 17 BC leads into a digression on the *XVviri sacris faciundis* which pursues that topic down to the end of Augustus.

Chapter 4, as noted above, deals with the consuls of the period from 16 to 7 BC, after a digression on the word *nobilis* (the chronological treatment resumes at p. 53).

Chapter 5, 'Monarchy and Concord', covers the same ten years. It was announced at the end of the previous chapter (63) as 'the achievement of the decade (on brief and selective treatment), urban occupations and habits of the aristocracy'—that is, social history, chosen no doubt in order to avoid 'Augustan' panegyric on the wars of conquest.

Chapter 6 is entitled 'Some Perturbations', referring to the withdrawal of 'Claudius Nero' to Rhodes in 6 BC and the Julia debacle in 2 BC.

Chapter 7 is 'Stability Restored'—by the deaths of Gaius and Lucius, the recall of Tiberius, and his adoption in AD 4. At the end of the chapter there is a rapid resumé of the years 4 to 6: Tiberius in Germany, and the revolt of Pannonia.

At the end of chapter 7 comes the unannounced turning point of the book, a very important passage (103):

> The great war in the North served to divert attention from discomfort and friction in the dynastic circle. The turn of events in the summer of the year 4 was sharp, and it seemed decisive. Some expectations were annulled, others enfeebled or deferred.
>
> Aemilius Paullus (*cos.* AD 1), married to Julia (the elder granddaughter), had been passed over. Hope did not abandon them. Fortune by opportune deaths had been generous to other persons whom they now saw installed in the power.
>
> Tiberius Caesar, at the seat of war, enjoyed robust health, long to defy the doctors and comfort his astrologer. Yet a variety of hazards threatened the survival of Tiberius and of others—battle and the plague, conspiracy or a casual assassin . . .

141

> Chance and usurpation conferred the supreme power, and the victor had to be aristocratic by name or by descent. If the campaign in Africa against Caesar the Dictator had gone otherwise, the world might have known a ruler with an appellation like 'Imp. Scipio Pius'. Scipiones and Aemilii were in close alliance at the time of the Hannibalic War, and their names thereafter occupy a large portion in Roman annals. The husband of Julia had Scipiones for ancestors.

There follow chapters 8 and 9, 'The Resplendent Aemilii' and 'The End of L. Aemilius Paullus'.

So this passage marks the point of transition, from the chronological treatment in chapters 3–7 to the discussion of families in the next twenty or so chapters. A climax to the narrative is implied but not stated—the disgrace and punishment of L. Paullus and the younger Julia in AD 8. It was that episode that had caught the attention of Tacitus, and made him resolve to deal with the late Augustan period at some time in the future; according to Syme, Tacitus should have begun the *Annals* not in AD 14, but ten years earlier.[16]

Chronologically speaking, then, the description of *The Augustan Aristocracy* as a supplement and sequel to *The Roman Revolution* and *Tacitus* makes very good sense. The narrative part of the former ran from 44 to 23 BC, and the implied narrative of the latter from AD 14 onwards (but it should have been AD 4). The narrative part of the new book runs from 29 BC to AD 4, with an implied extension to AD 8.

IV

All of that has to be worked out with little or no help from the author. The only thing Syme tells his readers is that the nucleus of the book consists of the consuls of 16–7 BC. Here are their names, with minimal annotation:

16. L. DOMITIUS AHENOBARBUS: husband of elder Antonia, *leg. Aug.* Illyricum, *leg. Aug.* Germany
    P. CORNELIUS SCIPIO: son of Scribonia, so half-brother of elder Julia
15. M. LIVIUS DRUSUS LIBO: nephew of Scribonia, stepbrother of Livia
    L. CALPURNIUS PISO *pontifex*: *leg. Aug.* Galatia/Thrace, *leg. Aug.* Syria?

14. M. LICINIUS CRASSUS FRUGI: *leg. Aug.* Tarraconensis
Cn. CORNELIUS LENTULUS *augur: leg. Aug.* Thrace?
13. [Ti. CLAUDIUS NERO]
P. QUINCTILIUS VARUS: husband of Vipsania (daughter of elder Marcella), *leg. Aug.* Syria, *leg. Aug.* Germany
12. M. VALERIUS MESSALLA APPIANUS: husband of younger Marcella
P. SULPICIUS QUIRINIUS
11. PAULLUS FABIUS MAXIMUS: husband of Marcia (cousin of Augustus), *leg. Aug.* Tarraconensis
Q. AELIUS TUBERO
10. AFRICANUS FABIUS MAXIMUS
IULLUS ANTONIUS: husband of elder Marcella (widow of Agrippa)
9. [NERO CLAUDIUS DRUSUS]
T. QUINCTIUS CRISPINUS SULPICIANUS
8. C. MARCIUS CENSORINUS: *leg. Aug.* Galatia?
C. ASINIUS GALLUS: husband of Vipsania (ex-wife of Tiberius)
7. [Ti. CLAUDIUS NERO II]
Cn. CALPURNIUS PISO: *leg. Aug.* Tarraconensis

Syme draws a careful distinction between significant and insignificant aristocrats. Contrast his comment on the Cornelii Lentuli—'Many of the problems that infest their stemma are trivial or antiquarian; such a plethora of nonentities' (249)—with what he has to say about the Iunii Silani, the subject of chapter 14: 'Equity demands that the Silani be put on review in a survey that takes life and substance from noblemen whom excellence or infamy commemorated' (188).

In the list of the consuls in Syme's central decade there is a high proportion who later became *legati Augusti*, commanding armies in dangerous provinces, or who were related by marriage to the imperial house, or both. Some of these men were demonstrably formidable characters, rivals as well as contemporaries of Tiberius.

Ambition and *adulatio* are the recurring themes. Were the Augustan aristocrats a threat to the *princeps*, or his subservient allies? Both ideas are present in another key passage, at the end of the 'Monarchy and Concord' chapter (81):

Consensus remained, and power changed into delegated authority. Aristocrats were not deceived by names and phrases, or by an ostensible antithesis. They knew the term 'principatus et dominatus',[17] and they refused legitimacy to the last of the dynasts. Fate or chance had produced him. Descendants of his rivals were extant.

Being 'Imperator Caesar divi f. Augustus', the ruler towered above them. They accepted him, for he was not one of themselves. The next Caesar might run into trouble.

Arrogant in comportment to those beneath, the *nobiles* showed deference to superior authority. The saving word is 'obsequium'. It was in danger of passing easily into 'adulatio'.

The Tacitean theme of aristocratic servility recurs constantly, and is particularly emphasized in the last two chapters. In the chapter on 'Nobiles in Velleius', for instance, 'pliant accommodation marks the renascent *nobilitas*, for personal and family advantage . . .' (432), while in the concluding chapter on the 'Apologia for the Principate', 'the apologia thus emerging was in large measure the creation of senators, and a product of tacit collusion' (441); 'subservient to power, the aristocrats decline to the level of clients and flatterers' (444).

Augustus offered co-operation, and they co-operated. 'Connivance is manifest between the Princeps and the governing class' (70). But Syme's point is that they accepted him because he was *not* one of themselves. 'The next Caesar [who *was*] might run into trouble.'

Tiberius was a patrician Claudius—indeed, doubly so, as Suetonius points out, since his maternal grandfather was a Claudius Pulcher who became Livius Drusus by adoption. But in *The Augustan Aristocracy* we find a Tiberius who was 'estranged in many ways from his own class' (145).[18] A conspicuous contrast is offered between the acquiescent *nobiles* and a man who 'cherished the aristocratic ideal of free speech' (117) and 'honoured all through an allegiance to the cause of the Republic and the families of the vanquished' (311). Here is the Syme view in a nutshell (100):

> Tiberius discerned ever more clearly the failings of the nobility now brought back to wealth, prestige, and public honour. He disliked their luxury and conceit, neglect of 'bonae artes', subservience to power.

Well and good—but subservience is only half the story. The aristocrats could not compete with Augustus because of his unique prestige, but there were real chances for them to exploit when Augustus grew old and his heirs were still young and vulnerable. 'Fate and chance' (81) had produced Augustus; 'chance and usurpation conferred the supreme power' (103).

This too is a recurring theme, and the phrases re-echo through the text (282, 312):

> Fate or chance awarded the principate. Men who bore the names of ancient or recent power saw usurpation in the primacy seized by Julii and Claudii and refused to surrender parity.

> The principate began in war and was maintained through matrimonial compacts, in spite of repeated deaths. Luck or accident or an armed proclamation might put it into contention again, with another ruler, of necessity from the high aristocracy.

That could have happened in AD 14, and it did happen when the principate was 'put into contention' in AD 41, 42 and 68. Syme never forgot the golden rule of history, to think away hindsight. *They* didn't know what was going to happen; but they did know what might.

In the post-Actium period, 'statesmen wrote their memoirs, salons opened, the social life of the aristocracy resumed its normal habits' (36); in 23 BC, 'the aristocracy seized the occasion to sharpen and reinforce verdicts normally confined to their clubs and conclaves' (38); after 6 BC, 'whatever estimate Caesar Augustus formed (and kept to himself), eager speculation in clubs and salons would fasten on the theme of "capax imperii"' (408); in AD 4, 'men of understanding or hardened intriguers found plenty to talk about in their clubs and circles' (341); and at all times, 'malice knew no restraint when men congregated at a club, a banquet, or a funeral' (441).

Those clubs and salons (*circuli*) are attested by Tiberius himself, in Tacitus' version of his letter to the Senate in AD 22.[19] The subject of discussion in the later years of Augustus may be easily imagined. 'What happens when the old man dies?'

That gives rise to another recurring theme in *The Augustan Aristocracy*: 'boy princes once again (or at least youthful), and the need for a regent, or a successor in the supreme power' (341, on AD 4); 'boy princes and a sexagenarian autocrat held out seductive prospects' (312, on AD 6). So too in the late years of Tiberius (324): 'Transmission of power through the line of Julii and Claudii had become precarious. The boys . . . might have no long survival.'

It was not inevitable that matters would turn out as in fact they did. The theme 'if things had gone otherwise' is of particular importance for

145

Syme. It occurs in the passage at the end of chapter 7 which we identified earlier as a turning point (103, 'if the campaign . . . had gone otherwise'), and it occurs again when Tiberius' survival is discussed (353):

> If the astrologer had miscalculated, other things being equal, Claudius Nero might never have left Rhodes, condemned to live out a long existence (he was very robust), or rather perhaps falling to the sword or mandate of a centurion, as happened on another island to Agrippa Postumus, the last grandson of Caesar Augustus.

Similarly in AD 8, 'a variety of hazards threatened the survival of Tiberius . . . battle and the plague, conspiracy or a casual assassin' (103).

That is why the notion of 'capax imperii' is so important, like the discussion in those clubs and salons of boy princes and sexagenarian autocrats. The consuls of 16 to 7 BC, as we have seen, were not only Tiberius' contemporaries but also his potential rivals. Syme is brilliant on Tiberius' enemies, whether as the nobiles celebrated in Horace (chapter 27) or as those conspicuously absent in Velleius (chapter 29). In particular, there were Paullus Fabius Maximus (chapter 28), L. Ahenobarbus the husband of Antonia, and Asinius Gallus the consul of 8 BC; at the time of his death in AD 33, Gallus 'was aged about seventy-three, close coeval to the ancient enemy, the recluse on the island Capreae' (63). The enmity of Gallus is attested by Tacitus;[20] that of Maximus is conjectural. Tiberius' hostility to Maximus, 'not stated by any author, is an inference or an assumption, yet not to be gainsaid' (409).

V

Much of The Augustan Aristocracy falls into the category of 'inference or assumption'. On the crucial period after 6 BC, for instance (112):

> Disturbed though not totally thwarted by the secession of his stepson, Augustus was now intent on conciliating the aristocracy and widening the ambit of his alliances. The situation is clear, the evidence largely missing or conjectural.

Or again, on the death of L. Paullus, husband of the younger Julia (122):

Speculation is baffled about the delinquency of Paullus and Julia . . . The main purpose of the present disquisition is to emphasize the singular dearth of information—and to offer compensation (by its nature inconclusive) for deficiencies in historians both ancient and modern.

Even where evidence does exist, Syme is prepared to reject it. In 2 BC, for instance (113), 'Caesar Augustus was imposing a tight regime. After the catastrophe of Julia, he appointed for the first time commanders of the Praetorian Guard.' After; but Dio puts it before, 'surely in error'. So too on the sources of Quinctilius Varus' wealth (328):

> Velleius declares the answer, in a sentence constructed with epithets in crude and conventional antithesis: he plundered the opulent province of Syria. Sober speculation will look to wealth blamelessly accruing from repeated matrimony and the bounty of Caesar.

Sober speculation is preferable, especially when opposed to crudity of style.

Syme was never afraid of speculation. 'The task,' he wrote in *Sallust*,[21] 'entails sundry hazards, and speculation cannot be avoided if one tries to put Sallust in his proper setting.' In *Tacitus*, he had used a different word:[22]

> The record being one of scraps and pieces, with many of the agents little more than names, and momentous transactions buried in deep obscurity, reconstruction is hazardous. But conjecture cannot be avoided, otherwise the history is not worth writing, for it does not become intelligible.

It was particularly necessary for the obscure period after Dio's continuous narrative breaks off in 6 BC. In his 1974 paper to the Bavarian Academy on the crisis of 2 BC, he put it plainly:[23]

> It is hardly possible to work out a satisfactory narrative. Mere paraphrase or amalgamation is not enough. Investigation of this obscure decade calls for various resources, and rational conjecture cannot be dispensed with.

If we think of *The Roman Revolution*, *The Augustan Aristocracy* and *Tacitus* as a trilogy, taking the Tacitean theme of *libertas et principatus* right through from Sulla to Hadrian, it is the narrative of the second volume that has by far the least satisfactory evidence,

147

especially for the period after 6 BC when the great dynastic issues became most acute. So it is there above all, even more than in the two earlier books, that Syme had to wrestle with the problem of turning accumulated data and inference into coherent history.

The two prefaces of *The Augustan Aristocracy* are dated to September 1982 and May 1985. It is a reasonable assumption that the book, and the issues involved in its composition, were much in Sir Ronald's mind when he gave the James Bryce Memorial Lecture at Somerville College on 10 May 1984.[24] Discussing Marguerite Yourcenar's *Mémoires d'Hadrien*,[25] he drew attention to

> a number of items or episodes where the dearth of reliable evidence encourages constructive fiction—or, as sober historians style the process, 'rational conjecture'. When other practitioners take that path, it becomes 'idle or barren speculation'.

Ten years before, he had used 'rational conjecture' of his own procedure in the reconstruction of the crisis of 2 BC. Now it is applied to a historical novel, in a lecture entitled *Fictional History Old and New*.

The Bryce lecture is an essential document for the study of Syme's views on the nature of historiography. But first, it will be expedient (as Syme used to say) to return for a moment to the theme of *The Augustan Aristocracy*.

VI

'The principate was formed in usurpation.' That is the first sentence of Syme's *Tacitus*—and it is a quasi-Shakespearean iambic pentameter (for the feminine ending, compare 'I come to bury Caesar, not to praise him'). It introduces a ferociously compressed history of the Principate from its origins to the start of his narrative in AD 96.[26]

'Urbem Romam a principio reges habuere.' That is the first sentence of Tacitus' *Annals*—and it is a quasi-Ennian dactylic hexameter. It introduces a ferociously compressed history of the government of Rome from its origins to the start of his narrative in AD 14.[27]

Syme tacitly identifies himself with the great exemplar. So too in *The Augustan Aristocracy*: in the third chapter—that is, at an early point in the narrative, just as in the *Annals*—he introduces the judgement of the *prudentes* on the achievements and shortcomings of Augustus. The context is not Augustus' death, but what might have been Augustus' death, at the time of his serious illness in 23 BC.[28] There is of course no indication of the parallel, just the assumption that the readers he wants will have picked it up.

Reviewing Syme's books, Arnaldo Momigliano repeatedly drew attention to the parallels between the author and the historians he wrote about: 'his images of Thucydides, Sallust, Livy, Tacitus and the anonymous author of the *Historia Augusta* have a common denominator, which is Syme himself.'[29] And it has become a commonplace to take the lapidary final sentence of *Tacitus*—another iambic pentameter, though with trochees in the first two feet—as a sort of motto for Syme's own work. 'Men and dynasties pass, but style abides.' The author who described Sallust's historical attitude in the same terms as his own,[30] and who in his seventies, discussing Ovid, observed that late work was often a writer's best,[31] is not likely to have been unconscious of the parallels.

In the light of that, it becomes particularly interesting to see how Syme defines the literary manner and method of Tacitus. Early Syme thought of him as a 'poet and dramatist'; there is a wonderful passage in *Tacitus* where the virtues of epic, tragedy and political oratory are all subsumed into the style of Tacitus, his manner of historiography effectively replacing those now obsolete genres.[32] Late Syme, at the time when *The Augustan Aristocracy* was being written, comments that Tacitus was 'moving towards drama and the novel'.[33] This analogy with the classic genre of modern narrative is, I think, something new.

In a public lecture in 1982, he spelt it out explicitly:[34]

> To become intelligible, history has to aspire to the coherence of fiction, while eschewing most of its methods. There is no choice, no escape.

Hence the Bryce Lecture two years later. In it he praised the purity of Mme Yourcenar's style:[35]

> Never a word or an expression to betray the middle years of the XXth century. A non-contemporary manner conveys advantage to historians in any age. They too are fabricators and creators of illusion.

Near the end of his discussion of fictional history and historical fiction, Syme appeals to those narrative historians whom he had named as his models more than twenty years before, and in terms which recall the preface to *Tacitus*:[36]

149

Diligence and accuracy, that is all that a man can claim, in the words of Edward Gibbon. More is required. The writing must be coherent and intelligible, otherwise the thing is not worth doing. There is more fabrication than meets the eye or is generally conceded by the practitioners. And it is unavoidable when the evidence is fragmentary and defective . . .

Historians in antiquity learned from epic and from tragedy. In the more recent time, prose fiction has become the dominant genre. Gibbon confessed that he owed not a little to the reading of novels, and one might wonder about Macaulay or Mommsen. Indeed, history, so it has been contended, needs to be as convincing as fiction.

'So it has been contended.' One of the footnote references is to a work of modern fiction, Anthony Powell's *Dance to the Music of Time*, in the final volume of which the novelist X. Trapnel makes the following statement:[37]

'People think that because a novel's invented, it isn't true. Exactly the reverse is the case. Because a novel's invented, it is true. Biography and memoirs can never be wholly true, since they can't include every conceivable circumstance of what happened. The novel can do that. The novelist himself lays it down. His decision is binding.'

The historian too is a creative artist, and his method is not dissimilar. In an earlier volume of the Powell sequence, Trapnel draws an analogy between the novelist and the spy, 'the point being that you don't suddenly steal an indispensable secret that gives complete mastery of the situation, but accumulate a lot of relatively humdrum facts, which when collated provide the picture'.[38] That, essentially, is what Syme did, and *The Augustan Aristocracy* is a particularly dense example.

Years before, observing in a review of *Tacitus* that 'the author is frequently speculative', A.N. Sherwin-White had given the reason; it was 'because his imagination is excited by a powerful creative effort'.[39] By the time he came to write the 'sequel and supplement', after long years working on the bogus history of the *Historia Augusta*,[40] Syme had thought deeply about the demands of historical creativity and come to define it by analogy with fiction.

My own 'rational conjecture', based only on inference from his *obiter dicta*, is that Syme's reflections in the eighties on fiction and

150

history and what they have in common were stimulated above all by his experience in writing *The Augustan Aristocracy*. Somehow, sense had to be made of that obscure but crucial period after 6 BC. There was no choice, no escape. To become intelligible, history had to aspire to the coherence of fiction.

VII

Here is a paradox. Syme appeals to fiction (as 'rational conjecture') in order to achieve a coherent and intelligible narrative in the absence of adequate evidence. But the work in which he presents his results—like all of 'late Syme'—conspicuously lacks the coherence and intelligibility of the novel.

However, what he says is '. . .aspire to the coherence of fiction while eschewing most of its methods'.[41] Syme knew the difference as well as the similarities. The analogy was in 'fabrication' and the handling of material, not in the way the material is presented. But there is a sort of parallel with modern fiction, in the hard work the reader is expected to do. As Powell's Trapnel observed on another occasion, 'reading novels needs almost as much talent as writing them'.[42] You might say that about reading 'late Syme'.

Nowadays, it is a critical commonplace to collapse the distinction between fiction and history. Syme would have had none of that. The difference between his position and that of the modern theorists is that he had *earned* the right to draw his conclusion, after a lifetime spent making sense of extraordinarily complex and intractable source material.

He is also more serious than the theorists. All the great historians have a sense of the responsibility of history: it matters that you get it right, or as near right as is humanly possible. Throughout his life, Syme explored the conflict of freedom and authority—most obviously in *The Roman Revolution*, but equally in *The Augustan Aristocracy*, with its closing chapter on the 'apologia for the Principate'. He concludes the book with reference to a classic text for that theme, Tacitus' *Dialogus* (454):

> Great eloquence (that of the Republic) was not compatible with stable government. Such is the conclusion of the *Dialogus*, not without gentle irony. The ruler now holds the arbitrament, he is the wisest, and men of good sense are quick to reach unanimity.

The language of Tacitus may have some relevance to the pronouncement of some unnamed sage in the recent time: 'in a true democracy there is no place for a serious difference of opinion on great issues.' The maxim clearly obtains when the issues are defined (or have been decided) by those who hold the power.

Syme's irony was not so gentle. Those final words of a book completed in 1982 carried a serious message for Mrs Thatcher's Britain.

Appendix A: Hermann Reich,
'On the Sources of Early Roman History
and Roman National Tragedy'

[*Festschrift zum siebzigsten Geburtstage Oskar Schade dargebracht von seinen Schülern und Verehren* (Königsberg 1896) 399–415. Translated by Hazel Harvey.]

I

As befits the status of the Roman Empire, with its enormous significance in world history and its long existence, the heroic figures of its history have seized the imagination of all succeeding nations. It is easy to conjure up before the mind's eye the figures of a Scipio, Cato or Cicero, of a Pompey, Antony or Caesar, of an Octavian, Nero, Titus, Marcus Aurelius, and Constantine the Great as well. But surprisingly enough, however great the deeds or the crimes of these men were, however much the results of their acts are still visible in our own time (when our heads of state still take their title from the name of Caesar), it is nevertheless true that we are at least equally familiar—perhaps more familiar—with the Roman names that pre-date the whole of real Roman history. Who has not heard of Romulus and Remus, the twin sons of Mars suckled by the she-wolf and fed by a woodpecker, of the rape of the Sabine women, of the fight between the Horatii and the Curiatii, of the dreadful end of the aged Servius Tullius, of the sinister Tarquin, the very type of a tyrant, of noble Brutus, liberator of Rome, who had his own sons executed! And the rape of Lucretia, the heroism of Horatius Cocles and Mucius Scaevola, the pride of Cn. Marcius Coriolanus and the tragic fate of Virginia are famous enough.

And these figures, of whom real history has nothing to say,[1] which appear to the historian as mere shadows that melt into the mist in the face of any attempt to fix them in history, should rightly be no more than shadowy figures to us as well, whereas in fact they are sharply drawn with individual Roman characteristics, as distinctly as art can portray anyone. That is why an uncritical eye regarded them as clearer and therefore almost more authentic than the truly historical figures.

Since these splendid, heart-warming pictures do not belong to history, one has to ask: what secret power has created them, and breathed such powerful life into them that they have continued to arouse as much interest as the great commanders and emperors of Rome's great history, and indeed are almost more memorable than these? This power, as we know since Perizonius, belongs only

153

to saga and poetry. But in what way did this act of creation occur? Niebuhr's answer, based on dubious evidence from Varro and Cato, was that there was a great Roman national epic, and from this epic all these poetic figures crossed over into history.[2]

This theory has enjoyed a great deal of support for a long time.[3] It inspired no less a figure than Macaulay to recreate the sort of lays of ancient Rome which Niebuhr imagined, in the Roman spirit, based on the narratives of Livy, Plutarch and Dionysius of Halicarnassus. He created ballads about Horatius Cocles, the battle of Lake Regillus, the death of Virginia, and the murder of Amulius by Romulus and Remus. He believed that to a certain extent he was recreating ancient Roman heroic lays. These Roman ballads of Macaulay's are not without poetic value, but for the historian and the philologist they are mere hollow concoctions. There never was a comprehensive ancient Roman epic such as Niebuhr and Macaulay imagined.

However, though this theory may be totally false, it cannot be called a deviation from the true path, for it has the merit of having pointed out with great energy that poetry alone can have created, or at least given the final form to, all the splendid stories from Rome's earliest history. This perception also accounts for the support given to Niebuhr's theory, misguided though it was.

But for some time now scholars have been on the right track and close to explaining this mystery.[4] Again and again, Greek and Roman historians, narrating the fables from Rome's prehistory—and regarding them as historical—express amazement that these fables have such a dramatic form. Thus Livy, after reporting the story of the conquest of Veii, which he expressly describes as a *fabula*, adds that such things are 'ad ostentationem scaenae gaudentis miraculis aptiora' [more appropriate to a stage show, for the stage delights in marvels]; that is, they would be more suitable in a drama than in a serious work of history. Similarly, Dionysius of Halicarnassus cannot stop expressing amazement at these stories, which resemble theatrical inventions and actual dramas more than historical narratives. And Plutarch rises up against certain critics who cast suspicion on *to dramatikon*, the dramatic element, in the tale of Romulus and Remus. He counters with *Tyche*, fortune or chance, which can produce events in real life identical to those portrayed in drama. This great Boeotian was never one of the great critics.[5]

Thus there was a widely held view in antiquity that many of these ancient fables are remarkably dramatic in form, indeed that they actually remind one of dramas. There is no denying that these fables are poetry, but the life that flows through the veins of most of them is not epic but dramatic.

This dramatic life in the fabulous figures of Roman prehistory is truly powerful. Again and again in recent times, albeit in modernised dramatic form, they have bestridden the Italian, Spanish, French and English stages, and have kept their power. I will mention only a few examples which I have to hand; an expert in this field could easily extend the list. The tragic fate of the aged Servius Tullius is portrayed in Gravina's *Servio Tullio*. Martelli wrote a *Tullia*. A *Brutus* was written by the Italians Pansuti, Costi and Alfieri, and the French Voltaire. A *Lucretia* was written by the Spaniard Juan Pastor and the Italian Delfino; there are plays with the title *Virginia* by the Italians Pansuti, Bianchi and Alfieri, and the Spaniard Juan de la Cueva. The tale of the Horatii and the Curiatii was dramatised by Corneille in his play *Les Horaces*, by Pietro Arretino in his *Orazia* and by Gigli in his tragedy *Gli Orazi e Curiazi*. Similarly, Pansuti composed a play called *Orazia*. The dramatic shade of Mucius Scaevola was also conjured up in the *Comedia de la libertad de Roma por Mucio Scaevola* of Juan de la Cueva. A *Coriolanus* was written by the Italian Crescentio and by Shakespeare. *The Fabii* was the title of an English drama from the end of the sixteenth century, and from our own century we have the *Fabier* of Gustav Freytag, a play by Martello called *Quinto Fabio* and a tragedy by Gravina called *Appio Claudio*.[6] There were also innumerable plays telling the story of Aeneas and Dido in English, Italian and Spanish.

Now why should the choice of so many poets, so varied in their nature, including the greatest heroes of the realm of poetry, fall so often upon these long-ago figures of ancient Roman prehistory, with whom we have no direct links and whose deeds do not touch our lives in the way that other heroes from history, particularly Romans, still do? The reason can only be that the modern dramatists could not resist the appeal of the dramatic vigour in these stories; they had no need to invent and shape dramatic figures, their imagination was free to play with existing plots.

But who were the ancient masters who first poured dramatic lifeblood into the figures of Tarquin and Brutus, Coriolanus, Virginia and Lucretia? Where are they, whose heirs include, among many other poets, even Shakespeare, when he wrote his *Coriolanus*?

Roman tragedy has long suffered from a lack of respect, although little of it is known and its highest achievements have all been lost. Critics are more inclined to respect the tradition of Roman comedy. Plutarch's evil mistress *Tyche*, who has condemned the better plays of the Romans to oblivion and preserved the poorer comedies, has thereby caused posterity—which takes Chance as the judgement of world history—to regard as worthless the worth of Roman tragedy.

But there was a century in Rome when tragedy blossomed, and that was the period of the Second Punic War. And it seems that the heroism of this epoch found an echo in the tragedies of Naevius, Ennius, Pacuvius, Accius, and many other less famous tragedians.[7] It is certain, however, that the consciousness of Roman strength and the feeling of Roman greatness inspired Naevius to create the *fabula praetexta*, the national tragedy of Rome, Rome's historical drama. And if the Romans for once are not to be regarded just as imitators and as mere second-raters in the field of poetry, it is mainly thanks to this great creation of Naevius', which has often been imitated in modern times.[8] In all, thirteen titles of *praetextae* have survived, of which the majority (nine) are from the period of the Republic, four from the Empire. If we estimate that there were originally 65–70 *praetextae* (an arbitrary guess),[9] this is doubtless a conservative estimate. The period which followed was particularly hostile towards the *praetexta*. In Horace's day the beginning of the so-called classical period of literature led to a lack of respect for the less well-shaped works of the old republican period, particularly the tragedies. But above all, the beginning of the imperial period was unfavourable to the true republican spirit which breathed through this old national drama, particularly in the tragedies of the founder of this genre, Naevius, with his strong sense of citizenship. From Tacitus' *Dialogus de oratoribus* we see how much the friends of Curiatius Maternus trembled for him when he composed a national tragedy, *Cato*, in the reign of Vespasian, who was regarded as a tolerant master.[10] And yet even in those times, so unfavourable to national tragedy, there were always new poets attracted to use the *praetexta*, so great was its ancient reputation.

Thus there was certainly a not inconsiderable number of Roman national tragedies, and they all deal with themes from Roman history. Sometimes they present contemporary events, as in Ennius' *Ambracia*, Naevius' *Clastidium*, Pacuvius' *Paulus*; sometimes fables from the prehistory of Rome, as in Pomponius' *Aeneas*, Naevius' *Alimonia Remi et Romuli*, Ennius' *Sabinae*, Accius' *Brutus*.[11] But the numerous *praetextae* of which even the titles are lost will hardly have treated themes of a very different kind.

So now we know the source of the poetry of the prehistory of Rome. It comes down not from a Roman national epic—there never was such a thing—but from Roman national tragedy, which created and shaped all these splendid tales. And we ought to applaud the happy naivety of the earliest Roman historians, who wove into their works everything they found about ancient Roman times in the historical national tragedies, since otherwise they had little or no information. It is thanks to them that we can now establish from historical sources more precise information about the form and content of these lost plays.

To judge by the poetic content of the stories from the prehistory of Rome, these Roman *praetextae* must have had no small value, for Macaulay is right when he says 'The early history of Rome is indeed more poetical than anything else in Latin literature'.[12] This means that in Latin literature these *praetextae* should occupy a very high rank.

It is true that we should not regard Roman saga as a whole as a product of the Roman national tragedy. The dryness of many of these stories makes that impossible, and their aetiological origin, which is clear to see. Alfred Schöne was right about this; see his perceptive and excellent discussion of the Roman *praetextae*, which contains ideas that lay the foundations for any examination of this field.[13] *Praetexta* material can be recognised by the stamp of Euripidean tragedy on it. This is because Euripides was the chief model for the earliest Roman tragedians.

So these old dramas in their historical disguise attracted modern tragedians, speaking to their spirit, leaving them no peace until they had rescued them from their prison of dry history and given them back a cloak of drama such as they must originally have had. In a certain sense we can regard all these historical dramas by English, French, Italian, Spanish and German writers, drawn form the Roman stories, as attempts to reconstruct Roman *praetextae*. And several of the few surviving *praetexta* titles do in fact overlap with the titles of modern historical plays about Rome, such as *Brutus* by Accius and by Conti, Alfieri and Voltaire, *Aeneas* by Cassius[14] and the dramas about Aeneas and Dido in English, Italian and Spanish.

The eagerness with which the modern dramatists have followed in the tracks of the ancient Roman national drama increases our desire to find out more about it, and to see what it was about the art of the Roman tragedians, otherwise so despised, that inspired so many others, including the greatest tragic poet of modern times, the author of *Coriolanus*. We shall see if we cannot, at least in one case, conjure up the ghosts of these great old tragedies.

If the attempt is successful in this one case, we shall see whether the ancient *praetexta* took the form of a structured drama in the style of Euripides, as Schöne presupposes, or whether, as Ribbeck believes, only the loose frame of a dramatic historical painting.[15] Once we have established the form of the ancient *praetexta* by examining one example, we shall have established a firm basis for our researches.

II

The Roman saga of the story of Romulus' and Remus' childhood is well known, in the form narrated by Dionysius (*Roman Antiquities* I 76–85) and Plutarch (*Romulus* 3–9).

I will briefly run through the main features of this story. When the Vestal Virgin Rhea Silvia has given birth to the sons of Mars, Romulus and Remus, her uncle Amulius throws her into prison and sets the twins adrift on the Tiber. Nourished at first by the she-wolf and the woodpecker, they are found by Faustulus and brought up by him. They become leaders of the herdsmen, get into a fight with the herdsmen of Numitor, and Remus is taken prisoner by them and brought before Amulius; the latter does not recognise Remus and hands him over to Numitor for punishment. But Numitor hesitates when he sees the youth's noble bearing, and is then told of the miraculous survival of his grandsons. They are both still at a loss as to what to do when Romulus appears, who knows from Faustulus the circumstances of their birth and rescue, and has been shown the original vessel as a token. There can be no doubt as to their identity. Meanwhile Faustulus has come hurrying to town full of anxiety for his foster-sons, carrying the vessel, the proof of identity (*gnorisma*), hidden under his toga. Amulius' men seize him. He has to confess to the tyrant that the twins were rescued. Thus there is a recognition scene here too. Amulius quickly sends his heralds out to find the brothers in the countryside, where Faustulus has cunningly alleged that they are to be found. He also sends for Numitor. He will hold him hostage until he has seized the brothers and killed them. But the exact opposite comes to pass. Amulius' plan is betrayed to Numitor, and Amulius is killed by Romulus and Remus and the herdsmen who come running to help.

All this is explained in remarkable detail. The scene between Mars and Rhea Silvia is described most precisely; we hear the Vestal lament and her mother advise her, we hear how the aged Numitor defends her before Amulius and the Senate, later we hear Amulius' judgement on Remus, and then the dialogue between Numitor and Remus and between Amulius and Faustulus. The action is played out in a well-ordered and lucid way, down to the smallest detail. This very explicit, well-ordered, well-arranged narrative is very different from a naive folk saga about the long-ago founders of an ancient city.[16]

The outer form is that of a drama; it is composed of dialogue throughout, and the action plays in speech and counter-speech. As in ancient dramas, the plot is based on recognition. As in Greek drama, once the recognition has occurred, what must follow is *nemesis* for past acts of cruelty, in this case those of Amulius. Thus the vessel plays a major role as proof of identity, in the manner of Euripides. It is described in detail, just like the basket in the *Ion* in which Creousa abandoned her son. Secret marks have been etched on the bronze hoops.[17]

Above all, however, the action of this so-called saga is constructed entirely according to a dramatic principle, that of the irony of fate. Numitor laments to his grandson Remus, standing alive in front of him, the murder of his grandsons. Numitor's herdsmen regard their master's grandson as his worst enemy and drag him before Amulius. The latter releases him, who was born to be his deadly enemy, but hands him over to be punished by his own grandfather. Faustulus wants to rescue Remus by showing the vessel, the proof of identity, to Numitor, but puts Remus in great danger when he falls into the hands of Amulius and has to confess that Remus and Romulus are alive. Amulius now seeks to get both the twins and Numitor into his power, but this leads not to the triumph he hopes for but to his own destruction.

The dramatic form of this story is so obvious to everyone that even Plutarch, who had no eye for such things, says (*Romulus* 8):

ὕποπτον μὲν ἐνίοις ἐστι τὸ δραματικὸν καὶ πλασματῶδες, οὐ δεῖ δὲ ἀπιστεῖν τὴν τύχην ὁρῶντας οἵων ποιημάτων δημιουργός ἐστι.

[Some suspect the dramatic and apparently fictional nature of the story, but we should not disbelieve it, seeing what works Fortune has created.]

So our opinion that this story is dramatic through and through is far from new and far from subjective, since it was already proposed by writers in ancient times. How would it be if this dramatic narrative of Remus and Romulus were truly nothing other than a poet's creation, a Roman drama?

It is true that the historians Dionysius and Plutarch consider this fable to be simply an ancient popular foundation-story, although we shall see that even they had a few slight reservations. But they refrain from vouching for the authenticity of the story. The one who does have to vouch for it is Fabius Pictor, who according to Plutarch[18] followed Diocles of Peparethos; thus the latter must be the final guarantor of its authenticity. But perhaps this examination of witnesses will help us to discover when this so-called saga crossed over into history, and who its true author was.

Fabius Pictor used Diocles. But he was writing at the end of the third century BC, and so Diocles, who lived in the third century at the earliest, must have written his ῾Ρώμης κτίσις, the work that Plutarch says is the first historical report of the foundation of Rome, in the second half of that century. Now Dionysius narrates (*Rom. Ant.* I 72.5) that Callias, who wrote the history of Agathocles, told the old story of the Trojan woman called Rhome, who came to Italy and married king Latinus. Their three sons, Romulus, Remus and Telegonus, founded a city and called it Rome after their mother. It is clear that Callias knew nothing of our story of the foundation of Rome, which was so detailed and later so generally known. He is familiar only with one of the numerous meagre and mutually contradictory stories about the foundation which were originally found in Greek authors. Yet as a Sicilian, and as a knowledgeable historian, he would surely have heard of so detailed and apparently reliable a story, with pretentions quite different from those of the other short and meagre versions of the foundation, if it had actually existed.[19] So it seems that when Callias was writing, in the first half of the third century, this story did not yet exist, or at least was not yet widely known. And since Diocles, writing in the second half of the third century, does know it, it must date to the middle of that century.[20]

Now this is the time when Cn. Naevius lived, the creator of Rome's national tragedy, the first to give bold dramatic form to material from Roman saga and history. He was the only one of his time to dare to do this. Thus he is the only one who can have been responsible for the perfecting in dramatic form of the story of Romulus and Remus. And in fact one of his pieces did carry the title *Alimonia Remi et Romuli*, 'The Childhood of Romulus and Remus', which seems tailored to the dramatic narratives of Dionysius and Plutarch. So the wholly poetic and dramatic narrative of what happened to the young Remus and Romulus, which Plutarch and Dionysius present as folk saga, is nothing but Naevius' *Alimonia Remi et Romuli* with a superficial discarding of its dramatic dress.

We shall make an experiment. Leaving aside the opening, we shall take the narrative of Dionysius and Plutarch, adding nothing and taking nothing away. The only change we shall make is to put some of the speeches into the order required by the drama, which was necessarily disturbed by telling the story in strictly chronological order. And we shall change indirect speech in the history to direct speech in the drama. If these small changes actually result in the construction of a drama, then we shall surely have rediscovered the outlines of the *Alimonia Remi et Romuli*.

I am far from believing it possible to reconstruct with any certainty the complete play Naevius wrote. In such attempts there are bound to be parts which are doubtful and subjective. But if I succeed in demonstrating, from one clear example, that a great deal of material from the ancient *praetexta* passed into early Roman history, then I feel that something has been gained for the study of both history and philology.

The Childhood of Remus and Romulus

The scene shows the palace of King Amulius, opposite
that of Numitor.[21]

Act 1, Scene 1

King Amulius stands on the steps which lead to his palace; before him are the ambassadors from king Vibe of Veii. Amulius asks what they desire. They reply:

'Vibe king of Veii greets Amulius king of Alba. He sends friendly greetings to you, wise old man. What is your reply, is it health?'[22]

The anxious question in the ambassadors' speech, 'Is it health?', already indicates that Vibe is in difficulties. He has been expelled by the Veientes. This is why Amulius then asks:

'Tell me how you have lost your great power so quickly?'[23]

And the ambassadors reply:

'New orators sprang up, a young and foolish crowd.'[24]
Amulius pledges support for king Vibe, who is as terrible a tyrant as himself. He thus declares war against the Veientes.[25] But the audience begins to suspect that the dreadful Amulius may suffer even more dreadful things than his friend king Vibe. The beginning of the exposition serves to reveal the sinister, tyrannical mind of Amulius.

Scene 2

A crowd of herdsmen fills the stage; they are leading a youth whom they have captured. Amulius steps down from his palace.

Herdsmen's spokesman: 'Hear us, o king! We, the herdsmen of your brother Numitor, were peacefully grazing our flocks when this Remus and his brother Romulus whipped up against us your own herdsmen, whose leaders they are, and drove us off our pastures. Many of us were injured, and we resolved to take vengeance. We laid an ambush and went to those young men's sheep-folds in the night. Romulus had gone with the chief herdsmen to Ardea, to make a sacrifice, but Remus quickly assembled some herdsmen and attacked us. We pretended to run away till we came to the ambush, where we halted, and there our men attacked him. We surrounded him and threw stones at him from every direction, until he sank down exhausted and we took him prisoner.[26] If this misguided youth is not punished, we will leave our herds and pastures for ever.'

The herdsmen display their injuries. Old Numitor appears and also asks for Remus to be punished, but the latter stands there proud and defiant. His behaviour irritates Amulius.

As befits a tyrant, he sentences him without a hearing and hands him over to Numitor, whose herdsmen were injured by the twins, for execution. His sentence concludes: 'It is just that anyone who does evil shall be punished by the victim of that evil.'[27] Remus is taken by Numitor's herdsmen to be executed in the palace of (unknown to him) his grandfather.

Act 2, Scene 1

Numitor stands in front of his palace. He delivers a monologue. Remus' appearance has affected him strangely, and he is touched by the youth's proud and bold bearing, going to his death without lament or fear. He has the captive brought to him, to ask about his origin.[28]

Numitor explains: a youth of such regal appearance cannot be of common parentage.

Remus replies: 'I will not conceal anything from you. You seem to have a more kingly mind than Amulius—for you investigate before you condemn, whereas Amulius sentenced me without a hearing. My twin brother Romulus and I are only the foster-sons of Faustulus. We were exposed on the Tiber in a vessel, found by Faustulus and brought up as if we were his children. The vessel is still in his house; there are bronze hoops on it with secret signs etched into them. Truly, we brothers have a fine proof of identity, which is no use to either us or our parents, for we shall die wretched and unrecognised.'[29]

Numitor begins to suspect that the twins could be his grandsons. He says: 'You know, Remus, that you have been put in my hands. However, if you do what I ask you to, and carry out a great deed, I will let you go free.'

Remus swears to do what Numitor asks; his bonds are unfastened.

Numitor: 'Now listen to the misfortunes of my house.[30] When our father died, Amulius seized the throne, although he was the younger. But not content with that, he was afraid of later vengeance and so tried to wipe out my whole house. He had my son Aegestes killed while hunting, and spread the story that he had been murdered by highwaymen. I had to keep silent for fear of my own life. He made my daughter Silvia become a Vestal, so that she would not be able to give me grandsons who might avenge my wrongs. When she had been three years in the goddess's service, she went to fetch water in the sacred grove of Ares, and there a miracle took place. The sun suddenly stopped shining and darkness covered the sky. The god of war himself came to Silvia and forced her to do his will. Then he comforted her, revealed who he was, and prophesied that Silvia would bear him twins who would excel all men in strength and wisdom. After these words, a cloud surrounded the god, and he went up to heaven. When Silvia's mother heard of this, she advised her to take no more part in the sacred rites in the Vesta temple. The other Vestals took over her share of the service, and she kept herself hidden. Amulius became suspicious and sent doctors to her, but the Vestals explained that she had an illness that men were not permitted to know about. But Amulius sent the queen to her, and she found out what had happened. The tyrant put an armed guard round Silvia, so that she could not give birth in secret. He then called me before the council and accused me of complicity in my daughter's wrongdoing. But I swore that I knew nothing of it at all, protested my innocence and requested time to discover the truth. Then, when I learned from Silvia what had happened, I went before the council again, told them what the god had said, and requested that it should be believed, if Silvia did indeed give birth to twins of outstanding strength and size. But Amulius would listen to none of this, although the council was beginning to believe that I was speaking the truth and that a miracle had happened. The tyrant's judgement was that the Vestal should be punished according to the law, flogged and executed, and that the children should be thrown into the river. But Antho, the daughter of Amulius, begged for Silvia's life, and so Amulius imprisoned her instead. When the babies were born, he handed them to a servant, who was supposed to throw them into the Tiber. Thus I was robbed of the grandsons who were to take vengeance on Amulius for the misfortunes of myself and of my house.' After these words Numitor weeps bitterly.[31]

Remus asks Numitor to send him immediately to take vengeance on the bloodthirsty tyrant.

Numitor rejoices at the youth's eagerness and says: 'I myself will decide on the moment of vengeance. You send a messenger immediately to your brother to tell him that you are saved and he is to come here.'[32]

Scene 2

Remus and Numitor are still standing in front of the palace when Romulus arrives. Faustulus, who has hitherto concealed from the youths their true parentage, has now revealed to Romulus that they are descended from Numitor, and has told him to hurry to Numitor to save Remus.

Romulus finds Numitor very willing to listen to him when he explains that he and Remus are his grandsons. When Numitor asks him to tell him the details of how he and his brother were saved, he says:[33] 'The servant who carried us to the Tiber found that it was flooded, and he put us in a vessel in the shallow water. But when the floods went down, the vessel bumped against a stone and tipped over. We lay in the mud and cried. And out of the wood came a she-wolf who had just had cubs; she suckled us and licked off the mud that covered us. And a woodpecker flew past and brought us food and kept watch over us. A herdsman saw this miracle, called the other herdsmen to come, and they all gazed in wonder at the she-wolf. But she took no notice at all and stayed with us. Finally she left, without any sign of anxiety, and disappeared into the sacred cave of Pan. Then the herdsmen came and picked us up. One of them was Amulius' chief herdsman, called Faustulus; he took us twins and gave us to his wife, who had just had a stillborn baby, and they kept us as their children. Thus we grew up as the sons of Faustulus.'

Numitor perceives that the twins were suckled by the she-wolf of Mars according to the god's provision. There is a touching scene of recognition between the grandfather and the grandsons he had believed dead.

Act 3, Scene 1

In front of the palace of king Amulius stand several soldiers surrounding a prisoner; it is Faustulus, the king's chief herdsman. One of the soldiers is carrying a vessel.[34] Amulius comes from the palace.

One of the soldiers: 'O king, we were guarding the gate as you commanded, because you feared an enemy attack.[35] There came this Faustulus, looking worried and carrying something hidden under his clothes. One of us asked what he was carrying, but he wouldn't say; then he was arrested and a vessel was found under his clothes. And when I looked at it, sir, I recognised the vessel in which, by your command, I once carried the sons of the Vestal to the Tiber. I recognised it by the writing which is engraved on the iron hoops.'

Amulius turns to Faustulus and threatens to have him stoned to death if he does not explain everything truthfully. Since he has the vessel, he must also know what has become of the twins. He must say whether they are still alive.

Faustulus confirms that they are, and briefly narrates their miraculous salvation.

Amulius: 'Very well, if you have told the truth, then say where the brothers are now. For it is not right that they should pass their lives unrecognised among herdsmen, since they are related to me and have been saved by the providence of the gods.'[36]

Faustulus sees through the king's cunning plan, and says: 'The boys are pasturing the cattle on the hillsides, as usual. But I was sent by them to their mother with news of them. When I heard that you are holding her in prison, I wanted to ask your daughter to bring me to her. I brought the vessel with me to vouch for the truth of what I say. Since you know now that the brothers are alive, rejoice, o king, and send messengers with me to give them your message.'[37]

Amulius calls the most reliable of his men and commands him to go with the herdsman and bring the young men to him, for he wants to kill them.

Faustulus leaves with this man.

Scene 2

Amulius alone; he debates with himself how to prevent Numitor from supporting the young men. He summons a trusted servant and commands him to fetch Numitor; he wants to keep him imprisoned until it is all over.

Act 4, Scene 1

Numitor and the messenger stand in front of his palace. The messenger reveals Amulius' treacherous plan and urges Numitor to outwit him; he himself will assist.

Numitor calls Romulus and Remus, and reveals that to ensure their own safety they must take vengeance now.

Scene 2

On one side Remus with Numitor's men, on the other side Romulus with the herdsmen, approaching Amulius' palace. Romulus and Remus force their way into the palace and kill the tyrant. Silvia is released from prison; she blesses her sons. Numitor praises the just vengeance of the gods. Romulus and Remus greet their grandfather as king.

Thus the drama closes with majestic pomp. That it is a true drama, in every way, cannot be denied. The choruses which must have been included have of course disappeared without trace in the superficial historical reworking of the drama.[38]

The poetic quality of the *Alimonia Remi et Romuli* cannot have been low, as far as one may judge from this rough reconstruction of the original drama. It is true that the splendour of Naevius' poetic diction shines only faintly, through the fine narration of Silvia's pregnancy, the exposure and rescue of the twins, and various pieces of dialogue. If a *Latin* writer had retold this so-called saga, we could have admired the rhythm of Naevius in the poetic expressions; it was said of him that since Naevius went to his grave the Romans had forgotten to speak Latin.

But the great art which the poet displayed in depicting the characters could not be entirely erased by the historian. How splendidly he portrayed Remus and Romulus, the sons of the god of war, predestined founders of Rome! How the Roman audience must have marvelled at these heroes in their godlike strength and beauty, recognised by the stubborn herdsmen as their natural leaders, prepared with unshaken resolve to descend to the land of the dead without complaint, as their fortune turned, who are so ready to fight for justice for the weak and oppressed, who gladly and voluntarily renounce the recovered crown in favour of their weak old grandfather! Opposed to them stands Amulius, the sly, cunning tyrant, whose robust conscience is not frightened by the most dreadful acts of cruelty. There stands Numitor, the weak, oppressed old man, who dares not act against his terrible brother. But he nurses his sorrow in his heart and hopes for a day of vengeance. There is Faustulus, the good herdsman, who comes to protect his foster-sons, deceives the cruel tyrant in order to save them, and would rather flee homeless to the mountains than betray his protégés. Finally, there are the cowardly servants of the sinister tyrant, who do not hesitate to carry out his commands.

But Naevius' dramatic art is seen most clearly in the structure of the action. We have seen how skilfully he uses the dramatic means of recognition (*anagnorisis*) and the irony of fate. Like Euripides, with tremendous effect, he links the recognition scene with the high point of the *peripateia*. By means of all these effects, he arouses in a truly artistic way the tragic passions of fear and pity. How the latter feeling reigns as we see the aged Numitor lamenting the misfortune of his house; how our hearts melt during the scene of recognition between the grandfather and his grandsons! And on the other hand, what dread seizes us as we fear that the sinister tyrant's cunning attack might yet succeed! Like Euripides, the Roman poet shows himself capable of portraying human passions and thus carrying the audience along with him. During scenes of this play many a Roman will have been moved to tears. Thus it is particularly in arousing pity, which was Euripides' great art, that Naevius too is so skilful. But over everything there hovers the visible working of the divine power, which seizes the guilty man when his atrocities reach the limit, and destroys him at the moment of his triumph. What is more, the threads of the action are spun marvellously fine with astonishing dramatic skill, and woven together lightly and surely with the perfect touch of a great master. The play thus belongs to the genre of 'interwoven' tragedy (τραγῳδία πεπλεγμένη), at which Euripides too excelled.[39]

So the Roman *praetexta* is not the 'loose frame of a dramatic historical painting', but a real, genuine drama; and Alfred Schöne perceptively saw the truth when he stated that Euripides was the model for the Roman *praetexta* poets.[40] It is true that there is no other field in which the Romans freed themselves so completely from their Greek model. If this drama had enjoyed the favour of the ages to the degree that the *Aeneid* has, it would doubtless have been highly esteemed in the Roman national consciousness. Indeed, it can also be compared with the *Aeneid* because of the major part played in it by fate, *fatum*, in true Roman fashion.

At the conclusion of this study I should like to recall the words of Macaulay: 'The early history of Rome is indeed more poetical than anything else in Latin literature.' And with that we must remember that everything that is so poetic about Rome's prehistory stems largely from the national tragedy of Rome, of which one example, and that not the poorest, is the *Alimonia Remi et Romuli* of Cn. Naevius.

Appendix B: The *ludi saeculares*

Our sources offer the following dates for the celebration of Secular Games during the Republic ('BC' dates are according to the Varronian era):

509 BC: AUC 245, 'exactis regibus' (Censorinus 17.10); 'Valerius Publicola qui primus consul fuit' (Val. Max. II 4.5); τῷ πρώτῳ μετὰ τοὺς βασιλέας ἔτει (Zosimus II 3.3).

504 BC: Publicola's fourth consulship (Plut. *Publ.* 21.1).

456 BC: AUC 299 [*sic*], 'M. Valerio Spurio Verginio coss.' (Cens. 17.10, from the *XVuirorum commentarii*). [The true date *ab urbe condita* is 298, and editors emend accordingly.]

452 BC: Year of Abraham 1565, Olymp. 82.1, AUC 302 (Jerome *Chron.* 112 Helm: MSS variants offer also 453 and 456/5).

348 BC: Μάρκου Ποπ<ι>λίου τὸ τέταρτον ὑπατεύοντος (Zosimus II 4.1); '<M. Valerio Corvo M.> Popilio Laenate <IV coss.>' (Festus 440L).

346 BC: AUC 408 (Cens. 17.10). [Lachmann emends to AUC 410 = 344 BC]

344 BC: AUC 410, 'M. Valerio Corvino II C. Poetelio coss.' (Cens. 17.10, from the *XVuirorum commentarii*). [Lachmann emends to AUC 408 = 346 BC, the date given by Livy and other sources for the consulship of M. Valerius Corvus and C. Poetelius.]

252 BC: AUC 502 (Livy *Per.* 49, Zosimus II 4.1).

249 BC: 'P. Claudio Pulchro L. Iunio Pullo coss.' (Cens. 17.10, from Antias [fr. 22P] and Livy [fr. 11W]; ps.Acro on Hor. *Carm. saec.* 8).

236 BC: AUC 518, 'P. Cornelio Lentulo C. Licinio Varo coss.' (Cens. 17.10, presumably from the *XVuirorum commentarii*, though the citation is lost in a textual lacuna).

149 BC: AUC 605, 'L. Marcio Censorino M'. Manilio coss.' (Cens. 17.11, from Antias [fr. 55P] and Livy [fr. 13W, *Per.* 49, *Per. Ox.* 49]; Zosimus II 4.2)

146 BC: AUC 608, 'Cn. Cornelio Lentulo L. Mummio Achaico coss.' (Cens. 17.11, from Piso [fr. 39P = 46.11 Forsythe], Gellius [fr. 28P] and Cassius Hemina [fr. 39P = 41 Santini]).

126 bc: AUC 628, 'M. Aemilio Lepido L. Aurelio Oreste coss.' (Cens. 17.11, from the *XVuirorum commentarii*).

Some of the variants—e.g. 456/452, 348/346/344, 252/249—may be merely the result of historians using a non-Varronian era for *ab urbe condita* dating.[1] But elsewhere deliberate manipulation is obvious: the Augustan *quindecimuiri*, who used a secular unit of 110 years rather than 100, evidently invented the games of 456, 346, 236 and 126 in order to justify Augustus' celebration of the *ludi saeculares* in 17 BC.

Similarly, Claudius must have had his own justification for the games of AD 47=AUC 800. Otto Hirschfeld brilliantly conjectured that Plutarch's date of 504 BC=AUC 250 was the result of counting back five 110–year *saecula* from Claudius' games,[2] with the happy coincidence that 504 was one of the dates handed down for the arrival in Rome of the founder of the Claudian *gens*.[3] Hirschfeld also believed that the 504 date went back to Valerius Antias.[4] But that is an unnecessary complication: not all Plutarch's material on Publicola was from Antias (see below), and it is more straightforward to suppose that the 504 date, with its implied sequence of *saecula*, was created by Claudius' *quindecimuiri* just as the 456–126 sequence had been created by those of Augustus.

Coarelli, in his important recent discussion,[5] rightly insists on the historicity of the *ludi saeculares* of 146, guaranteed by three contemporary sources. Antias' 'games of 149' are therefore spurious; and Coarelli may well be right to attribute to Antias a sequence 348–249–149, which was then taken over by Varro.[6] If so, then he and Varro must have had 49 BC in mind for the next *ludi saeculares*;[7] moreover, counting back from Valerius Corvus' consulship in 348, Antias might even have attributed Secular Games to the consulship of Valerius Potitus in 449, certainly an epoch-making year.

The year 509 was even more epoch-making, and it is natural to assume that Antias would want the greatest of the Valerii to have given Secular Games as well. That would involve either a short *saeculum*, from 509 to 449, or a long one, from 509 to 348. But that is not an argument against Antias' authorship; it is equally true, and equally problematic, whoever attributed the games to Publicola. Perhaps it was possible to think of Publicola's games as not strictly *saeculares*, with the hundred-year interval being introduced only later. Certainly Jerome says that the games he reports in 452 were the first ('agon centenarius *primum* actus').

Coarelli believes both that Antias dated Publicola's games to 504, and that the date was authentic. The latter argument seems to depend on the belief, which I do not share, that the 'Cumaean chronicle'—the authoritative source for Aristodemus of Cumae and his war against Arruns Porsenna—was sufficiently interested in the internal affairs of the Roman Republic to report the events of Publicola's fourth consulship.[8] Failing that, I think the state of our knowledge about the real events of the late sixth century makes it impossible to claim with any confidence that *only* in 504 BC would the phrase 'uti Latinus obtemperassit' (attested in the liturgy of the Secular Games) be appropriate to the historical context.

As for Coarelli's assumption that Antias dated Publicola's games to 504,[9] that is apparently plausible, in that Plutarch must have used Antias extensively in his life of Publicola. But he did not use Antias alone: his reports of events that showed Publicola in a poor light, for instance, show that he had other sources available.[10] It may be more significant that Censorinus, who used Antias specifically for the Secular Games, does not know about the '504' variant.

Coarelli indeed alleges that Censorinus' date of 509 'è solo il risultato di una correzione dei codici, in cui appaiono varie cifre'; but he cites no evidence for his statement that 'nei codd. si trova CCLV e CCXL'[11] (no variants are reported in the apparatus criticus of either Jahn [1845] or Rapisarda [1991]), and in any case those alleged variants would refer to 499 or 514, which would not help his case. Censorinus is explicit: he says 'exactis regibus', not 'anno post reges exactos sexto'.

Plutarch's date is unique to him, and best explained by Hirschfeld's hypothesis that it was necessary for the calculation of the Claudian Secular Games. I conclude (unlike Hirschfeld and Coarelli) that Plut. *Publ.* 21.1 comes not from Antias but from a Claudian source, no earlier than AD 47; and therefore that Antias is available as the hypothetical source for the 509 BC Secular Games, and thus also for the inscription on the altar of Dis quoted by Zosimus.

Notes

Introduction

1. See most recently T.J. Cornell, *The Beginnings of Rome* (London 1995) 93–6; C. Smith, *Early Rome and Latium* (Oxford 1996) 100–3.
2. E. Badian, in T.A. Dorey (ed.), *Latin Historians* (London 1966), 2–7; fragments and *testimonia* at *FGrH* 809 and 810 = F. Jacoby (ed.), *Fragmente der griechischen Historiker* III C (Leiden 1958) 845–80.
3. Jupiter temple: L. Richardson jr, *A New Topographical Dictionary of Ancient Rome* (Baltimore 1992) 221–4. Walls: Cornell, op. cit. (n. 1 above) 198–9; Richardson, op. cit. 262–3. Roads: T.P. Wiseman, *Roman Studies* (Liverpool 1987) 144–8, 379. Aqueducts: A.T. Hodge, *Roman Aqueducts and Water Supply* (London 1992). Land and colonies: T.J. Cornell, in *Cambridge Ancient History* VII.2 (ed. 2, Cambridge 1989) 403–5.
4. C.E., *Times Literary Supplement* 4767 (12 August 1994) 25; T.J. Cornell, *Times Higher Education Supplement* 1246 (20 September 1996) 27; W.V. Harris, *London Review of Books* (23 May 1996) 22; E. Gabba, *Athenaeum* 85 (1997) 309; J. Van Sickle, *Bryn Mawr Classical Review* 8.6 (1997) 574–5. *Contra*: J.W. Rich, *Classical Review* 45 (1995) 368; M. Beard, *Times Literary Supplement* 4854 (12 April 1996) 3.
5. H.I. Flower, *Ancestor Masks and Aristocratic Power in Roman Culture* (Oxford 1996) 91–127.

Chapter 1

1. *Monatsberichte der k. Preussischen Akademie* (1849) 3, 238: 'Zur Kritik des Dionysius von Halikarnass', repeated at a session of the full Academy on 25 October.
2. So C. Trieber, *Rheinisches Museum* 43 (1888) 569, and W. Soltau, *Die Anfänge der roemischen Geschichtschreibung* (Leipzig 1909) 21 n. 1, citing Ranke's paper as if it were a published text. Ranke's *Weltgeschichte* III.2 (*Analekten: Kritische Erörterungen zur alten Geschichte*, Leipzig 1883) ch. 3, 'Ueber die römischen Alterthümer des Dionysius von Halicarnass' (pp. 92–150), is presumably an updating of his 1849 argument; see 108–115 ('Romulus und Remus') for the drama theory. I am very grateful indeed to

Prof. Dr Ulrich Muhlack of Frankfurt for expert guidance on this complex matter.
3. For Niebuhr's theory, its origin and its reception, see A. Momigliano, *Journal of Roman Studies* 47 (1957) 104–14 = *Essays in Ancient and Modern Historiography* (Oxford 1977) 231–51.
4. A. Schwegler, *Römische Geschichte* I (Tübingen 1853) 53–73; Sir G. Cornewall Lewis, *An Enquiry into the Credibility of Early Roman History* I (London 1855) 202–37.
5. G. Linker, *Die älteste Sagengeschichte Roms* (Vienna 1858) 5 ('seit Niebuhr's unsterblichem Werke'), 22 (Tullia, Lucretia), 27 ('es ist das Verdienst Niebuhr's . . . das Wort der Lösung gesprochen zu haben').
6. Ranke, op. cit. (n. 2) 110, on Dion. Hal. I 79.2 and 82.3–5; 111, on I 83.3; 112–3, on Euripides etc; 111, 113 (drama, not saga); 115, on Naevius.
7. O. Ribbeck, *Die römische Tragödie im Zeitalter der Republik* (Leipzig 1875) 63–75, esp. 72 on Dion. Hal. I 84.1 (ὡς δραματικῆς μεστὸν ἀτοπίας) and Plut. *Rom.* 8.7 (δραματικὸν καί πλασματῶδες). See n. 11 below for his successive editions of the fragments.
8. Ribbeck, op. cit. 63; Trieber, op. cit. (n. 2) 569–82.
9. O. Jahn, *Der Tod der Sophoniba auf einem Wandgemälde* (Bonn 1859) 12–13: '[D]ie immer wieder erneuerten Versuche ihrer tragischen Dichter in der Prätexta legen ein schlagendes Zeugniss dafür ab, wie tief gefühlt das Verlangen nach einer nationalen Tragödie war.'
10. O. Ribbeck, 'Ein historisches Drama', *Rheinisches Museum* 36 (1881) 321–2: Livy V 21.8–9 ('haec ad ostentationem scaenae gaudentis miraculis aptiora'); cf. 19.1–2 (*fata*), 21.15 (nemesis anticipated). Cf. also O. Ribbeck, *Geschichte der römischen Dichtung* I (Stuttgart 1887) 191.
11. O. Ribbeck, *Tragicorum Romanorum reliquiae* (Leipzig 1852) 233–40 = ed. 2 (Leipzig 1871) 275–86 = *Tragicorum Romanorum fragmenta* (Leipzig 1897) 319–31, 335.
12. Varro *De ling. Lat.* VII 107, IX 78: for Marcellus, cf. Diomedes *Gramm. Lat.* I 490K.
13. Varro *De ling. Lat.* VII 54, 107.
14. Festus 334L, Cic. *De sen.* 20(?); J.G.F. Powell, *Cicero, Cato maior de senectute* (Cambridge 1988) 145–6.
15. Donatus on Ter. *Adelphi* 537. Note that nos. 2, 3 and 4 may be one play, or two, or three.
16. Nonius 125L, 269L, 753L, 756L.
17. Julius Victor *Rhet. Lat.* 402H.
18. Gellius *NA* IX 14.13, Nonius 816L, 820L, Priscian *Gramm. Lat.* II 196K, Macrobius *Sat.* VI 5.14.
19. Nonius 32L, 105L, 139L, 177L, 203L, 256L, 272L, 295L, 332L, 393L, 777L, 811L; cf. Diomedes *Gramm. Lat.* I 490K.
20. Cic. *De div.* I 43–5, *Sest.* 123; Varro *De ling. Lat.* V 80; cf. Diomedes *Gramm. Lat.* I 490K.
21. Pollio in Cic. *Ad fam.* X 32.3.
22. Varro *De ling. Lat.* VI 7, VII 72. The author's name is often emended to Accius, quite unnecessarily; see Porphyrio on Hor. *Epist.* I 4.3 and *Sat.* I 10.61 for the tragedies of Cassius Parmensis.

23. Charisius *Gramm.* 163B.
24. Tac. *Dial.* 2.1, 3.2–3.
25. Tac. *Dial.* 3.4.
26. The only surviving *praetexta* text, wrongly attributed to Seneca and transmitted with his tragedies.
27. Varro *De ling. Lat.* VI 18; above, pp. 8–11.
28. Ovid *Fasti* IV 291–349 ('mira sed et scaena testificata loquar', 326); see further chapters 2 and 3.
29. Hor. *Ars poetica* 285–8: 'Nil intemptatum nostri liquere poetae, nec minimum meruere decus uestigia Graecae ausi deserere et celebrare domestica facta, uel qui praetextas uel qui docuere togatas.'
30. Homer *Odyssey* I 350–2, Telemachus on Phemius' song of the heroes' homecoming from Troy. For games vowed by a commander (and no doubt put on at the time of his triumph), see for instance Livy XXXVI 2.2–5 (M'. Acilius Glabrio, 191 BC). Festus (Paulus 249L) defines *praetextae* as 'quae res gestas Romanorum continent scripta'.
31. K. Meiser, *Ueber historische Dramen der Römer* (Munich 1887) 36–8; A. Schöne, *Das historische Nationaldrama der Römer: die Fabula praetexta* (Kiel 1893) 3, 18. Meiser accepted the Niebuhr theory of lost epics as one reason for the poetic nature of early Roman history, but sought to show that 'drama too had exercised a similar influence and left its mark behind' (op. cit. 22–3).
32. Meiser, op. cit. 21–5; Schöne, op. cit. 6–8, 11–13.
33. Meiser, op. cit. 23 on Dionysius and Plutarch (cf. n. 7 above). Schöne, op. cit. 13–17: Dion. Hal. III 18.1 (θεατρικαῖς ἐοικότα περιπετείαις), 22.10 (θαυμαστὰς καί παραδόξους περιπετείας), IX 22.3 (πλάσμασιν ἔοικε θεατρικοῖς).
34. Schöne, op. cit. 17; Meiser, op. cit. 25–7 (Livy XXIII 2–10), 27–31 (Livy XL 2–16, 20–4, 54–6), 32–6 (Plut. *C. Gracchus* 14 etc, on which see chapter 5).
35. Diomedes *Gramm. Lat.* I 490K; partial translation in T.P. Wiseman, *Historiography and Imagination* (Exeter 1994) 140–1.
36. Cf. Ribbeck, op. cit. (1852, n. 11 above) 351: 'Et haec sunt, quae de nobilissima praetextarum poesi ad nos peruenerunt, exigua scilicet regum imperatorumque quasi ossa, quorum animus utinam redimere possent uel Medeae et Atrei tenebris redditae!'
37. G. Boissier, 'Les *fabulae praetextae*', *Revue de philologie* 17 (1893) 101–8, esp. 101–2 (portrayal of *res gestae*), 106–8 ('left the public cold'). Boissier assumed that 'il y avait quelque chose de choquant à voir les faits et les personnages de l'histoire romaine présentés de la même manière et sous le même jour que les évènements et les héros des légendes antiques' (op. cit. 106); but that seems to be no more than an arbitrary reflection of nineteenth-century taste.
38. Schöne, op. cit. (n. 31) 9–10: 'Es ist darum kein müssiges Spiel des Scharfsinne, wenn die Philologie bemüht ist, dem nationalen historischen Drama dieser grossen Periode Roms näher nachzugehen, erloschene oder verwischte Spuren, die es in der Litteratur hinterlassen haben kann, sorgfältig aufzusuchen, und ihm als sein Eigenthum Manches zuzuweisen,

was bisher als geistiges Besitztum anderer Literaturgebiete, insbesondere der Geschichte und der Geschichtschreibung gegolten hat.'

39. Op. cit. (n. 37) 107: 'c'étaient des pièces de circonstance, comme on vient de le voir, et le plupart n'ont pas dû survivre aux circonstances mêmes pour lesquelles on les avaient faites.'

40. W. Reich, in *Festschrift zum siebzigsten Geburtstag Oskar Schade dargebracht* (Königsberg 1896) 399–415: pp. 153–64 above. Cf. Ribbeck (op. cit. n. 8 above) for the play as Euripidean; Trieber (op. cit. n. 8 above) and W. Soltau, *Archiv für Religionswissenschaft* 12 (1909) 105–111, took it as a rewriting of Sophocles' *Tyro*.

41. W. Soltau, op. cit. (n. 2) 17–59, 92–131.

42. Op. cit., first paragraph of the Introduction (page not numbered): 'Dieses Buch wird zeugen, dass alle lebensvollen und individuellen Züge der älteren römischen Geschichte auf *Dichtung* und *Erfindung* beruhen. Nicht Mythus, nicht Volkssage, sondern literarische Erfindung ist alles das, was an geschichtlich erscheinenden Berichten einer gleichzeitigen Geschichtsüberlieferung vorangeht.' (The italics represent Soltau's emphatic spaced type.)

43. Op. cit. 263–4 (*Anhang* I: *Die nachweisbaren Praetextae*).

44. W. Soltau, *Livius' Geschichtswerk, sein Composition und seine Quellen* (Leipzig 1897).

45. H. Peter, *Berliner philologische Wochenschrift* 30.2 (8 Jan. 1910) 51: 'Sein Temperament hat ihn oft zu nicht zwingenden Schlussfolgerungen geführt . . .'

46. F. Münzer, *Cacus der Rinderdieb* (Basel 1911) 4: 'Man müsste annehmen, dass . . . bestimmte Bühnenwerke, deren Verfasser wohl bekannt waren, künstlich eine Tradition erzeugt hätten, die sofort und ganz allgemein von dem römischen Volke als die Geschichte seiner eigenen Vergangenheit anerkannt wurde, obgleich gerade dieses Volk mit grosser Zähigkeit an der Vergangenheit haftete.'

47. Münzer, op. cit. 4: 'Also nicht nationale, sondern graecisierte Poesie, nicht epische, sondern dramatische Poesie, nicht Volkspoesie, sondern Kunstpoesie!' Peter, op. cit. (n. 45) 52: 'Was in einer Erzählung dramatisch ist, stammt darum nicht aus einem Drama, ebensowenig wie, was poetisch, aus einer Dichtung.'

48. F.M. Litto, 'Addison's *Cato* in the Colonies', *William and Mary Quarterly* 23 (1966) 431–49, and C.J. Richard, *The Founders and the Classics: Greece, Rome, and the American Enlightenment* (Harvard 1994) 57–60.

49. H.B. Wright, *The Recovery of a Lost Roman Tragedy: a Study in Honor of Bernadotte Perrin, PhD LLD, Professor in Yale University 1893–1909* (New Haven 1910), quotations from pp. 25 and 30.

50. Livy I 46.3, 'sceleris tragici exemplum'; Wright, op. cit. 39.

51. Livy I 46.4–5 (1); 46.5 (2); 46.6 (4); 46.7 (6); 46.7–8 (7); 46.9 (8); Dion. Hal. IV 28.1–2 (1); 28.3 (3–4); 28.4 (5); 29.1–7 (7); 30.1 and 4 (8).

52. Accius fr. 655–6R = 699–700 Dangel (Cic. *Orator* 156): '. . . mulier una duom uirum', 'uideo sepulcra dua duorum corporum'.

53. E.S. Duckett, *Studies in Ennius* (Bryn Mawr 1915) 6–7: '[Ranke's]

suggestion was infectious, and quickly attacked other parts of this body of folk-lore . . .'

54. Ibid. 7–22.
55. C.C. Coulter, *Classical Journal* 35 (1939–40) 460–70, quotation from p. 462.
56. Ibid. 465 (Ranke), 467–8.
57. A.K. Michels, *Latomus* 10 (1951) 13–24, differing from Wright in her view of Dionysius.
58. Ibid. 17, 19 (Livy I 41.4, 47.7, 59.13); ibid. 24 on Pollio, whose tragedies are mentioned by Horace (*Odes* II 1.9–12, *Sat.* I 10.42–3) and Virgil (*Ecl.* 8.10).
59. H. Bardon, *La littérature latine inconnue* I (Paris 1952) 326–7 (p. 53 above); R.M. Ogilvie, *A Commentary on Livy Books 1–5* (Oxford 1965) 186, 189, 196, 219 (p. 31 above).
60. J. Heurgon, 'Tite-Live et les Tarquins', *L'information littéraire* 7 (1955) 56–64, at 58: 'quand les *scriptores Tusci* l'avaient rédigée, la Melpomène d'Eschyle et d'Euripide était à leurs côtés.'
61. Varro *De ling. Lat.* VI 18. Poplifugia, 5 July; Nonae Caprotinae (or Capratinae) 5 or 7 July: sources in *Inscriptiones Italiae* XIII.2 (Rome 1963) 476–81, but see also N. Robertson, *Museum Helveticum* 44 (1987) 18–20, and now above all F. Coarelli, *Il campo Marzio dalle origine alla fine della repubblica* (Rome 1997) 17–61.
62. Most recently R.G. Kent (Loeb ed. 1938), A. Traglia (Turin 1974) and P. Flobert (Budé ed. 1985); the MS reading, first admitted by L. and A. Spengel in 1885, appears in the Teubner edition of G. Goetz and F. Schoell (1910). The emended reading is insisted on (wrongly, in my view) by Coarelli, op. cit. 38–9.
63. Coarelli's evasiveness is revealing (op. cit. 39, 55): 'quando alle *mulieres* viene consegnata la *toga praetexta* . . . la distribuzione della *toga praetexta* alle *mulieres* . . .', without comment or explanation; ibid. 44–5, where he assumes that the women concerned were prostitutes (which would account for the toga, but cf. n. 78 below). Similarly P. Flobert, in J. Collart et al., *Varron: grammaire antique et stylistique latine* (Sorbonne Études 14, Paris 1978) 47, assumes that the *mulieres* were the maidservants, to whom the Senate gave the right to wear the dress of free women on that day (Macrobius *Sat.* I 11.38 and 40); he thinks that 'toga praetexta data eis Apollinaribus ludis' can mean 'le droit qui leur a été accordé de porter la toge aux Jeux Apollinaires'.
64. *Fabulam dare*: e.g. Terence *Eun.* 23–4, Cic. *Brutus* 73, *Tusc.* I 3, Gellius *NA* XVII 21.45. *Praetextae* and *togatae*: Horace *Ars poetica* 288, with C.O. Brink, *Horace on Poetry: the 'Ars Poetica'* (Cambridge 1971) 319–20. Defined by Roman subject-matter: Varro fr. 306 Funaioli (*togatae*), Festus (Paulus) 249L (*praetextae*). *Praetextae* (or *praetextatae*) as tragedy, *togatae* as comedy: Donatus *De com.* 6.1, Lydus *De mag.* I 40, Diomedes *Gramm. Lat.* I 482K, 489K. *Togatae* as 'between tragedy and comedy': Seneca *Epist.* 8.8, 89.7. *Praetextae* (or *praetextatae*) as a type of *togatae*: Diomedes *Gramm. Lat.* I 489–90K.

65. P. Drossart, 'Le théâtre aus Nones Caprotines (à propos de Varron, *De linua latina* 6,18)', *Revue de philologie* 48 (1974) 54–64; Ribbeck, op. cit. (1897, n. 11 above) 335.
66. Polyaenus VIII 30. Also Plut. *Romulus* 29.3–6, *Camillus* 33.2–6, ps.Plutarch *Parallela* 30 (Aristides of Miletus *FGrH* 286 F1), Macrobius *Sat.* I 11.35–40, Polemius Silvius on 7 July (*CIL*² 1.269); cf. Ovid *Ars am.* II 258. The Latin leader was Postumus Livius, dictator of Fidenae (Macrobius, Plut. *Rom.*); in Ovid and ps.Plutarch the enemy were Gauls. The heroine's name was either Philotis or Tutula (Plutarch, Macrobius); ps.Plutarch calls her Rhetana.
67. In the Campus Martius (Historia Augusta *M. Aurelius* 13.6); Coarelli, op. cit. (n. 61) 56, cf. 21, 180, 198, 218.
68. Soltau, op. cit. (n. 41) 48, 120; cf. 98, 130 on the analogous 'intermezzo' of the Faliscan schoolmaster (Livy V 27).
69. P. Flobert, *Varron, La langue latine, livre VI* (Paris 1985) 89: despite the complexity of the evidence (n. 64 above), Flobert takes it as given that a *togata* was a comedy and a *praetexta* a tragedy; the inconvenient evidence of Diomedes (*Gramm. Lat.* I 490K) is dismissed as 'factice'. The same argument at greater length in Flobert, op. cit. (n. 63) 46. Coarelli (op. cit. [n. 61] 38) states without argument that 'una togata praetexta non dà senso'.
70. Cf. Flobert, op. cit. (n. 63) 47: 'Enfin, il faut avouer que l'histoire de *Tutela/Philotis* relève plutôt du vaudeville ou de la mascarade que de la tragédie: le travestissement, l'ivresse des ennemis, les signaux lumineux et le retour triomphale des servantes fidèles constitueraient un sujet de prétexte assez étrange, reconnaissons-le.' For the argument to work, 'prétexte' has to be coterminous with 'tragédie'.
71. See n. 17 above. The insertion into the Sabine story of Latin girls from Caenina, Crustumerium, Antemnae and Fidenae (Dion. Hal. II 32.2, Livy I 9.8, Plut. *Rom.* 17.1) was no doubt to make the parallel more exact.
72. Actaeon: Varro *Menippean Satires* fr. 513 Astbury (Nonius 563L); cf. Ovid *Met.* III 138–252 for the story. *Mimae*: see pp. 70–74 above; for some suggestions about their Roman repertoire, analogous to the *Nonae Caprotinae* scenario, see T.P. Wiseman in C. Kondoleon and B. Bergmann (eds), *The Art of the Ancient Spectacle* (Studies in the History of Art, Washington D.C. 1998).
73. See for example (respectively) Seneca *Epist.* 8.8–9 and Ovid *Tristia* II 497–8; E. Rawson in H.D. Jocelyn and H. Hurt (eds), *Tria Lustra* (Liverpool 1993) 255–60. The complex interrelations of the dramatic genres are illustrated by an inscription of AD 169 honouring a *nobilis archimimus* who was also a *tragicus* and *comicus*, or perhaps honoured by the tragic and comic actors' guilds (*CIL* XIV 2408=*ILS* 5196); for the latter interpretation see E.J. Jory, *Philologus* 109 (1965) 307–8.
74. ἱλαροτραγῳδία (Suda s.v. *Rhinthon*), cf. Nossis *Anthologia Palatina* VII 414; for *Rhinthonica* on the Roman stage, see Donatus *De com.* 6.1, Evanthius *De com.* 4.1, Lydus *De mag.* I 40; for knowledge of Rhinthon at Rome, cf. Cic. *Ad Att.* I 20.3).

75. Sibylline oracle on the Secular Games, quoted by Phlegon of Tralles *FGrH* 257 F37.v.4 (line 35): σπουδῇ δὲ γέλωτι μεμίχθω.
76. H. Funaioli, *Grammaticae Romanae fragmenta* (Leipzig 1907) 182— followed by Varro's four books of *Satires*, which were in some sense a 'stage genre' (fr. 304B, 'hic modus scaenatilis')
77. Cic. *Pro Q. Gallio* fr. 4 Puccioni (Jerome *Ep. ad Nepotianum* 52.8); tentatively classified as mime by M. Bonaria, *Romani mimi* (Rome 1965) 87–8, and F. Giancotti, *Mimo e gnome* (Messina 1967) 119–28.
78. Briefly suggested by Goetz and Schoell, op. cit. (n. 62) 65 app. crit., 248. The toga was thought to have been worn by women in the distant past (Varro *De vita populi Romani* fr. 44 Riposati), but became the characteristic dress of prostitutes (p. 69 above); it would better suit a slave girl at a dramatic date in the early fourth century than citizen women at the *ludi Apollinares* (founded in 212 BC).
79. B. Gentili, *Lo spettacolo nel mondo antico* (Universale Laterza 379, Bari 1977) 3: 'Le pagine che seguono affrontano il problema istituzionale del teatro romano arcaico in rapporto alle istituzioni teatrali dell'età ellenistica . . .'
80. Ibid. 6–23, on the increased importance of music and song, and of virtuoso solo performers. See further n. 95 below.
81. Ibid. 5–6, 23–4, 89–97 (esp. 90–5 on the difference between the archaic and Hellenistic forms of Greek influence on Rome).
82. Ibid. 39–40: 'I modi che gli autori del teatro romano suguirono nel rielaborare i modelli greci non vanno giudicati con criteri puramente letterari, come se fossero opere di letterati da tavolino che scrivessero per un ristretto pubblico di persone colte ed erudite: il loro interesse era essenzialmente di soddisfare le esigenze del pubblico, un interesse prima di tutto teatrale e spettacolare, proprio di chi opera nel teatro e per il teatro.'
83. Ibid. 41–3; Gellius *NA* X 18.7, Stobaeus *Flor.* 51.21, Suda s.v. *Lykophron*.
84. N. Zorzetti, *La pretesta e il teatro latino arcaico* (Forme materiali e ideologie del mondo antico 14, Naples 1980) 11–16, cf. 17 for the effect on study of the Roman theatre: '[L]a frattura tra la parte preletteraria e la parte letteraria si risolve così nella contrapposizione tra una deteriore e ideologica antropologia del primitivo e la critica del prodotto letterario colto. E ciò rumpe l'unità culturale delle esperienze teatrali . . .'
85. Ibid. 80–1, 83 ('manifestazioni culturali, in cui il popolo romano era sollecitato ad esprimere, per mantenerla o adattarla, la coscienza della propria tradizione'), 91 n. 12 (*praetexta* and *ludi*). For the other elements, see Zorzetti's later articles: 'Poetry and the Ancient City: the Case of Rome', *Classical Journal* 86 (1990–1) 311–29, and 'The *carmina convivalia*', in O. Murray (ed.), *Sympotica: a Symposium on the Symposion* (Oxford 1990) 289–307 ('What we see is the cultural model of an archaic *polis*', 297).
86. Pol. VI 56.8 (ἐκτετραγῴδηται), 56.11 (τραγῳδία); Pacuvius *Paulus* fr. 1R (Gellius *NA* IX 14.9), Accius *Aeneadae sive Decius* fr. 4R (Nonius 272L); Zorzetti, op. cit. (n. 82) 64–5, following S. Mazzarino, *Il pensiero storico classico* II (Bari 1966) 61–2. Mazzarino defined the whole period of the late third and second centuries BC as 'the age of the *praetexta*' (op. cit. 59–60).

87. F. Dupont, *L'acteur-roi, ou le théâtre à Rome* (Paris 1985) 20, 21; cf. also 312 ('Les textes dramatiques ne sont qu'une part minime à Rome du théâtre . . .').
88. Ibid. 291, cf. 222 for the 'contradictory' confusion of the opposites in the *praetexta*.
89. Ibid. 65, cf. 56, 178; because 'les jeux ont toujours été le lieu du luxe, du superflu, de la consommation somptueuse' (72).
90. Ibid. 215–28 (esp. 224, 'si le public ne prenait pas de plaisir aux prétextes, les gens de bien les détestaient . . .'). Note in particular the slide from 'la plus vraisemblable' to 'fort probable' to 'en réalité' (222–3); also the confident assertion of aristocratic ideology in the *Octavia* (226–7), despite the evidence of the text, for which see P. Kragelund, *Prophecy, Populism and Propaganda in the 'Octavia'* (Opuscula Graecolatina 25, Copenhagen 1982).
91. Ibid. 217, cf. pp. 4–5 above (Boissier's article was one of the only two items of bibliography Dupont cited on the *praetexta*).
92. N. Horsfall, 'The Prehistory of Latin Poetry: Some Problems of Method', *Rivista di filologia* 122 (1994) 50–75, quotations from pp. 66–7 and 68.
93. Wiseman, op. cit. (n. 35) 13.
94. Ibid. 13–14, on Heraclides Ponticus fr. 102 Wehrli (Plut. *Camillus* 22.2), Callimachus *Aetia* fr. 106 Pfeiffer, etc.
95. See for instance K. Neiiendam, *The Art of Acting in Antiquity* (Copenhagen 1992) 15–93; O. Taplin, *Comic Angels, and Other Approaches to Greek Drama through Vase-Paintings* (Oxford 1993); J.R. Green, *Theatre in Ancient Greek Society* (London 1994); R. Green and E. Handley, *Images of the Greek Theatre* (London 1995); J.R. Green in A. Griffiths (ed.), *Stage-Directions: Essays in Ancient Drama in Honour of E.W. Handley* (BICS Supplement 66, London 1995) 93–121; J.R. Green, *Bulletin of the Institute of Classical Studies* 41 (1996) 17–30.
    Cf. R.C. Beacham, *The Roman Theatre and its Audience* (London 1991) ch. 1, which I think is vitiated by a false view of the Romans' relationship with their Greek neighbours (e.g. 7–8): 'It is most unlikely that Rome of the mid-fourth century was in any position either geographically or culturally to benefit directly from such a sophisticated theatrical culture. Roman visitors may possibly have been bemused observers from time to time of performances in Greek theatres, but they would have brought back only travellers' tales of practices, entertaining perhaps to recount to their families and friends, but aesthetically too advanced to be understood or to influence the growth of whatever crude drama was germinating at Rome.' I do not think that can be true of the society that produced the 'Ficoroni *cista*': Wiseman, op. cit. (n. 35) 13–16.
96. See for instance C.W. Dearden in Griffiths, op. cit. (previous note) 81–6, esp. 85. Satyr-play: T.P. Wiseman, *Journal of Roman Studies* 78 (1988) 1–13 = op. cit. (n. 35) 68–85, esp. 8–10 = 79–81 on cross-genre influence. Mime: Beacham, op. cit. (previous note) 129–53; E.J. Jory in Griffiths, op. cit. 139–52, and in W.J. Slater (ed.), *Roman Theater and Society* (E. Togo Salmon Papers 1, Ann Arbor 1996) 1–27.

So I venture to disagree with Alessandro Barchiesi (*The Poet and the Prince: Ovid and Augustan Discourse* [Berkeley 1997] 247) when he finds it 'impossible to believe that the audience Ovid is writing for was accustomed to seeing publicly active "Roman kings and generals" alternate with satyrs and "other ridiculous characters" in a literary context that makes it hard to distinguish between the serious and the playful, between responsibility and entertainment. No common language or socially acceptable container can exist for a mixture of themes and styles which amounts to a breakdown of the conventional hierarchies.' So dogmatic an assertion is very uncharacteristic of Barchiesi.

97. Zorzetti in Murray, op. cit. (n. 85) 303. For Rhinthon, see n. 74 above.

98. H.I. Flower, '*Fabulae praetextae* in Context: When Were Plays on Contemporary Subjects Performed in Republican Rome?', *Classical Quarterly* 45 (1995) 170–90, quotation from p. 170; pp. 173–5 were a critique of Wiseman, op. cit. (n. 35) 1–22. Like Dupont, whose methodology she approved (170 n. 5), Flower assumed that *praetextae* were rarely performed; she attributed it to 'state control of aristocratic competition' (190). And yet she rightly pointed out the reason for the paucity of information about *praetextae*: 'their meaning and importance was inextricably connected to the spectacle itself in the context of the immediate political climate, and this helps to explain their ephemeral interest and the few fragments quoted by later authors' (190, cf. p. 5 above).

99. See n. 53 above.

100. Op. cit. 181–3; cf. 177–81 for an attempt (unnecessary, I think) to disqualify funerary and triumphal games as possible contexts.

101. Varro *De ling. Lat.* VI 18: 'Cur hoc, togata praetexta ... docuit populum.'

102. 'There is an almost total lack of ancient evidence to support Wiseman's wide-ranging and speculative theories ...' (Flower, op. cit. [n. 98] 173); on 'speculation', see the introduction to Wiseman, op. cit. (n. 35), esp. xii-xiii.

103. 'Kaum war durch Livius Andronikus ein dramatische Literatur bei den Romern begründet, so versuchte sich schon der kühnaufstrebende Geist seines Nachfolgers Nävius an nationalen Stoffen' (Meiser, op. cit. [n. 31] 5). For Naevius as the inventor of the *praetexta*, see Ribbeck, op. cit. (n. 7) 63; taken for granted ever since, as for instance by W. Beare, *The Roman Stage* (ed. 3, London 1968) 39. Beare's treatment of the *praetexta* (ibid. 39–44) seems to me wholly inadequate.

Chapter 2

1. M. Beard, 'Looking (harder) for Roman Myth: Dumézil, Declamation and the Problems of Definition', in F. Graf (ed.), *Mythos in mythenloser Gesellschaft: das Paradigm Roms* (Stuttgart 1993) 44–64; quotation from p. 56.

2. J.P.V.D. Balsdon, *Life and Leisure in Ancient Rome* (London 1969) 245–8; A. Degrassi (ed.), *Inscriptiones Italiae* XIII.2 (Rome 1963) 372–6.
3. E. Rawson, *Roman Culture and Society: Collected Papers* (Oxford 1991) 581, and in H.D. Jocelyn and H.V. Hurt (eds), *Tria Lustra: Essays and Notes presented to John Pinsent* (Liverpool 1993) 260.
4. Varro *Ant. div.* frr. 7–10 Cardauns, in Augustine *Civitas Dei* VI 5 (translation by H. Bettenson, Penguin Classics).
5. Augustine *Civitas Dei* VI 6, 'ab dis poeticis theatricis ludicris scaenicis'.
6. Ibid. IV 26, 27, VI 6.
7. Ibid. IV 27 ('multa de dis fingantur indigna'), VI 8 ('de dis indigna'); cf. also VI 1 ('de his quos deos immortales uocant falsa atque indigna'), 6 ('de dis talibus maiestati indigna diuinae'), 7 ('theologia fabulosa theatrica scaenica, indignitatis et turpitudinis plena').
8. Plautus *Amphitruo* 41–5: 'nam quid ego memorem (ut alios in tragoediis uidi, Neptunum, Virtutem, Victoriam, Martem, Bellonam commemorare quae bona uobis fecissent) quis benefactis meus pater, deorum regnator, architectust omnibus?'
9. Ibid. 59–63.
10. Ibid. 86–95, *novom* at 89.
11. Augustine *Civitas Dei* IV 27 ('Iouem ipsum conuerti in bouem aut cygnum ut cum aliqua concumbat'); cf. VI 25 ('iste alienarum adulter uxorum') and 26 ('ludi scaenici ubi haec dictitantur cantitantur actitantur').
12. Ibid. VI 7.
13. Arnobius *Adversus nationes* IV 35, 'indignas de diis fabulas'.
14. For Attis on the stage, see the painting in the house of Pinarius Cerealis at Pompeii illustrated in M.J. Vermaseren, *Cybele and Attis: the Myth and the Cult* (London 1977) plate 47.
15. Augustine *Civitas Dei* IV 27; Lucian *Dearum iudicium* 9–13 (Loeb ed. vol. III pp. 397–403). Actresses undressing on stage were characteristic of the *ludi Florales* (Valerius Maximus II 10.8, Seneca *Epist.* 97.8, Lactantius *Inst.* I 20.10).
16. Arnobius V 1 = Valerius Antias fr. 6P; cf. Livy XXXIX 43.1 on Antias, 'ut qui . . . fabulae tantum sine auctore editae credidisset'.
17. Plutarch *Numa* 15.3.
18. Arnobius V 2, 'omnia et excogitata at comparata derisui'.
19. Ovid *Fasti* III 259–392.
20. H.H. Scullard, *Festivals and Ceremonies of the Roman Republic* (London 1981) 85–6; Degrassi, op. cit. (n. 2) 417–18.
21. Ovid *Fasti* III 262: 'nympha, Numae coniunx, ad tua facta ueni!'
22. ibid. 346: 'imperii pignora certa dabo.'
23. Varro *De ling. Lat.* VI 94, Livy I 20.7, Ovid *Fasti* III 327–30.
24. Degrassi, op. cit. (n. 2) 422: Servius on *Aeneid* VII 188, Lydus *De mensibus* IV 49.
25. Compare R. Seaford, *Reciprocity and Ritual: Homer and Tragedy in the Developing City-State* (Oxford 1994) 276–7, on Athenian drama.
26. Festus (Paulus) 117L: 'unaque edita uox omnium potentissimam fore civitatem quamdiu id in ea mansisset.'

27. Ovid *Fasti* III 370.
28. Ibid. VI 612, cf. Livy I 46.3 (see above, pp. 32–3).
29. Dion. Hal. IV 29.7, Eur. *Phoenissae* 524–5; Ovid *Fasti* VI 617–20.
30. Ovid *Fasti* IV 326: 'mira, sed et scaena testificata, loquar.'
31. For different angles on the subject, see J.C. McKeown, *Proceedings of the Cambridge Philological Society* 25 (1979) 75–6; E. Fantham, *Harvard Studies in Classical Mythology* 87 (1983) 196–201; T.P. Wiseman, *Journal of Roman Studies* 78 (1988) 10–13 = *Historiography and Imagination* (Exeter 1994) 79–84. [A. Barchiesi, *The Poet and the Prince: Ovid and Agustan Discourse* (Berkeley 1997) 238–51.]
32. Ovid *Fasti* I 391–438: 'omnibus ad lunae lumina risus erat' (438).
33. A. Richlin, *Pornography and Representation in Greece and Rome* (New York 1992) 169–72; cf. Fantham, op. cit. (n. 31) 190–1.
34. Ovid *Fasti* II 583–616; see T.P. Wiseman in B. Bergmann and C. Kondoleon (eds), *The Art of the Ancient Spectacle* (Washington DC, forthcoming).
35. Ovid *Fasti* II 586: 'multa tulit tanto non patienda deo.'
36. Ibid. 605 ('miserataque nuptas').
37. Prop. IV 9.32 ('verba minora deo').
38. McKeown, op. cit. (n. 31) 77–8. [For a very different, non-comic reading of the episode, see now A. Staples, *From Good Goddess to Vestal Virgins: Sex and Category in Roman Religion* (London 1998) 24–28.]

Chapter 3

This chapter is the expanded text of a paper given at Exeter, Belfast and Leeds in 1997. I am very grateful for the comments and suggestions made on all three occasions, and particularly to Matthew Leigh for ongoing advice and help.

1. A. Muñoz, *Campidoglio* (Rome 1930) 20: 'Oggi, per voluntà del Duce, prontamente interpretata dal Governatore di Roma, l'isolamento, vorremmo dire la redenzione del Campidoglio, è in massima parte compiuta. Si erge maestoso, libero da ogni superfetazione con la sua massa fulva il sasso Tarpeo, da cui si gettavano, fuori della città, i corpi impuri dei traditori; e lo cinge una corona di allori, di mirti, di olivi, verdi simboli della giovinezza eterna della Patria.' See A. Cederna, *Mussolini urbanista: lo sventramento di Roma negli anni del consenso* (Rome 1979) 121–56.
2. Ovid *Fasti* VI 480, 569, 625–8. They were destroyed in the great fire of 213 BC and rebuilt the following year: Livy XXIV 47.15–16, XXV 7.5–6; cf. V 19.6, 23.7 (Mater Matuta temple earlier rebuilt by Camillus). Details and bibliography in G. Pisani Sartorio, *Lexicon Topographicum Urbis Romae* II D-G (Rome 1995) 281–5, 450–1.
3. Ovid *Fasti* VI 569–636.
4. Dion. Hal. IV 2.1–3 (Hephaistos or 'the hero of the house'); Pliny *Nat. Hist.* XXXVI 204 (*Lar familiaris*); Plut. *Mor.* 323b–c (a 'hero of the house' or Hephaistos); Arnobius *Adv. nat.* V 18 (*Di conserentes*).
5. Promathion *FGrH* 817 F1 (Plut. *Rom.* 2.3–6); cf. T.P. Wiseman, *Remus: a Roman Myth* (Cambridge 1995) 57–61.

6. He ignores the rival version that the statue was of Fortuna herself: Varro *De vita populi Romani* fr. 17 Riposati (Nonius 278L). Cf. F. Coarelli, *Il foro boario* (Rome 1988) 265–73.
7. E.g. Livy I 26.13 ('id hodie quoque ... manet'), II 4.1 ('usque ad nostram aetatem ... manet'), etc. See S.P. Oakley, *A Commentary on Livy Books VI–X* I (Oxford 1997) 128.
8. Op. cit. (n. 6) 304–13, followed by Pisani Sartorio, op. cit. (n. 2) 281.
9. E.g. the idea of a window leading to a subterranean chamber (Coarelli, op. cit. 311–2).
10. Equally explicit in Plutarch: *Mor.* 322e (*De fortuna Romanorum* 10).
11. Plut. *Mor.* 273b-c (*Quaest. Rom.* 36).
12. Livy I 41.4; cf. Pliny *Nat. Hist.* XXXIV 29 (citing the unknown Annius Fetialis) on the palace opposite the Jupiter Stator temple as that of Tarquinius Superbus.
13. Solinus 1.24: 'ad Mugoniam portam supra summam nouam uiam.' Dion. Hal. II 50.3 for the Jupiter Stator temple at the Porta Mugonia.
14. E.g. Porta Carmentalis=Scelerata (Festus 450–1L), Porta Collina=Agonensis (Festus [Paulus] 9L), Porta Saturnia=Pandana (Solinus 1.13).
15. Varro *De ling. Lat.* V 164 ('intra muros ... in Palatio'); Livy I 12.3 ('uetus porta Palatii'), cf. Dion. Hal. II 50.3.
16. Coarelli, op. cit (n. 6) 13–59, esp. 20–5, 50–2.
17. Cic. *Ad Att.* VII 3.9 (50 BC); cf. Livy XXXV 9.3, 21.5 ('*circa* portam Flumentanam').
18. A. Carandini, in *La grande Roma dei Tarquini* (Rome 1990) 97–9, plan at p. 97; C. Smith, *Early Rome and Latium: Economy and Society c.1000–500 BC* (Oxford 1996) 177–8, plan at p. 252.
19. Ovid *Fasti* VI 579 (*voltus*), 580 (*ora*), 619 (*ore*), 623 (*caput*).
20. Gluttony and lust: Seneca *De vita beata* 13.2. Brothel: e.g. Petronius *Sat.* 7, Juv. 6.118, Lucian *Dial. mortuorum* 20.11 (374), Hist. Aug. *Verus* 4.6, *Elagabalus* 32.9, Isid. *Orig.* XIX 26. Tavern: e.g. Cic. *Pis.* 13, Pliny *Ep.* III 12.3.
21. E.g. Hor. *Sat.* II 7.55, Juv. 6.330, Philostratus *Soph.* I 25.25, Apuleius *Met.* VIII 20, IX 20, Fortunat. *Rhet.* I 6 (85H).
22. For his wife Gegania, see Valerius Antias fr. 12P (Plut. *Mor.* 323c).
23. Sen. *Epist.* 114.6: 'non aliter quam in mimo fugitiui diuites [diuitis?] solent.'
24. Ovid *Tristia* II 497–514; see R.W. Reynolds, *Classical Quarterly* 40 (1946) 77–84 on the 'adultery mime'.
25. Gods in mime: Augustine *Civitas Dei* VI 7 (Priapus), VII 26 (Venus); see above, pp. 20–21. Window scenes conveniently collected by J.R. Green in A. Griffiths (ed.), *Stage Directions: Essays in Ancient Drama in Honour of Eric Handley* (BICS Supplement 66, London 1995) 109f and Plate 10.
26. So A. Barchiesi, *The Poet and the Prince: Ovid and Augustan Discourse* (Berkeley 1997) 229: 'a story of clandestine love affairs that could make good material for a mime show.'
27. E.g. *Fasti* I 25, II 360, IV 10.
28. E.g. *Fasti* II 3–8, 119–26; IV 3, 9–12, 948; VI 21.
29. Ennius *Annals* frr. 137–49 Skutsch; Dion. Hal. IV 6.1, 7.1 (Fabius Pictor

FGrH 809 F7), Piso frr. 21–4 Forsythe, Gellius fr. 18P, Valerius Antias fr. 12P, Licinius Macer fr. 8P, Livy I 34–II 21.

30. A. Klotz (ed.), *Scaenicorum Romanorum fragmenta* I (Munich 1953) 365–7, J. Dangel, *Accius: Oeuvres (fragments)* (Paris 1995) 237–9; esp. fr. iv (Cic. *Sest.* 123), 'Tullius qui libertatem civibus stabiliverat'. *Pace* Klotz and Dangel, fr. v (Varro *De ling. Lat.* VI 7, VII 72) is evidently from another *Brutus*, by Cassius Parmensis.

31. Livy I 46.2–3.

32. R.M. Ogilvie, *A Commentary on Livy Books 1–5* (Oxford 1965) 186, 196, 219.

33. H.B. Wright, *The Recovery of a Lost Roman Tragedy: a Study in Honor of Bernadotte Perrin* (New Haven 1910), cf. pp. 6–7 above; A.K. Michels, 'The Drama of the Tarquins', *Latomus* 10 (1951) 13–24; listed by Ogilvie, op. cit. 187.

   A comparison of the texts is instructive. Wright, op. cit. 47: 'What is Tullia Ferox but a Romanized Clytemnestra, Arruns Tarquinius but an unsuspecting Agamemnon, Lucius Tarquinius but a remodeled Aegisthus, and Brutus but an adapted Orestes?' Michels, op. cit. 23: 'Tanaquil is a less terrible Clytemnestra, and Tullia a less noble Electra. Tarquinius is a less heroic Agamemnon, Servius a more moral Aegisthus and the younger Tarquin a less sympathetic Orestes.' Ogilvie, op. cit. 186: 'L. Tarquinius is a less scrupulous Orestes, Tullia a less noble Electra, and so Servius Tullius has to be Aegisthus, the intruder.' (Servius as *Aegisthus*? Tullia as *Electra*? Duncan and Lady Macbeth would be better analogies.)

34. Livy I 46.9, Dion. Hal. IV 30.1, Ovid *Fasti* VI 587.

35. Wright (op. cit. 33–4, 44–5) assumes that the murders happened 'behind the scenes', and the bodies were then brought on stage; Michels (op. cit. 17) prefers to have the murders happen before the drama begins: 'the story of their previous crime would come out in the conversation' between Tullia and Tarquin. Wright adduces Accius' unattributed lines 'video sepulcra duo duorum corporum' and 'mulier una duum virum' (frr. 655–6R = 700–1 Dangel: Cic. *Orator* 156); Dangel, however (op. cit. [n. 30] 378), thinks them more appropriate to the house of Atreus, e.g. Agamemnon and Aegisthus.

36. E.g. F. Bömer, *P. Ovidius Naso, Die Fasten* I (Heidelberg 1957) 26; R. Schilling, *Ovide, Les Fastes* II (Paris 1993) 192; C.E. Newlands, *Playing with Time: Ovid and the Fasti* (Ithaca 1995) 222–3. Note however Bömer, op. cit. II (1958) 378: 'Hauptquelle ist heute Livius, dem vielleicht die jüngerer Annalistik oder die Bühne (oder beide zugleich) vorangingen.'

37. *Fasti* IV 326; see above, p. 23.

38. Ovid *Fasti* VI 595, Livy I 46.3.

39. Cic. *Rab. Post.* 29, cited by M. Leigh, *Proceedings of the Cambridge Philological Society* 42 (1996) 186: 'One of the central functions of Roman tragedy was to offer a commentary on the ills of monarchy.' Ibid. 187f for the consequent sensitivity of tragic themes under the principate.

40. *Fasti* VI 592; cf. II 4, IV 3, VI 23. Also IV 948 (*grandius opus*), of Vesta and Augustus.

41. N. 28 above.
42. *Fasti* II 6, 'cum lusit numeris prima iuuenta meis'; *Amores* III 1.27–8, 'quod tenerae cantent lusit tua Musa puellae, primaque per numeros acta iuuenta suos'; J.F. Miller, *Ovid's Elegiac Festivals* (Studien zur klassischen Philologie 55, Frankfurt 1991) 22–3.
43. Ovid *Amores* III 1.24, cf. 13 (*sceptrum regale*), 40 (*regia*).
44. *Amores* III 1.70, 15.18 (cf. *Fasti* VI 585–6); III 15.17 (*thyrso grauiore*) refers back to Tragedy's reproach at 1.23, just before *maius opus*.
45. For its quality, see Quintilian *Inst.* X 1.98.
46. Ovid *Her.* 12.214; A. Barchiesi, *Harvard Studies in Classical Philology* 95 (1993) 344–5.
47. Livy V 21.8–9: 'haec ad ostentationem scaenae gaudentis miraculis aptiora quam ad fidem.'
48. Ovid *Fasti* VI 612, cf. III 370 (above, p. 23); that event too was followed by the voice of a god (Festus 117L, Jupiter).
49. E.g. Livy I 31.3, V 22.6, 32.6, Val. Max. I 8.3, Suet. *Nero* 46.2, Tac. *Hist.* V 13.
50. E.g. Ovid *Fasti* II 435, IV 268, Livy I 31.3, VI 33.5, Cic. *De div.* I 101. Cf. also Livy II 7.2 and Val. Max. I 8.5 for Silvanus *ex silva*.
51. Plaut. *Amph.* 41–4 (pp. 19–20 above).
52. Livy I 59.13; cf. ps.Sen. *Octavia* 304–5, 'dedit infandi sceleris poenas'.
53. Livy I 46.5; the cross-reference is to 42.1–2. Fortuna Populi Romani: Ovid *Fasti* V 729; *Inscr. Ital.* XIII.2.11 (*Fasti Antiates*), 67 (*Fasti Caeretani*), 87 (*Fasti Esquilini*), 91 (*Fasti magistrorum vici*).
54. Livy XXV 7.5–6, XXXIV 53.5 (see above, nn. 2 and 53).

Chapter 4

1. J.A. North in *Cambridge Ancient History* VII.2 (ed. 2, Cambridge 1989) 574–6; A.K. Michels, *The Calendar of the Roman Republic* (Princeton 1967) 119–30, 207–20. Michels dates the calendar to the Decemvirs in the mid-fifth century; Mommsen had preferred a date in the regal period, and this is accepted by T.J. Cornell, *The Beginnings of Rome: Italy and Rome from the Bronze Age to the Punic Wars (c.1000–274 BC)* (London 1995) 104–5.
2. The *terminus ante quem* is a bronze *cista* in Berlin featuring eleven gods, including 'Leiber': *ILLRP* 1198; G. Bordenache Battaglia and A. Emiliozzi, *Le ciste prenestine* I.1 (Rome 1979) 50–54, no.5.
3. Tac. *Ann.* II 49.1, Dion. Hal. VI 94.3. The three-name formula occurs in the calendar *fasti* for the Cerealia (19 April) and at Livy III 55.7, XXXIII 25.3, XLI 28.2.
4. See pp. 86–7 above, on the Dioscuri story of 168 BC and the praetor M. Aebutius Helva, whose name is given to Postumius' *magister equitum* at Lake Regillus.
5. Dion. Hal. VI 10.1, 17.2.
6. Dion. Hal. VI 17.2–4, 94.3.

7. Ps.Cyprian *De spect.* 4.1: 'Cum urbem fames occupasset, ad auocationem populi adquisiti sunt ludi scaenici et Cereri et Libero dicati postmodum.'

8. E.g. Livy XXVI 26.5, XXXI 5.2, XXXIII 43.1 (210, 200, 195 BC). Anna Perenna: pp. 64–7 above.

9. The intervening Equirria days in honour of Mars (27 February, 14 March) may have been associated with the confiscation of the royal estate and its dedication to Mars (Livy II 5.2, Plut. *Publicola* 8.1); cf. Ovid *Fasti* II 860, 'quae deus in campo prospicit ipse *suo*'.

10. W.R. Connor, 'City Dionysia and Athenian Democracy', *Classica et Mediaevalia* 40 (1989) 7–32; quotation from R. Seaford, *Reciprocity and Ritual: Homer and Tragedy in the Developing City-State* (Oxford 1994) 244, whose whole chapter 'Dionysos and the Polis' is relevant to the question.

11. Alexander Polyhistor *FGrH* 273 F109 (Plut. *Mor.* 289A = *Quaest. Rom.* 104); cf. F. Altheim, *Terra Mater: Untersuchungen zur altitalischen Religionsgeschichte* (Religionsgeschichtliche Versuche und Vorarbeiten XXII.2, Giessen 1931) 23–7. Tarquins and Pisistratids: Pliny *Nat. Hist.* XXXIV 17.

12. Gorgasos and Damophilos: Pliny *Nat. Hist.* XXXV 154. The Ceres cult was entrusted to priestesses from the Greek cities of Velia and Naples (Cic. *Balb.* 55).

13. P.S. Lulof, *The Ridge-Pole Statues from the Late Archaic Temple at Satricum* (Scrinium 11, Amsterdam 1996) 54–6, 104–7 (identifying her as Aphrodite or Ino-Leucothea), 203–8 ('500–490 BC').

14. T.H. Carpenter, *Dionysian Imagery in Archaic Greek Art: its Development in Black-Figure Vase Painting* (Oxford 1986), and *Dionysian Imagery in Fifth-Century Athens* (Oxford 1997), esp. 62–9.

15. Both deifications are already in Hesiod (*Theogony* 940–2, 947–9); see M.L. West, *Hesiod Theogony* (Oxford 1966) 416, 418.

16. Semele: Ovid *Fasti* VI 503, *CIL* VI 9897; for the site of the Lucus Stimulae see O. de Cazanove, *Mélanges de l'École française de Rome* 95 (1983) 56–66. Ariadne: Ovid *Fasti* III 507–14, Hyginus *Fabulae* 244; cf. Pliny *Nat. Hist.* XXXVI 29.

17. For the etymology, see Ovid *Fasti* III 777–8, Seneca *De tranq. animi* 17.8, Servius on *Georgics* I 116 and *Aeneid* IV 638, Festus (Paulus) 103L.

18. Servius on *Aeneid* III 20, IV 57: 'apte urbibus libertatis est deus; unde etiam Marsyas, minister eius, per ciuitates in foro positus uel libertatis indicium est . . .' For examples in provincial cities see P. Veyne, 'Le Marsyas 'colonial' et l'indépendance des cités', *Revue de philologie* 35 (1961) 87–98.

19. See F. Coarelli, *Il foro romano: periodo repubblicano e augusteo* (Rome 1985) 91–119; M. Torelli, *Typology and Structure of Roman Historical Reliefs* (Ann Arbor 1982) 98–106. The Marsyas from Paestum (Coarelli, op. cit. 98–9) provides a *terminus ante quem* in the first half of the third century BC. For fragments of a probable third-century Marsyas statue at Alba Fucens, see D. Liberatore, *Ostraka* 4 (1995) 249–55. (The colonies at Alba Fucens and Paestum were founded in 303 and 273 respectively.)

20. *Lex de Aventino publicando* (456 BC): Dion. Hal. X 32.4. Aediles: Livy III

55.13 (449 BC), X 23.13 (296), XXVI 6.19 (210), 36.9 (208), XXXIII 25.2–3 (197).

21. Publicii: Ovid *Fasti* V 277–94, Tac. *Ann.* II 49.1; they also built the Clivus Publicius to the Aventine (Varro *De ling. Lat.* V 158, cf. Festus 276L). Neighbouring temples: Tac. *Ann.* II 49.1 (cf. Ovid *Fasti* V 335–46 for Flora and Bacchus). Senate: Ovid *Fasti* V 295–330.

22. Notes 7 and 10–11 above; Festus (Paulus) 103L, Tertullian *De spect.* 10, Ausonius VII 7.29.

23. Gellius *NA* III 3.15 (from Varro?); for possible examples, cf. Gellius *NA* VII 8.5 (Scipio Africanus?), ps.Asconius 215St (Metelli).

24. E.S. Gruen, *Studies in Greek Culture and Roman Policy* (Cincinnati Classical Studies 7, Leiden 1990) 92–106, esp. 102–4 on the prison story.

25. Cic. *De rep.* IV 10–13 (Augustine *Civitas Dei* II 9); Gruen, op. cit. 98, 101.

26. Cic. *De legibus* III 7, 11, 29, 46–7; *De rep.* IV 6, 10.

27. Naevius fr. 113R = Festus (Paulus) 103L. Noted but not discussed by Gruen, op. cit. (n. 24) 95. Quotation: E.S. Gruen, *Culture and National Identity in Republican Rome* (Cornell Studies in Classical Philology 52, Ithaca 1992) 183.

28. Livy XXV 1.6–12, 12.2–15. For the tradition of prophecy in Rome, see T.P. Wiseman, *Historiography and Imagination* (Exeter 1994) 49–67, and pp. 103–4 above.

29. Livy XXV 12.2–3; cf. Cic. *De div.* I 89, 115, II 113, Festus 162L; see nn. 18–19 above.

30. Apollodorus I 4.2, Hyginus *Fab.* 165, Ovid *Fasti* VI 707–8, Pliny *Nat. Hist.* XVI 240; a version sympathetic to Marsyas at Diodorus III 58.3–59.5.

31. Livy XXV 12.15 ('victoriae ergo', cf. Macrobius *Sat.* I 17.25), XXVII 23.5.

32. 'Iussis vatum': Arnobius *Adv. nat.* VII 49. Sibylline books: Varro *De ling. Lat.* VI 15, Livy XXIX 10.4, Ovid *Fasti* IV 255–60. For the diplomatic background, see Gruen, op. cit. (n. 24) 5–33.

33. Marsyas and Cybele: Diodorus III 58.3, 59.1. Apollo: Livy XXIX 11.5–6, Val. Max. VIII 15.3, Ovid *Fasti* IV 261–4 etc.

34. *Megalesia*: Livy XXIX 14.14 (204 BC), XXXIV 54.3 (194), XXXVI 3.4 (191). Senators' seats: Cicero in Asconius 69C, Livy XXXIV 54.3–8, Val. Max. II 4.3 (*ludi Megalenses*); Valerius Antias fr. 37P, Livy XXXIV 44.4 (*ludi Romani*); Asconius 70C (*ludi votivi*). See J. Briscoe, *A Commentary on Livy Books XXXIV-XXXVII* (Oxford 1981) 118, 134.

35. Livy XXXIX 8–19, esp. 8.3 ('sacrificulus et vates'), 17.6 (seven thousand 'conspirators'), 18.4 (executions etc); *CIL* I² 581 = *ILLRP* 511.

36. See n. 16 above. Semele became the goddess Thyone, whose name means in Greek what Stimula means in Latin: Schol. on Pindar *Pyth.* 3.177, Suda s.v. Thyone (παρὰ τὸ θύειν, ὅ ἐστιν ὁρμᾶν).

37. Livy XXXIX 15.3 ('prauis et externis religionibus'); they drive the mind to crime and debauchery 'uelut furialibus stimulis', an evident allusion to Semele-Stimula.

38. Cic. *De nat. deor.* II 62 (Loeb translation by H. Rackham).

39. Liber *pater*: Servius on *Georgics* II 4, *ILLRP* 206–7, etc.

40. Dion. Hal. VI 17.2, 94.3 (Kore), p. 35 above; also Cic. *Verr.* V 187, Arnobius *Adv. nat.* V 21.

41. Ampelius 9.11. Editors emend *Merone* to *Melone*, on the strength of the parallel passage in Lydus *De mensibus* IV 51: κατὰ δὲ τοὺς ποιητὰς Διόνυσοι πέντε· πρῶτος Διὸς καὶ Λυσιθέας, δεύτερος ὁ Νείλου ὁ καὶ βασιλεύσας Λιβύης καὶ Αἰθιοπίας καὶ ᾿Αραβίας· τρίτος Καβείρου παῖς κτλ. Melo was another name for Nilus (the Nile), according to Festus (Paulus) 7L, 16L, 111L. But Lydus' second Dionysus seems to have nothing in common with Ampelius' second Liber, and when Ampelius (in the previous paragraph, 9.10) refers to a daughter of Nile, he uses the normal name Nilus. So I see no reason to alter the MS reading.
42. Some editors emend *Saturno* to *Saturnio*, but 'the son of Saturn' seems an unlikely way to refer to Jupiter in this context.
43. See n. 21 above. In the first version, where Proserpina cannot be the daughter of Ceres, she may be thought of as Flora (Pliny *Nat. Hist.* XXXVI 23).
44. μηροτραφής as epithet of Dionysus: *Orphic hymns* 52.3, *Anth. Pal.* XI 329, Strabo XV 1.7 (687); at XV 1.8 Strabo refers to Mt Meron above Dionysus' birthplace at Nysa (also Pliny *Nat. hist.* VI 79, Pomponius Mela III 7.66, Curtius Rufus VIII 10.13, Appian *Alex.* V 1.6, *Indica* 1.6), no doubt the result of a similar rationalisation.
45. Hesychius I 390 Latte: γρήνη, ἄνθη σύμμικτα· Γρήνικος, ποταμός.
46. Ovid *Fasti* III 785–6. M. Volteius' series of denarii illustrating the main *ludi scaenici* show Liber and Ceres on the same coins: M.H. Crawford, *Roman Republican Coinage* (Cambridge 1974) 399, 402 (no. 385.3). The *ludi Cereales* are first attested in 201 BC (Livy XXX 39.8).
47. Livy XL 51.3, XLI 27.5; Ovid *Fasti* V 311–30. On the Livy passages, see F. Coarelli, *Il Campo Marzio dalle origini alla fine delle repubblica* (Rome 1997) 603–6.
48. Livy *Epit.* 48, Val. Max. II 4.2, Velleius I 15.3, Orosius IV 21.4, Augustine *Civitas Dei* I 31–3. See J.A. North in *Apodosis: Essays presented to Dr W.W. Cruickshank* (London 1992) 75–83; also Gruen, op. cit. (n. 27) 205–10, esp. 208: 'nothing in the previous history of the institution [the theatre] suggests that it had served as outlet for popular discontent or sedition.' Not sedition, but perhaps discontent.
49. Most recently J.-M. Pailler, *Bacchanalia: la répression de 186 av. J.-C. à Rome et en Italie* (BEFAR 270, Rome 1988), previous bibliography at 831–4; R. Rousselle in C. Deroux (ed.), *Studies in Latin Literature and Roman History* V (Collection Latomus 206, Brussels 1989) 55–65; A. Scafuro, 'Livy's Comic Narrative of the Bacchanalia', *Helios* 16 (1989) 119–42; R.A. Bauman, 'The Suppression of the Bacchanals: Five Questions', *Historia* 39 (1990) 334–48; Gruen, op. cit. (n. 24) 34–78; P.G. Walsh, 'Making a Drama out of a Crisis: Livy on the Bacchanalia', *Greece and Rome* 43 (1996) 188–203; W. Nippel, 'Orgien, Ritualmorde und Verschwörung? Die Bacchanalien-Prozesse des Jahres 186 v. Chr.', in U. Manthe and J. von Ungern-Sternberg, *Grosse Prozesse der römischen Antike* (Munich 1997) 65–73.
50. Livy XXXIX 13.9 (Annia Paculla and her sons Minius and Herennius Cerrinius), 17.6 (M. and C. Atinius, L. Opicernius, Minius Cerrinius); G. Tarditi, *Parola del passato* 37 (1954) 266–8.

51. P.G. Walsh, *Livy Book XXXIX* (Warminster 1994) 5; ibid. 27–35 for the translation. I am very grateful to Professor Walsh for allowing me to quote so extensively. I have marked the five 'acts' he identifies (Walsh, op. cit. [n. 49] 195–8) and added paragraphing *ad libitum*.

52. Livy XXXIX 14.3 ('quae ab se inquisita foret'). G. Méautis, *Revue des études anciennes* 42 (1940) 477: 'vérité officielle' in the form of a 'roman-feuilleton'. H. Jeanmaire, *Dionysos: histoire du culte de Bacchus* (Paris 1951) 457–8: 'Le rôle attribué au jeune Aebutius et à sa maîtresse . . . a toute l'apparence d'une mise-en-scène policière.' A.J. Festugière, *Mélanges de l'École française de Rome* 66 (1954) 83 = *Études de religion grecque et hellénistique* (Paris 1974) 93: 'Le récit . . . doit se fonder en dernier ressort sur le procès-verbal de cette affaire.' Pailler, op. cit. (n. 49) 264, 598: 'C'est par lui [Postumius] que nous connaissons le contenu des interrogatoires.' Erich Gruen (op. cit. [n. 24] 64–5) even suggests that the whole scenario was a 'staged operation' set up by the consul.

53. E.g. P.V. Cova, 'Livio e la repressione dei Baccanali', *Athenaeum* 52 (1974) 82–109; Scafuro, op. cit. (n. 49).

54. Pailler, op. cit. (n. 49) 597–612, with previous bibliography at 600–1; Walsh, op. cit. (n. 49) 192–3, 201–2.

55. Most probably Valerius Antias, named as a source at Livy XXXIX 22.9, 41.6, 43.1, 56.7; see pp. 86–7 above for a likely case of Antias taking over, and elaborating, a scene from Postumius.

56. Lake Regillus: pp. 35–6 and 85–7 above. Cf. Walsh, op. cit. (n. 49) 201: 'a dramatic version which would titillate a Greek audience reared on the conventions of New Comedy.'

57. See nn. 5 and 40 above.

58. It is possible that a dramatic element was involved in the Bacchanalia ritual itself: cf. Livy XXXIX 13.13, with Walsh, op. cit. (n. 51) 122, and de Cazanove, op. cit. (n. 16) 105–11.

59. Ovid *Fasti* VI 483–550. Ovid uses 'Liber' and 'Bacchus' interchangeably (e.g. *Fasti* III 410/414, 461/465, 479/481, 733/736).

60. Stimula (VI 503) and *instimulat* (VI 508, cf. n. 37 above): see de Cazanove, op. cit. (n. 16) 88–93. Post-186 ideology: A. Mastrocinque, *Lucio Giunio Bruto* (Trento 1988) 268–70.

61. Apart from the invocation (VI 483–4), the cakes aetiology alludes to Liber (VI 531, cf. III 733–4); and who was Carmentis' god (VI 538)?

62. E.g. *Fasti* II 585–616 (p. 24 above).

63. See pp. 8–11, 22–4, 27–30 above. No doubt the play about Quinta Claudia (Ovid *Fasti* 326) was another example.

Chapter 5

1. O. Ribbeck, *Die römische Tragödie im Zeitalter der Republik* (Leipzig 1875) 72–5, 207–11, 326–34.

2. E.g. W. Beare, *The Roman Stage* (ed. 3, London 1964) 41–44: 'we must conclude that the introduction of the historical play by Naevius proved comparatively sterile' (p. 43).

3. Diomedes in *Gramm. Lat* I 490K: 'togata praetextata a tragoedia differt, quod in tragoedia heroes inducuntur, . . . in praetextata autem quae scribitur Brutus uel Decius, item Marcellus.' For *praetextae* at the dedication of temples, see H.I. Flower, *Classical Quarterly* 45 (1995) 182–90.

4. Pollio in Cic. *Ad Fam.* X 32.3, 'de suo itinere ad L. Lentulum proconsule sollicitandum'.

5. K. Meiser, *Ueber historische Dramen der Römer* (München 1887) 23–36: Livy XXX 12–15; Livy XXIII 2–10; Livy XL 2–16, 20–4, 54–6; Plut. *C. Gracchus* 14–17.

6. H. Bardon, *La littérature latine inconnue* I (Paris 1952) 327.

7. For 'tragic history', see the classic study of F.W. Walbank, *Historia* 9 (1960) 216–34 = *Selected Papers: Studies in Greek and Roman History and Historiography* (Cambridge 1985) 224–41.

8. Compare Tac. *Ann.* XIV 63 ('meminerant adhuc quidam Agrippinae a Tiberio, recentior Iuliae memoria obuersabatur a Claudio pulsae') with the observations by the chorus of citizens at *Octavia* 924–57.

9. E.g. Suet. *Aug.* 89.3 (Augustus), Pliny *Paneg.* 54.1–2 (Domitian).

10. Livy I 46.3 (on Tullia): 'tulit enim et Romana regia sceleris *tragici* exemplum'. Cf. Tarquin and Lucretia in the *Brutus* plays of Accius (Cic. *De div.* I 43–5) and Cassius (Varro *De ling. Lat.* VI 7), respectively.

11. *Valuae regiae*: Vitr. *Arch.* V 6.3. My argument here is much indebted to comments by Roland Mayer at a seminar in London in January 1995.

12. Plut. *C. Gracchus* 14.4–16.5.

13. See C.B.R. Pelling, 'Truth and Fiction in Plutarch's *Lives*', in D.A. Russell (ed.), *Antonine Literature* (Oxford 1990) 19–52, esp. pp. 43 and 49 on 'true *enough*'.

14. Plut. *Thes.* 28.2; cf. C. Gill and T.P. Wiseman (eds.), *Lies and Fiction in the Ancient World* (Exeter 1993) 130f.

15. Plut. *Cic.* 48.1, cf. Sen. *Contr.* VII 2.8; Pliny *Nat. Hist.* VII 141, cf. Sen. *Contr.* II 4; T.P. Wiseman, *Clio's Cosmetics* (Leicester 1979) 31–7.

16. Tac. *Ann.* III 19.2, IV 11.2 ('fabulosa et immania'), 11.3 ('ueris in miraculum corruptis'), XI 27 ('fabulosum . . . miraculi causa').

17. Thucydides I 21.1 (τὰ πολλὰ . . . ἐπὶ τὸ μυθῶδες ἐκνενικηκότα); F.M. Cornford, *Thucydides Mythistoricus* (London 1907) 130–1: his italics.

18. Herodotus I 8–12 (8.2 for eyes); *Oxyrhynchus Papyri* XXIII 2382; E. Lobel, *Proceedings of the British Academy* 35 (1949) 207–16. Play predates Herodotus: B. Snell, *Zeitschrift für Papyrologie und Epigraphie* 12 (1973) 197–205. *Contra*: J.A.S. Evans, *Greek Roman and Byzantine Studies* 26 (1985) 229–33, etc.

19. W. Soltau, *Die Anfänge der roemischen Geschichtschreibung* (Leipzig 1909) 53–4: 'Auch wird man billig fragen können, ob der Senat und die Beamten der Reaktion die Aufführung eines solchen Dramas gestattet haben würden. Derartiges konnte doch nur die soeben mit Gewalt unterdrückten Gefühle, welche die Volksmassen zur Revolution getrieben hatten, aufs neue entfachen, und einem neuen Umsturz den Weg bahnen.' The answer to the question was taken for granted by H.B. Wright, *The Recovery of a Lost Roman Tragedy: A Study in Honor of Bernadotte Perrin* (New Haven

1910) 29 n. 2: 'The officials at Rome in the times of the late Republic would never have permitted the presentation or publication of a drama dealing with the revolutionary story of the Gracchi as related by Plutarch.'

20. A. Keaveney, 'The Three Gracchi: Tiberius, Gaius and Babeuf', in *La storia della storiografia europea sulla rivoluzione francese* (Rome 1990) 417–32. For Babeuf's own self-mythologising, cf. his father's supposed dying words as reported in V. Advielle, *Histoire de Gracchus Babeuf et du Babouvisme* I (Paris 1884) 13: 'Voici le seul trésor que je puisse vous léguer: c'est le grand Plutarque; sa lecture a fait toute la joie et les malheurs de ma longue et pénible carrière. C'est à vous de choisir, parmi la vie des hommes de l'antiquité, le rôle que vous désirez suivre. Les grandes pensées viennent du coeur et vous n'en manquez pas. Vous assisterez à de terribles révolutions. Votre génie vous dira quelle lumière vous devez suivre. Celle du peuple, depuis les siècles, a presque toujours été méconnue. Pour moi, celui auquel j'aurai voulu le plus ressembler est Caïus Gracchus, quand même j'aurais du périr comme lui et les siens, pour la cause la plus belle, celle du bonheur commun!'

21. Sall. *Iug.* 41.2–7; *Hist.* I 11–12M, IV 45M (= I 10, 12, IV 40 McGushin); Tac. *Ann.* IV 33.2. For a balanced analysis of the nature of late-republican politics, see P.A. Brunt, *The Fall of the Roman Republic and Related Essays* (Oxford 1988) 12–68.

22. Ps.Asconius 217St (on Cic. *Verr.* 1.31): 'Plebeii ludi, quos exactis regibus pro libertate plebis fecerunt. An pro reconciliatione plebis post secessionem in Auentinum?' Source unknown: possibly Varro's *De scaenicis originibus* (frr. 70–77 Funaioli).

23. Livy VI 42.12–14, VII 2.1–3; T.P. Wiseman, *Remus: a Roman Myth* (Cambridge 1995) 135–6, cf. 107–8.

24. Livy XXV 1.6–12, 12.2–16; T.P. Wiseman, *Historiography and Imagination* (Exeter 1994) 64.

25. Ovid *Fasti* V 277–330, esp. 312 'me quoque Romani praeteriere patres'.

26. Cic. *Sest.* 105, 115–23; *Ad Att.* II 19.3, XIV 3.2, *Ad fam.* VIII 2.1, etc; C. Nicolet, *The World of the Citizen in Republican Rome* (London 1980) 361–73; cf. Wiseman, op. cit. (n. 24) x-xii.

27. Ps.Sen. *Octavia* 291–308, 676–82, 877–95; for the People under Nero's tyranny, cf. 455–61, 572–9, 683–9, 780–4, 820–57; P. Kragelund, *Prophecy, Populism, and Propaganda in the 'Octavia'* (Copenhagen 1982) 38–43.

28. Plut. *C. Gracchus* 13.3–14.3; contrast Appian *Bell. Civ.* I 25.

29. Cf. Soltau, op. cit. (n. 19) 53: 'Hier ist die Geschichte selbst zu einem ergreifenden Drama geworden, welches auf der Bühne zu wiederholen ein Dichter kaum die Fähigkeit gehabt haben würde.'

30. Sall. *Iug.* 16.2 (Opimius), 31.7–9 (Memmius' speech), 42.4 ('plusque in relicuom sibi timoris quam potentiae addidit').

31. Memmius' speech in Sallust (*Iug.* 31) may well be essentially authentic; a C. Memmius contemporary with the historian, probably the tribune's grandson, was eager to publicise his family history (G.V. Sumner, *The Orators in Cicero's Brutus: Prosopography and Chronology* [Toronto 1973] 88–9 on his coins, stemma at p. 87).

32. Sall. *Iug.* 40; Cic. *Sest.* 140, *Brut.* 128.
33. Sall. *Iug.* 5.1: 'tunc primum superbiae nobilitatis obuiam itum est.'

Chapter 6

1. Plut. *Caes.* 32, *Pomp.* 60, App. *Bell. civ.* II 35, Suet. *Jul.* 31. For ἀνερρίφθω κύβος—a proverb, not just a quotation from Menander—see A.W. Gomme and F.H. Sandbach, *Menander: a Commentary* (Oxford 1973) 690–1.
2. H. Peter, *Historicorum Romanorum reliquiae* II (Stuttgart 1906, repr. 1967) lxxxxiii; J. André, *La vie et l'oeuvre d'Asinius Pollion* (Études et commentaires 8, Paris 1949) 58.
3. E.g. fr. 2P, the 'hoc uoluerunt' speech at Pharsalus.
4. Caes. *Bell. civ.* I 8.1: 'cognita militum uoluntate Ariminum cum ea legione proficiscitur . . .'.
5. E. Badian (*Gnomon* 62 [1990] 30) takes it as Caesar's own self-publicizing: 'for the record, and no doubt, as Asinius Pollio seems to have thought, for posterity.'
6. Pol. III 47.6–9 (Chaereas, Sosylus, Silenus?).
7. Livy V 20.8–9, Ovid *Fasti* IV 326; see above, pp. 2, 23.
8. For Pan playing a *harundo*, see for instance Ovid *Met.* XI 154.
9. Vitr. *Arch.* V 6.9, VII 5.2; Hor. *Ars poetica* 220–50; T.P. Wiseman, *Historiography and Imagination* (Exeter 1994) 68–85.
10. Python's *Agen*: Athenaeus XIII 596a; B. Snell, *Scenes from Greek Drama* (Berkeley 1967) 99–138.
11. M.H. Crawford, *Roman Republican Coinage* (Cambridge 1974) 346, 464; nos. 342.1–2, 449.1a-c; plates xliv.15–16, liii.10.
12. T.R.S. Broughton, *The Magistrates of the Roman Republic* III (Atlanta 1986) 220–1.
13. Cicero *Pro Gallio* fr. 4 Puccioni (Jerome *Ep. ad Nepotianum* 52.8): 'his autem ludis . . . unus quidam poeta dominatur . . . quantos plausus et clamores mouet!' Full text (with translation) and discussion in T.P. Wiseman, *Historiography and Imagination* (Exeter 1994) 80.
14. 'The poem is a dramatic mime': I.M. Le M. Du Quesnay, *Papers of the Liverpool Latin Seminar* 3 (Liverpool 1981) 36. For the *Eclogues* as stage performance, see J. Van Sickle, *Poesia e potere: il mito Virgilio* (Rome 1986) 17–23; Donatus *Vita Vergilii* 90, Servius on *Ecl.* 6.11; cf. Tac. *Dial.* 13.2 (popular acclaim for Virgil in the theatre).
15. Tityrus: Virg. *Ecl.* 1.1–5, 6.4, 8.55, *Georg.* IV 566; Propertius II 34.72, Ovid *Amores* I 15.25, Martial VIII 55.8. τίτυρος: Aelian *Var. hist.* III 40, Strabo X 3.15 (466).
16. Appian *Punica* 66; cf. Dion. Hal. *AR* VIII 72.10 and 12 (*satyristai*).

Chapter 7

1. Ovid *Fasti* I 1: 'tempora cum causis Latium digesta per annum'.
2. I 63–288 (Janus), II 267–452 (Lupercalia), II 685–852 (Regifugium), IV

179–372 (Megalensia), IV 393–620 (Cerealia), IV 721–862 (Parilia), V 183–379 (Floralia), VI 249–468 (Vestalia).

3. III 523–696, 697–710.
4. III 545–656; Stephen Hinds, in A.J. Boyle (ed.), *Imperial Roman Literature* I (= *Ramus* 16, Victoria 1987) 14–17, and in J.F. Miller (ed.), *Reconsidering Ovid's Fasti* (= *Arethusa* 25, Baltimore 1992) 108. See also J.C. McKeown, in T. Woodman and D. West (eds), *Poetry and Politics in the Age of Augustus* (Cambridge 1984) 169–87; and R.J. Littlewood, in C. Deroux (ed.), *Studies in Latin Literature and Roman History* II (Collection Latomus 168, Brussels 1980) 301–21.
5. *Fasti Vaticani* on 15 March: *Inscr. Ital.* XIII.2.172f.
6. Mart. IV 64.16f: 'et quod uirgineo cruore gaudet Annae pomiferum nemus Perennae.' M. Guarducci, *Studi e materiali per la storia delle religioni* 12 (1936) 25–50; G. Pugliesi Caratelli, *Parola del passato* 6 (1951) 68–75; P.E. Arias, *LIMC* I (1981) 795. I do not believe that Martial's reference was to some archaic rite of passage for the start of menstruation, nor to the defloration of girls at the riverside festival: these are the only two possibilities admitted by N. Boëls-Janssen, *La vie religieuse des matrones dans la Rome archaïque* (Coll. de l'École française de Rome 176, Rome 1993) 23–39, q.v. for bibliography.
7. Macrobius *Sat.* I 12.6; also Lydus *De mens.* IV 9, ὑπὲρ τὸν ὑγιεινὸν γενέσθαι τὸν ἐνιαυτόν. Cf. Varro *Menippean Satires* fr. 506B (Gell. *NA* XIII 23.4) for a prayer invoking 'Anna ac Peranna'.
8. *Fasti* III 145f, part of the proof that the year used to begin in March; Sil. It. VIII 200. Cf. also *Fasti Praenestini* on 15 March(?): *Inscr. Ital.* XIII.2.122f, 143, 423. The classic article of H. Usener is still fundamental on this: *Rheinisches Museum* 30 (1875) 182–229 = *Kleine Schriften* IV (Leipzig 1912) 93–143.
9. Cf. F. Ahl, *Metaformations* (Cornell 1985) 291 on *annus* and *anus* at *Met.* X 414.
10. Hes. *Theog.* 901, ἣ τέκεν ῞Ωρας.
11. For Sicily, see L. Pearson, *The Greek Historians of the West: Timaeus and his Predecessors* (APA Monographs 35, Atlanta 1987) 53–90: Hercules, the Argonauts, Diomedes, Odysseus, etc.
12. *Latium* from *latere*: Virg. *Aen.* VIII 322f, Ovid *Fasti* I 238, etc.
13. Varro *De ling. Lat.* V 42, Virg. *Aen.* VIII 357f, Festus 430L, Justin XLIII 1.5, etc.
14. Aesch. *Suppl.* 531–89, [Aesch.] *PV* 707–849.
15. Servius on *Aeneid* II 116; Ovid *Fasti* VI 485–550.
16. Apollodorus *Bibl.* II 1.3 (cf. 1.2 for Argus); full details in N. Yalouris, *Lexicon Iconographicum Mythologiae Classicae* V.1 (1990) 661–4.
17. Virg. *Aen.* VIII 345; see A. Heubeck, S. West and J.B. Hainsworth, *A Commentary on Homer's Odyssey* I (Oxford 1988) 79.
18. Ovid *Fasti* II 585–616; cf. T.P. Wiseman, *Remus: a Roman Myth* (Cambridge 1995) 70f. Temple of Mercury founded in 495 BC (Livy II 21.7, 27.5–6) 'facing the Circus' (Ovid *Fasti* V 669).
19. Servius on *Aeneid* VIII 345: their versions make the murdered Argus either (i) a treacherous guest of Evander, killed by the king's *socii*, or (ii) a son of

Danae, killed by the Aborigines, or (iii) the son of an Etruscan *haruspex*, killed by his father.
20. For Argiletum as a *nemus* (Virg. *Aen.* VIII 345), cf. Soph. *Electra* 5 (ἄλσος) on Io's captivity.
21. Ovid *Fasti* III 791f.
22. Apollodorus *Bibl.* II 1.2–3.
23. Varro *De ling. lat.* V 45, VII 44, Dion. Hal. I 37, Ovid *Fasti* V 621–62, Festus 18L, Macrobius *Sat.* I 11.47.
24. Herodian I 347.30 Lentz; Malalas II 28 (ravished by Zeus Picus, king of the West, on whom see Diodorus VI 5, probably from Euhemerus).
25. *Hom. Hymn to Hermes* 99f on Selene: daughter of Pallas, the eponym of Pallantion.
26. Dion. Hal. I 31.1–3, 32.3, 40.2, II 1.3; Plut. *Mor.* 277c = *Quaest. Rom.* 56 (otherwise known as Nikostrate or Carmenta); Pausanias VIII 43.2 (nymph, daughter of the river Ladon). Nikostrate: Strabo V 3.3 (C230), Plut. *Rom.* 21.2, Servius on *Aeneid* VIII 51, 130, 336, Solinus 1.10, *Origo gentis Romanae* 5.2, Isid. *Orig.* I 4.1. Carmenta/Carmentis: Livy I 7.8, Virg. *Aen.* VIII 336–40, Ovid *Fasti* I 467, 499, etc. According to Eratosthenes (Schol. Plato *Phaedrus* 244b, n. 29 below), she was 'the Italian Sibyl'.
27. For Azan, son of Arkas and the nymph Erato, see Pausanias VIII 4.3–5; cf. V 1.8, X 9.5, Diodorus IV 33.1.
28. Pausanias VIII 38.2–3 (eponyms of two Arcadian towns and an Arcadian river). The story was clearly a challenge to the Cretan legend of the birth of Zeus: Hesiod *Theog.* 477–84 (with M. West, *Hesiod Theogony* [Oxford 1966] 290–3), Ovid *Fasti* III 443–6, etc.
29. Quoted by a scholiast on Plato *Phaedrus* 244b: C.F. Hermann (ed.), *Platonis Dialogi* vol. VI (Teubner ed., Leipzig 1853) 270; the relevant phrase is relegated to the apparatus criticus ('add. vulg.') by G.C. Greene, *Scholia Platonica* (APA Philological Monographs VIII, Haverford PA 1938) 79f. Cf. T.P. Wiseman, *Journal of Roman Studies* 85 (1995) 3.
30. Op. cit (n. 18) 77–9, 86–8 (on Dion. Hal. I 79.8, 80.1); cf. 39–42 (suggesting a sixth-century origin).
31. Dion. Hal. I 32.3–33.1: Victory (Nike) was a daughter of Pallas, and thus sister of Selene (n. 25 above).
32. Luna: Tac. *Ann.* XV 41.1. Mercury: above, n. 18.
33. Ovid *Fasti* III 543, 662: 'quoniam rumoribus errat ... fama nec a ueri dissidet illa fide.' Hinds, op. cit. (n. 4).
34. Festus (Paulus) 519L; Paulinus of Nola *Carm.* 32.138f; cf. also Tibullus II 5.97f (harvest festival) for clothes as *umbraculae*. For non-Roman parallels, including the Jewish 'feast of tabernacles', see W. Warde Fowler, *The Religious Experience of the Roman People* (London 1911) 473–7.
35. *Per. Ven.* 5; also 43, 'floreas inter coronas, myrteas inter casas'; Littlewood, op. cit. (n. 4) 303f. Cf. Ovid *Fasti* I 423, 'sub acernis ramis', though that may be just beneath the trees. [At Alciphron *Epist.* IV 13.8 the girls break off yew and myrtle branches and spread their cloaks over them at the start of their amorous symposium.]
36. Plut. *Rom.* 29.6 (ἑστιῶσι δὲ τὰς γυναῖκας ἔξω, συκῆς κλάδοις σκιαζομένας), *Cam.* 33.6 (ἑστιώμεναι δὲ καθέζονται κλάδοις συκῆς σκιαζόμεναι). The best

recent accounts of the Nonae Caprotinae (or Capratinae) are by N. Robertson, *Museum Helveticum* 44 (1987) 8–41, and Bremmer in J.N. Bremmer and N.M. Horsfall (eds), *Roman Myth and Mythography* (BICS Suppl. 52, London 1987) 76–88; see esp. Robertson 18–20 for the date, Bremmer 79 for the suggestion that the mistresses waited on the slaves in a 'rite of reversal'. [Robertson and Bremmer are now superseded by the detailed analysis in F. Coarelli, *Il Campo Marzio dalle origini alla fine della repubblica* (Rome 1997) 21–46.]

37. Plut. *Rom.* 29.3–5, *Cam.* 33.2–5, Macrobius *Sat.* I 11.35–40, Polyaenus VIII 30, Polemius Silvius on 7 July (*CIL* I² p. 269); Ps.Plutarch (*Mor.* 313a = *FGrH* 286 F1) and Ovid (*AA* II 258) tell the story with Gauls, not Latins, as the enemy. Distribution to tents: Macrobius *Sat.* I 11.39.

[In the original publication of this chapter I allowed myself the rash guess that the wild fig-tree where the ritual took place was in the area now occupied by the Villa Borghese—i.e., where an army advancing from Antemnae on the Via Salaria might be expected to have camped before the walls of Rome. I was aware of Plutarch's reference to the Palus Caprae in the Campus Martius (Plut. *Rom.* 29.2), but thought that might have referred to a separate ritual on the day of Poplifugia. But Filippo Coarelli has now shown that there was a *caprificus* in the Campus Martius (Hist. Aug. *M. Aurelius* 13.6); he argues very convincingly for an archaic cult site of Juno Caprotina in the fields next to the 'Goat-marsh', at the far end of the Villa Publica area where the Porticus Minucia was created at the end of the second century BC (i.e. the Largo Argentina): Coarelli, op. cit. (n. 36) 56–60, 180–1, cf. 164–75 (Villa Publica), 296–345 (Porticus Minucia).]

38. The Latin version of her name (Tutula, cf. Tutunus) may also have had a sexual significance: G. Wissowa, *RE* 3 (1899) 1552. Cf. Augustine *Civitas Dei* II 6 on the 'Fugalia' (i.e. Poplifugia, 5 July?), 'effuse omni licentia turpitudinum'.

39. Plut. *Cam.* 33.4, *Rom.* 29.5; cf. Ausonius VII 24.10, 'stola matronis dempta teget famulas'.

40. Nonius 653L, 'vestimentum quo in foro amicimur'; Seneca *Epist.* 18.2, Pliny *Epist.* V 6.45, VII 3.2f (*toga=molestiae*), Juvenal III 127, 172 etc, Martial I 49.31, VI 24, X 47.5, XIV 142, Dio IX fr. 39.7.

41. *Plebs* as *pullati*: Suet. *Aug.* 44.2 (theatre), Quint. *Inst. or.* II 12.10, Pliny *Epist.* VII 17.9. Exceptions: *salutatio* (Martial IX 100, X 96.11, XIV 124 etc—a burdensome duty); Augustus' insistence on the toga in the forum and at the circus games (Suet. *Aug.* 40.5, cf. Juvenal XI 204 for the circus).

42. Nonius 867L (citing Afranius fr. 182R), Varro *De vita p.R.* fr. 44 Riposati; Servius on *Aeneid* I 282.

43. Festus 284L, Prop. IV 11.33; Pliny *Nat. Hist.* VIII 194.

44. Plut. *Cor.* 14.1, *Quaest. Rom.* 49 (*Mor.* 276d, quoting Cato fr. 112P). Normally, of course, one wore a tunic under the toga.

45. Cic. *Phil.* II 44, Hor. *Sat.* I 2.63 and scholiasts, Sulpicia [Tib.] III 16.3, Martial II 39.2, X 52, Juvenal II 68–70. Contrast with *stola*: Ovid *Ars am.* I 3.2 (= *Trist.* II 247–52), II 600, *Trist.* III 3.52, *Fasti* IV 134.

46. N. Horsfall, *Greece and Rome* 21 (1974) 195–7, on Appian *Bell. civ.* II 481, Dio XLIV 16.2, Nic. Dam. *Caes.* 98, Plut. *Caes.* 65.2.

47. Ovid *Fasti* III 539–42.
48. III 526, 'cum pare quisque sua'; cf. 534f (*qui . . . quae*), 542.
49. *Culta amica* also at Ovid *Ars am.* II 175; cf. I 97, III 51, *Amores* II 4.37, III 7.1, Propertius I 2.26, Juvenal XI 202.
50. Ovid *Fasti* III 643–8 (cf. 649–56 for the river-bank *aition*). He used the same phrase at *Amores* I 5.9 (had Corinna left her toga in the lobby?) and *Ars am.* I 529.
51. Ovid *Ars am.* III 311–52, cf. Propertius II 3.17–22, etc.
52. See J. Griffin, *Latin Poets and Roman Life* (London 1985), esp. 26–8, 54f, 112–8, 204–8.
53. Cic. *Pis.* 8, Asconius 7C, Macrobius *Sat.* I 7.34.
54. Prop. II 22a.3–8, with W.A. Camps, *Propertius Elegies Book II* (Cambridge 1966) 151–2: stages at the Compitalia?
55. Statius *Silv.* I 6.67–71. *ludiae* is Scaliger's emendation for *Lydiae*: for the etymology, cf. Dion. Hal. II 71.4, Appian *Pun.* 259, Tertull. *De spect.* 5.
56. For which see (e.g.) Plaut. *Casina* 1016–8, *Truc.* 965f, Alciphron III 29.2, Tertull. *De spect.* 17, Isid. *Orig.* XVIII 42.2.
57. Val. Max. II 10.8, 'ut mimae nudarentur'; Sen. *Epist.* 97.8, 'nudandarum meretricum'. Cf. also Ovid *Fasti* V 349, 'turba meretricia'; Lactantius *Div. inst.* I 20.10, 'meretrices quae tunc mimarum funguntur officio'; Arnobius VII 33, 'migratum ab lupanaribus in theatra'.
58. Ovid *Fasti* V 331–54, Martial I pref., 35.8–9, Hist. Aug. *Elagab.* 6.5, Ausonius VII 24.25f ('quae spectare uolunt qui uoluisse negant'). [See T.P. Wiseman in B. Bergmann and C. Kondoleon (eds), *The Art of the Ancient Spectacle* (Studies in the History of Art, Washington D.C., forthcoming).]
59. *ILLRP* 803 = *CIL* I² 1214 ('quae modo nobilium ludos decoraui choro'); Festus 436L, cf. Diomedes *GL* I 490K (in the *orchestra*). For private engagements, cf. T.P. Wiseman, *Catullus and his World* (Cambridge 1985) 44–8.
60. Lucr. IV 978–82; cf. 788–93 for the dancers.
61. Sir J.G. Frazer, *Publii Ovidii Nasonis Fastorum libri sex* (London 1929) I 271 = *Ovid's Fasti* (Loeb trans., London 1931, 1989²) 287, on V 349.
62. Gellius *NA* I 5.3, Cic. *Rosc. com.* 23.
63. Plut. *Mor.* 318c, *Sulla* 2.4; cf. Nic. Dam. *FGrH* 90 F75 (Athenaeus VI 261c).
64. Varro *Men.* 136B = 125 Cèbe, Plut. *Pomp.* 2.2–4; she may be the Flora of Philodemus 12G-P (*Anth. Pal.* V 132). Her portrait was dedicated in the temple of Castor by a Metellus (Plut. *Pomp.* 2.4).
65. Cic. *Verr.* III 83; cf. III 78–9, V 31, 40.
66. Antony: Cic. *Ad Att.* X 10.5, 16.5, *Phil.* II 20, 58, 62, 69, 77, Plut. *Ant.* 9.4–5, Pliny *Nat. Hist.* VIII 55. Gallus: Servius on *Eclogue* 10.1, *De vir. ill.* 82.2 (also M. Brutus). Cic. *Ad fam.* IX 26.2 for her presence at dinner when Cicero was a guest.
67. Josephus *Ant. Iud.* XIX 32–6, cf. Suet. *Gaius* 16.4—a grim story, for which the freedwoman's gentile name (cf. Cic. *Phil.* II 58 for Volumnia Cytheris) is appropriately used.
68. Statius *Silv.* I 6.73, cf. *Cod. Theod.* XV 13 ('plebeii scaenici'). At *Fasti* V 352 the girls at the Floralia are called *plebeius chorus*—mistranslated by Frazer (loc. cit. n. 61 above) as 'the common herd'.

69. *Fasti* III 543f, 661f: 'nec a ueri dissidet illa fide' (662).
70. Ovid *Fasti* III 761-70 (cf. 726, where part of the textual tradition has *vilis anus*).
71. III 693f, cf. I 437f, II 355f, III 759; see J.C. McKeown, *Proceedings of the Cambridge Philological Society* 25 (1979) 75-6; E. Fantham, *Harvard Studies in Classical Philology* 87 (1983) 189f, 200f. The laughter motif is noted, without any inference about mime, by Amy Richlin, in *Pornography and Representation in Greece and Rome* (New York 1992) 169-72.
72. Laberius fr. 2R = 10 Bonaria (Nonius 129L), cf. Ovid *Fasti* III 691 ('oscula sumpturus subito Mars aspicit Annam'); F. Giancotti, *Mimo e gnome: studio su Decimo Laberio e Publilio Siro* (Florence 1967) 61-3.
73. III 677 ('nuper est dea facta'), 684 (addressed by Mars as 'comis anus').
74. J. Barsby, *Ovid Amores Book I* (Oxford 1973) 91. See also M. Willcock, in *Papers of the Leeds International Latin Seminar* VIII (Arca 33, Leeds 1995) 22: 'She had been a *meretrix* herself when younger, and is now the helper, adviser, confidante, more like a madame in an upper class brothel.'
75. E.g. Herodas 1.48-66; see J.C. McKeown, *Ovid Amores: Text, Prolegomena and Commentary* II (Arca 22, Leeds 1989) 198-9.
76. Tib. II 6.41-54, cf. I 5.47-68, Prop. IV 5, Ovid *Amores* I 8.
77. *Fasti* II 571-82; J.F. Miller, *Ovid's Elegiac Festivals* (Studien zur klassischen Philologie 55, Frankfurt 1991) 105-6.
78. Varro *Ant. div.* fr. 7 Cardauns, *De gente p.R.* fr. 18 Fraccaro (Augustine *Civitas dei* VI 5, XVIII 10); cf. Augustine *Civitas Dei* II 27, VI 1, 6, 7, 8, Arnobius IV 35, VII 33, Tertull. *Apol.* 15.1-3; pp. 18-21 above.
79. E.g. Virg. *Aen.* IV 216, IX 616 (Lydians, Phrygians), Propertius IV 7.62 (Lydians), Pliny *Nat. Hist.* VI 162 (Arabs).
80. *Copa* 1-3, 9-10: 'Copa Syrisca, caput Graeca redimita *mitella*, crispum sub crotalo docta mouere latus, ebria *fumosa* saltat lasciua taberna . . . en et Maenalio quae garrit dulce sub antro, *rustica* pastoris fistula in ore sonat.'
81. Tavern-keepers: Lucilius fr. 128M = 123W, *IG* XIV 24 (Syracuse), cf. Juv. VIII 159-62. Dancing girls (*ambubaiae*): Horace *Sat.* I 2.1 and Porph., Petronius *Sat.* 74.13, Juvenal III 62-6, Suet. *Nero* 27.2.
82. For freedwomen called Anna, see *CIL* X 355, 3030, 8402a, XIV 1748 (Atina, Puteoli, Tarracina, Ostia).
83. Ulpian *Digest* XXIII 2.43.9: 'si qua cauponam exercens in ea corpora quaestuaria habeat (ut multae adsolent sub praetextu instrumenti cauponii prostitutas mulieres habere), dicendum hanc quoque lenae appellatione contineri.' Also 2.43 pref.: prostitutes include 'si qua (ut adsolet) in taberna cauponia uel qua alia pudori suo non parcit.'
84. *CIL* IX 2689 = *ILS* 7478. For *tabernae* and prostitution in general, see T. Kleberg, *Hôtels, restaurants et cabarets dans l'antiquité romaine* (Uppsala 1957) 89-91.
85. *Archimimae*: e.g. *CIL* VI 10106-7.
86. N. 5 above; Festus 442-4L.
87. Fr. 49 Wehrli; cf. Wiseman in C. Gill and T.P. Wiseman, *Lies and Fiction in the Ancient World* (Exeter 1993) 128-31.
88. Philochorus *FGrH* 328 F17, Demon *FGrH* 327 F5 (Plut. *Thes.* 16.1,

19.2–3), Hdt I 110.1, 122.3, Licinius Macer fr. 2P (Malalas VII 7 = 178–9D).
89. Aetiologies for Bovillae as Cowtown: Nonius 176L, Schol. Pers. 6.55. Cf. D. Porte, *L'étiologie religieuse dans les Fastes d'Ovide* (Paris 1985) 381–5, who implausibly suggests that Ovid's reference may be an allusion to Augustus: Bovillae was the origin of the *gens Iulia* (Tac. *Ann.* II 41.1), and Octavian's enemies alleged that his maternal grandfather had been a baker at nearby Aricia (Cassius Parmensis ap. Suet. *Aug.* 4.2).

Chapter 8

1. Title: Dion. Hal. VII 71.1 on Fabius (παλαιότατος γὰρ ἀνὴρ τῶν τὰ Ῥωμαικὰ συνταξαμένων), cf. Diodorus VII 5.4 (Φάβιος ὁ τὰς Ῥωμαίων πράξεις ἀναγράψας); M. Gelzer, *Hermes* 69 (1934) 129 = *Kleine Schriften* III (Wiesbaden 1964) 51. Latin equivalents: *Res gestae* (Nonius 835L, on the Latin Fabius), *Res Romanae* (Gellius *NA* XI 8.2, on Postumius), *Res populi Romani* (Sall. *Hist.* I 1M, Livy pref. 1). Cincius as contemporary with Fabius: Dion. Hal. I 6.2.
2. Pol. IX 2.2 (Ian Scott-Kilvert's Penguin translation).
3. Livy pref. 1: 'noui semper scriptores aut in rebus certius aliquid allaturos se aut scribendi arte rudem uetustatem superaturos credunt.'
4. Dion. Hal. I 6.2: τὰ δὲ ἀρχαῖα τὰ μετὰ τὴν κτίσιν τῆς πόλεως γενόμενα κεφαλαιωδῶς ἐπέδραμεν.
5. The classic treatment of this 'expansion of the past' is E. Badian in T.A. Dorey (ed.), *Latin Historians* (London 1966) 11–23. Gellius and Antias evidently wrote on a scale similar to that of Dionysius.
6. T.P. Wiseman, *Clio's Cosmetics* (Leicester 1979) 7–8, 31–37; id., *History* 66 (1981) 388–90 = *Roman Studies* (Liverpool 1987) 257–9.
7. T.J. Cornell in I.S. Moxon, J.D. Smart, A.J. Woodman (eds), *Past Perspectives: Studies in Greek and Roman Historical Writing* (Cambridge 1986) 83–4, and in K.A. Raaflaub (ed.), *Social Struggles in Archaic Rome: New Perspectives on the Conflict of the Orders* (Berkeley 1986) 58, 73–4; cf. T.P. Wiseman, *Roman Studies* (Liverpool 1987) 294–6, 384.
8. A. Carandini, *Boll. arch.* 1–2 (1990) 159–65; R. Ross Holloway, *The Archaeology of Early Rome and Latium* (London 1994) 101–2.
9. C.M. Stibbe et al., *Lapis Satricanus* (Scripta minora 5, The Hague 1980); Ross Holloway, op. cit. 149–55. [For a classic example of unjustified inference, see J.A.K.E. de Waele, *Ostraka* 5 (1996) 231: 'No longer can this first period of Republican history be regarded as shadowy and its main characters a product of later annalist historiography. Neither [do] the first *fasti consulares* and *fasti triumphales* turn out to be reconstructions or falsifications by later historiographers, as 19th-century ancient historians of the positivist school would like us to believe, but the years after the expulsion of the kings in 509 BC provide a series of historical 'facts' in their main essentials. With the discovery of the Satricum stone doubts about the historical veracity of the Early Republic might be eliminated.']

10. M.H. Crawford, *Roman Republican Coinage* (Cambridge 1974) 713-25 and 725-44, on public and private types respectively. See esp. 726: 'From the idea of issues for which they were responsible the moneyers seem to have moved to the idea of issues which were *theirs*.'

11. T. Hölscher, *Monumenti statali e pubblico* (Rome 1994) 144 = *Staatsdenkmal und Publikum* (Xenia 9, Konstanz 1984) 13. However, I am not convinced by Hölscher's explanation, that in the late Republic the *nobiles* were no longer addressing the Roman public, but only each other (op. cit. 143-52 = 12-19).

12. One of the contributory factors was probably the ballot law of 139 BC, and the consequent need to advertise oneself to the voters: T.P. Wiseman, *New Men in the Roman Senate 139 BC-AD 14* (Oxford 1971) 4, 148, 204; cf. Crawford, op. cit. (n. 10) 710, 728. For the quality of one's ancestry as a criterion in political competitiveness, see Lucretius II 11, Horace *Odes* III 1.10-14.

13. Accius' *Brutus* is the classic example; and what L. Balbus did at Cordoba in 43 BC (Pollio in Cic. *Ad fam.* X 32.3) his equals no doubt regularly did at Rome. Cf. T.P. Wiseman, *Catullus and his World* (Cambridge 1985) 30-34 on *nobilium ludi* (*ILLRP* 803.12).

14. Cic. *De fin.* V 51-2, with T.P. Wiseman, *History* 66 (1981) 383-4 = *Roman Studies* (Liverpool 1987) 252-3; Dion. Hal. *Thuc.* 50, with C. Schultze in Moxon, Smart and Woodman, op. cit. (n. 7) 134-6; cf. also Pliny *Nat. Hist.* pref. 6.

15. Plut. *Numa* 21.2, ὡς χαριζομένων τοῖς γένεσι καὶ προστιθέντων οὐκ ἀληθῆ στέμματα τῆς ἀπὸ Νομᾶ διαδοχῆς. See G. Forsythe, *The Historian L. Calpurnius Piso Frugi and the Roman Annalistic Tradition* (Lanham 1994) 202-6.

16. Wiseman, *Clio's Cosmetics* (n. 6 above), chapters 5-6. [S.P. Oakley, *A Commentary on Livy Books VI-X* I (Oxford 1997) 98 n. 292: 'That this [hostile] portrayal of the Claudii was started by the systematic perversion of the record by one individual is likely enough, but he cannot now be identified.' The final phrase seems to be based on a reluctance to accept the evidence for a late date for Antias (Oakley, op. cit. 89 n. 250), for which see n. 111 below.]

17. Livy VII 9.5, 'quaesita ea propriae familiae laus'.

18. F. Münzer, *De gente Valeria* (Opollae 1891) 70-1.

19. For the traditions on the Rape and its consequences, see T.P. Wiseman, *Classical Quarterly* 33 (1983) 445-50 = *Roman Studies* (Liverpool 1987) 285-90.

20. Livy I 13.1-2; Ovid *Fasti* III 215-24, Plut. *Rom.* 19.1-2, Dio I fr. 5.5.

21. Dion. Hal. II 45.3-6 (cf. 31.1 for Gellius); Gellius fr. 15P (Gell. *NA* XIII 23.13); cf. Appian *Reg.* fr. 5, *Ital.* 5.5 (n. 108 below). The women first get approval for their embassy from the Senate.

22. Comitium: Plut. *Rom.* 19.7, Dio I fr. 5.7 (*comitium* from *coire*); Dion. Hal. II 45.6 (συνελθόντας), 46.1 (συνελθόντων). Cloacina: Pliny *Nat. Hist.* XV 119, cf. Lactantius *Inst.* I 20.11; Dion. Hal. II 46.3 (altars set up 'about the middle of the Sacra Via'). See F. Coarelli, *Il foro romano: periodo arcaico* (Rome 1983) 84-5, 97. The Sacra Via was named from the *foedus* (Festus

372L, Appian *Reg.* fr. 5), and the *sacellum* of Janus symbolised the union of the two peoples (Servius on *Aeneid* XII 198).

For Virgil's revisionist version (*Aen.* VIII 639–41, an altar of Jupiter), see A.J. Woodman in J. Diggle, J.B. Hall, H.D. Jocelyn (eds), *Studies in Latin Literature and its Tradition in Honour of C.O. Brink* (Philological Society supp. vol. 15, Cambridge 1989) 135–7.

23. Dion. Hal. II 46.3, cf. IV 67.3, V 12.3. The other two were Mettius Curtius, the hero of the battle in the Forum (II 42.2–6), and a mysterious 'Tallus, surnamed Tyrannus'.

24. *En masse*: Cic. *De rep.* II 13 (*orantibus*), 14 (*oratrices*), Livy I 13.2 (*orantes*), Ovid *Fasti* III 217–24, Appian *Reg.* fr. 5. Hersilia: Gellius fr. 15P (*oraret*), Dion. Hal. II 45.6 (δεήσιν), Plut. *Rom.* 19.2–5 (ἱκεσίαν καὶ δεήσιν), Dio I fr. 5.5–7.

25. σύγκρασις, κοινωνία etc: Plut. *Rom.* 14.2, 14.6, 19.7, *Numa* 6.4, Dion. Hal. II 46.3.

26. Plut. *Publ.* 1.1.

27. Cf. n. 22 above.

28. Cic. *De rep.* II 25, Livy I 17.7–11, 18.5 (*populus* chooses on Senate's authority); Dion. Hal. II 58, Plut. *Numa* 3.1–3 (Senate chooses, informs *populus*).

29. Plut. *Rom.* 3.3, 5.1; Dion. Hal. II 60.1.

30. Dion. Hal. II 60.1 (cf. 58.2 for Pompon, Plut. *Numa* 3.4 for the brothers); Plut. *Numa* 5.2, 6.1.

31. Plut. *Numa* 5.1. Julius Proculus: Cic. *De rep.* II 20, *De leg.* I 3, Livy I 16.5–8, Ovid *Fasti* II 499–510, Plut. *Rom.* 28.1–3, *Numa* 2.3, Dio LVI 46.2.

32. According to Plut. *Numa* 6.1, the Roman embassy pleaded with Numa to save them from strife and civil war.

33. Brutus is Collatinus' cousin (Dion. Hal. IV 68.1–2, Diod. Sic. X 22.1) and Lucretia's maternal uncle (Serv. *ad Aen.* VIII 646). [For a suggestion about why and how Brutus' presence came to be part of the tradition, see T.P. Wiseman, *Greece and Rome* 45 (1998) 19–26.]

34. Livy I 58.5–6. Zonaras too (VII 11) has Brutus and Valerius accompany Lucretia's husband and father, though they are not mentioned in the Dio extract from *De virtutibus et vitiis* (Dio II fr. 11.18).

35. Dion. Hal. IV 66.1–3, 67.1–4, 70.1–2, 71.5–6. For Brutus as *tribunus celerum* see also Livy I 59.7, Pomponius *Digest* I 2.2.15, Servius on *Aeneid* VIII 646.

36. He is not present in Diod. Sic. X 20.3, Ovid *Fasti* III 815–52, Florus I 9.1, Dio II fr. 11.18 (cf. n. 34 above), Servius on *Aeneid* VIII 646, or *De vir. ill.* 9.4–5.

37. Plut. *Publ.* 1.3, 1.5–2.1.

38. Dion. Hal. V 6.4, Plut. *Publ.* 3.3–4; cf. Livy II 4.1.

39. F. Zevi in A. Storchi Marino (ed.), *L'incidenza dell'antico: studi in memoria di Ettore Lepore* (Naples 1995) 291–314. For the 'Cumaean chronicle' see A. Alföldi, *Early Rome and the Latins* (Ann Arbor 1965) 56–72; for Tarquin at Cumae, see Livy II 21.5, 34.4, Dion. Hal. VI 21.3.

40. Suet. *Vit.* 2.1 (from Cassius Severus); however, the chronology is not easy,

since the informer's eldest grandson (ibid. 2.3) was praetor in the final years of Augustus. Cf. Suet. *Vit.* 1.2 on the 'patrician Vitellii' (supposed ancestors of the Augustan *novi homines*), who must derive from the annalistic story of the conspiracy.

41. Dion. Hal. V 5–6, Plut. *Publ.* 3; the common source evidently made great play with Brutus' name, 'stupid and cruel' or 'inflexible and unyielding' (Dion. Hal. V 8, cf. 9.3; Plut. *Publ.* 3.4, 6.4, cf. 3.1).
42. Plut. *Publ.* 4.1; cf. Sall. *Cat.* 22.1–2, Dio XXXVII 30.3, Tertull. *Apol.* 9.9.
43. Dion. Hal. V 7.1–4, Plut. *Publ.* 4; for Valerius' φιλανθρωπία, Plut. *Publ.* 1.2, 4.4.
44. Dion. Hal. V 7.5; Plut. *Publ.* 5 (where Marcus finds more letters at the *regia*).
45. Possibly a fourth-century story to explain the absence of consular Iunii before 317 BC? See T.P. Wiseman, *Remus: a Roman Myth* (Cambridge 1995) 109–10.
46. Dion. Hal. V 8–12, Plut. *Publ.* 6–7; also Zonaras VII 12. In Dionysius (V 11.2–12.1), Sp. Lucretius persuades Brutus to let Collatinus resign voluntarily. [Cf. Wiseman, op. cit. (n. 33), on the multiplicity of consuls: a result of the combination of originally independent stories?]
47. Piso fr. 26 Forsythe = 19P; Cic. *De rep.* II 53 (cf. I 62), *De off.* III 40, *Brut.* 53; so too Florus I 9.3, Augustine *Civitas Dei* II 17, III 16. See Forsythe, op. cit. (n. 15) 249–52.
48. Collatinus: Livy II 2.3–10, cf. Eutropius I 9.4. Conspiracy: Livy II 3.2–4.7, cf. *De vir. ill.* 10.5.
49. Virg. *Aen.* VI 817–23.
50. Livy II 5.1–4, Dion. Hal. V 13.2–4, Plut. *Publ.* 8.1–3: aetiological explanation of the Tiber island. Cf. Servius on *Aeneid* IX 272: the land granted to Tarquin *pro honore*.
51. Zosimus II 3.3, with C.B. Pascal, *American Journal of Philology* 100 (1979) 532–7: not later than Augustan, because misinterpreted by Valerius Maximus (II 4.4) or his source. For πυροφόρον πεδίον, cf. Homer *Iliad* XXI 602.
52. Censorinus *De die nat.* 17.10 (cf. Antias frr. 18P, 55P), Val. Max. II 4.5 *ad fin.*; I.B. Pighi, *De ludis saecularibus* (Milan 1941 = Amsterdam 1965) 38, 52. Cf. also Festus 440L, as supplemented by F. Castagnoli, *Mem. Lincei* (ser. 8) 1.4 (1946) 105–9.
   The complex question of the Republican *ludi saeculares* has been put on a completely new footing by F. Coarelli, 'Note sui *ludi saeculares*', in *Spectacles sportifs et scèniques dans le monde étrusco-italique* (Coll. de l'École française de Rome 172, 1993) 211–45. Much of his argument I find wholly convincing, but I differ from him on the question of Valerius Antias' contribution to the tradition: see Appendix B, pp. 165–7 above.
53. Zosimus II 3.2: Manius Valerius Tarantinus, because the site of the altar was called Tarentum (or Terentum, Festus 478–9L).
54. Val. Max. II 4.5, Sulpicia [Tib. IV] 8; A. Degrassi in J. Bibauw (ed.), *Hommages à Marcel Renard* II (Coll. Latomus 102, Brussels 1969) 174–5. On Valerius Maximus' name and status, see C.J. Skidmore, *Practical Ethics*

for Roman Gentlemen: the Work of Valerius Maximus (Exeter 1996) 113–7.

55. Dio XLI 14.5, Servius auctus on *Eclogue* 9.46, Virg. *Ecl.* 4.4 etc; S. Weinstock, *Divus Julius* (Oxford 1971) 191–7; I.M.LeM. DuQuesnay in F. Cairns (ed.), *Papers of the Liverpool Latin Seminar 1976* (Arca 2, Liverpool 1977) 39–43.

56. Second: Livy II 8.9–9.1, Plut. *Publ.* 16.1–2. Third: Dion. Hal. V 21.1.

57. Livy II 10.1, cf. 10.4, Dion. Hal. V 23.2; E. Gjerstad in *Opuscula Romana* VII (Acta Inst. Rom. Regni Sueciae 30, Lund 1969) 149–61; Wiseman, *Clio's Cosmetics* (n. 6 above) 44. For the wall by the river, perhaps made obsolete in the third century BC, see F. Coarelli, *Il foro boario* (Rome 1988) 35–42, 104–5; the later incorporation of the Janiculum into the circuit is implied by Appian (*Bell. civ.* I 68, III 91, 94).

58. Plut. *Publ.* 16.3–4: evidently two engagements, involving each of the consuls.

59. Polybius VI 55 (Cocles sacrifices his life); Cic. *De leg.* II 10, *De off.* I 61, *Paradoxa* I 12; cf. Val. Max. III 2.1, the first example in the section *de fortitudine*. There was a 'statue of Cocles' at the Volcanal (Plut. *Publ.* 16.7, Dion. Hal. V 25.2, Gellius *NA* IV 5.1, *De vir. ill.* 11.2), otherwise identified as Romulus (Dion. Hal. II 54.2) or as 'the actor's statue' (Festus 370L); cf. Coarelli, op. cit. (n. 22) 161–2, 174–5.

60. Livy II 10.11, 'rem plus famae habituram ad posteros quam fidei'. Cicero (*De off.* I 61) lists it with the battles of the Persian Wars, Leuctra, the Decii, the Scipiones and M. Marcellus.

61. Dion. Hal. V 22.5, 23.1; Plut. *Publ.* 16.3, 17.1.

62. Dion. Hal. V 24.3, Plut. *Publ.* 16.6–7; also Servius on *Aeneid* VIII 646, [and Appian *Reg.* fr. 10, where his lameness explains why he was never consul.] Contrast Livy II 10.11 and Val. Max. III 2.1, where he is miraculously unscathed. Cf. also Plut. *Publ.* 16.5 on his grotesque appearance, a variant explanation of his *cognomen*.

63. Cf. Florus I 10.3, 'illa tria Romani nominis prodigia atque miracula, Horatius, Mucius, Cloelia'. Cf. L. Arcella, 'Il mito di Cloelia e i Valerii', *Studi e materiali di storia delle religioni* 51 (1985) 21–42, for an interpretation quite different from mine: it depends on a synchronic and quasi-Dumézilian approach to the evidence which totally ignores the 'palimpsest' phenomenon.

64. Livy II 13.11 ('in summa sacra via'), Dion. Hal. V 35.2 ('on the sacred Way that leads to the Forum'), Seneca *Cons. Marc.* 16.2 ('in sacra via'), Plut. *Publ.* 19.5 ('on the Sacred Way as you go to the Palatine'), Annius Fetialis ap. Pliny *Nat. Hist.* XXXIV 29 ('contra Iovis Statoris aedem'); cf. *De vir. ill.* 13.4 ('in foro'). Annius Fetialis identifies the site as 'in uestibulo Superbi domus'; cf. Livy I 41.4, Solinus 1.24 for Tarquinius Priscus' house at the Porta Mugonia at the top of the Nova Via (fig. 2).

65. Val. Max. III 2.2, Plut. *Publ.* 19.2, 19.4 ('some say'), Florus I 10.7, *De vir. ill.* 13.1.

66. Swimming: Livy II 13.6, Virg. *Aen.* VI 651, Dion. Hal. V 33.1, Plut. *Publ.* 19.1, Polyaenus VIII 31. Gift: Dion. Hal. V 34.3, Plut. *Publ.* 19.4, Dio IV fr. 14.

67. Servius on *Aeneid* VIII 646, 'ut ei aliquid uirile decerneretur'. Exemplary: cf. Val. Max. III 2.2 ('uiris puella lumen uirtutis praeferendo'), Seneca *Cons. Marc.* 16.2.
68. Livy II 13.10 (*impubes*); cf. *De vir. ill.* 13.4 (*uirgines puerosque*), Servius on *Aeneid* VIII 646 (*uirgines*).
69. Dion. Hal. V 30.1–2, 32.4; Plut. *Publ.* 18.1–2. Cf. Dion. Hal. V 36.1–2 for the death of Arruns at Aricia the following year.
70. Dion. Hal. V 33.1–4, Plut. *Publ.* 19.1–3; Polyaenus (VIII 31) has the Dionysius-Plutarch version but without Valeria and the ambush. [For the suggestion that the Dionysius–Plutarch version ultimately derives (via Antias) from a scenario for the *ludi Florales*, see T.P. Wiseman in *The Art of the Ancient Spectacle* (Studies in the History of Art, Washington D.C., forthcoming).]
71. Plut. *Publ.* 19.5; for a further development, cf. Annius Fetialis ap. Pliny *Nat. Hist.* XXXIV 29, who alleges that Valeria alone swam the Tiber, and the other hostages were killed in the ambush.
72. [E.g. T.J. Cornell, *The Beginnings of Rome* (London 1995) 157, 174–5, 245, 306;] cf. also the references to the episode in *Cambridge Ancient History* VII.2 (ed. 2, Cambridge 1989) 24 (A. Drummond), 90, 98 (A. Momigliano), 261, 270, 292 (T.J. Cornell).
73. Virg. *Aen.* VII 708–9, Suet. *Tib.* 1.1; Wiseman, *Clio's Cosmetics* (n. 6 above) 59–61.
74. Livy II 16.2–5, Dion. Hal. V 40, Plut. *Publ.* 21.
75. Plut. *Publ.* 20.1. According to Dionysius (V 40.2, cf. Appian *Reg.* fr. 12), the Sabines were stirred up against Rome by Sex. Tarquinius; in Livy (I 60.2), Sextus was killed in 509.
76. Plut. *Publ.* 21.4–6, cf. Zonaras VII 13. For the favourable and hostile traditions on the founder of the *gens Claudia* see Wiseman, *Clio's Cosmetics* (n. 6 above) 62–4.
77. Cic. *De rep.* II 56 ('decem fere annos post primos consules'), Livy II 18.4–5 (501), Dion. Hal. V 73.1, 75.1 (498), Eutropius I 12.3 (501), Jerome *Chron.* sub anno 502/1; Lydus *De mag.* I 37, 38, Suda s.v. *hipparchos.*
78. Festus 216L; Livy II 18.6, contrasting it with the *veterrimi auctores* who named T. Larcius.
79. Livy II 18.4: '... quibus consulibus quia ex factione Tarquiniana essent—id quoque enim traditur—parum creditum sit.'
80. Livy II 18.7: 'patrem multo potius M. Valerium spectatae uirtutis [cf. n. 75 above] et consularem uirum legissent.'
81. Dion. Hal. V 50.3, cf. Thucydides I 72.2. This author evidently constructed the origins of the Latin War on the model of the Peloponnesian War: cf. Livy II 18.2 (501 BC) on the kidnapping of *scorta*, just as in Aristophanes' version of the cause of the war (*Acharnians* 523–9).
82. R.M. Ogilvie, *A Commentary on Livy Books 1–5* (Oxford 1965) 282–3.
83. Livy II 19.5; see J. Sihvola in E.M. Steinby (ed.), *Lacus Iuturnae* I (Rome 1989) 78–82.
84. Dion. Hal. VI 11.2 (in polemic with Gellius and Licinius Macer) insists that Tarquin himself was too old to take part; on the other hand, unlike Livy he has both T. and Sex. Tarquinii at the battle (cf. n. 75 above).

85. Livy II 20.8 (cf. 10.2), Dion. Hal. VI 12.3 (cf. V 23.2).
86. Livy II 19.6, 19.7–9, 20.7–9; Dion. Hal. VI 11.2 (cf. n. 84 above), 11.3, 12.4.
87. Livy II 20.1–3; Homer *Iliad* III 15–37. The Homeric parallels are noted by Ogilvie, op. cit. (n. 82) 286.
88. Livy II 20.3, cf. Homer *Iliad* IV 104–47; Dion. Hal. VI 12.2 (Publius and Marcus). [Accepted without question as historical by de Waele, op. cit. (n. 9) 234–5. The nearest he comes to an argument is at 237: 'It is high time that these remnants of modern hypercritical historiography are cleared up once and for all.']
89. Cic. *De nat. deor.* II 6, *Tusc.* I 28; Dion. Hal. VI 13.1–3, Val. Max. I 8.1, Frontinus *Strat.* I 11.8 (a rationalizing version), Plut. *Marcius* 3.4, Lactantius *Inst.* II 7.9, *De vir. ill.* 16.3.
90. Livy II 20.12, 42.5, Dion. Hal. VI 13.4.
91. Livy IX 46.15, Val. Max. II 2.9, *De vir. ill.* 32.3 (Q. Fabius Rullianus as censor). Sihvola, op. cit. (n. 83) 85–6, following M. Sordi, *Contributi dell'Istituto di storia antica* I (Milan 1972) 62–5; [*contra* Cornell, op. cit. (n. 72) 293–4, for whom the story dates back to the battle itself.]
92. Cic. *De nat. deor.* II 6, Val. Max. I 8.1, Pliny *Nat. Hist.* VII 86, Florus I 28.14–15, Lactantius *Inst.* II 7.10, Minucius Felix *Octavius* 7.3; Sihvola, op. cit. (n. 83) 86–7.
93. Livy XLIV 17.5 (Helva), XLV 28.11 (Postumius); Pol. XXXIX 1 on the historian (*FGrH* 812), cf. F.W. Walbank, *A Historical Commentary on Polybius* III (Oxford 1979) 726–8; Crawford, op. cit. (n. 10) no. 335.10b. For the Dioscuri on Roman coins, see J. Välimaa in Steinby, op. cit. (n. 83) 110–26, esp. 120–1 on the A. Albinus S.f. type, possibly issued for the 400th anniversary of the battle of Lake Regillus.
94. Cf. L. Harri in Steinby, op. cit. (n. 83) 177–98, on the archaizing statue-group of the Dioscuri at the Lacus Iuturnae; she dates it to the second half of the second century BC—i.e. soon after the publication of Albinus' history.
95. Livy II 20.1: 'domestica etiam gloria accensus, ut cuius familiae decus eiecti reges erant, eiusdem interfecti forent.'
96. Livy II 6.6–9, Dion. Hal. V 15.1–2.
97. Sall. *Hist.* I fr. 11, Livy II 21.5–6.
98. See Forsythe, op. cit. (n. 15) 278–96; Wiseman, op. cit. (n. 45) 114.
99. Livy II 30.5, Dion. Hal. VI 39.2 (cf. 40.1); *ILS* 50 = *Inscr. Ital.* XIII.3.8 ('Volusi f.').
100. Livy II 32.8–12 (cf. 33.10–11), Dio IV fr. 17.10–12, Zonaras VII 14; Ogilvie, op. cit. (n. 82) 312–3.
101. Cic. *Brut.* 54, cf. Plut. *Pomp.* 13.7; Val. Max. VIII 9.1. According to Zonaras (VII 14), 'Marcus' Valerius was called Maximus for his victory over the Sabines.
102. *Inscr. Ital.* XIII 3.60, cf. 78 (*ILS* 50). For the honour of the *sella curulis* in the Circus, see Festus 464L; Antias (fr. 17P) provided some others as well.
103. Dion. Hal. VIII 39.2, Plut. *Marcius* 33.1 (sister); Appian *Ital.* 5.3 (daughter).
104. Plut. *Marcius* 32.3–33.2.

105. Dion. Hal. VIII 39.4–5 (Loeb translation).
106. Dion. Hal. VIII 40.1–43.2 (persuading Veturia), 55.3–4 (temple and priestess).
107. Livy II 40.1–9, Val. Max. I 8.4, V 2.1, V 4.1, Florus I 22.3, Polyaenus VIII 25.3, Dio V fr. 18.7, *De vir. ill.* 19.4, Zonaras VII 6.
108. Appian (*Ital.* 5.3) compares the deputation to Coriolanus with that of Hersilia to T. Tatius (n. 21 above); cf. Ovid *Fasti* III 205–6, Hersilia and the women in the temple of Juno.
109. Plut. *Numa* 5.1–2, 6.1; Dion. Hal. VIII 41.1, 43.1–2.
110. Cf. also n. 55 above (item 5) for the forties BC.
111. Livy I 26.5–7, with J.D. Cloud, *Liverpool Classical Monthly* 2 (1977) 205–13; cf. ibid. 225–7 on the weakness of the traditional dating of Antias to the Sullan period. [On Cicero's silence about Antias, which is hard to explain if one accepts the early dating, see now M. Fleck, *Cicero als Historiker* (Beiträge zur Altertumskunde 39, Stuttgart 1993) 209–24.]
112. Items 5 and 11: see above, nn. 52 and 102.

Chapter 9

1. Cic. *Ad Att.* IX 6.1, Hor. *Epist.* I 18.20, Strabo 3.7 (C282); for conjectures about its date, see T.P. Wiseman, *Papers of the British School at Rome* 38 (1970) 131 = *Roman Studies* (Liverpool 1987) 135.
2. Augustus *Res gestae* 20.5: 'consul septimum uiam Flaminiam ab urbe Ariminum refeci pontesque omnes praeter Muluium et Minucium.' Cf. Cic. *Ad Att.* I 1.2 for a Minucius Thermus as *curator viae Flaminiae* in 65 BC.
3. Vell. Pat. II 8.3; cf. Cic. *Phil.* II 84, Fasti Praenestini 22 Dec. (*Inscr. Ital.* XIII 2.138f), Hist. Aug. *Commodus* 16.5.
4. Regionary Catalogue under regio IX: 'Minucias duas ueterem et frumentariam.' *ILS* 6071 (Claudian), Apuleius *De mundo* 35; *ILS* 1128, 1186, 1191, 1223 for the *curatores*.
5. Identified as the *p.M. frumentaria* by F. Coarelli in *L'area sacra di Largo Argentina* I (Rome 1981) 34–6, as the *p.M. uetus* by L. Richardson jr, *A New Topographical Dictionary of Ancient Rome* (Baltimore 1992) 315–6, and F. Zevi, *Mélanges de l'École française de Rome* 105 (1993) 661–708, who identifies the *p.M. frumentaria* as the building in the Via dei Calderari (E. Nash, *Pictorial Dictionary of Ancient Rome* [London 1961] I 297–300). [For a definitive account, see now F. Coarelli, *Il Campo Marzio dalle origini alla fine della repubblica* (Rome 1997) 296–345.]
6. The Porta Naevia on the Aventine was named not after the Naevii (best known for a praetor and a tribune in 184 BC), but after the notorious *nemora Naeuia* nearby: Varro *De ling. Lat.* V 163, Festus 170L.
7. Festus (Paulus) 109L, 131L.
8. Varro *De re rust.* III 5.12 (aedes Catuli); Pliny *Nat. Hist.* XXXVI 26 (delubrum Cn. Domitii), cf. XXXIV 57 (aedes Pompei Magni), XXXVI 40 (aedes Metelli), 163 (aedes . . .Seiani).
9. For examples of the normal usage, cf. Livy XXVIII 11.4 (ara Neptuni), Val. Max. II 4.5 (ara Ditis patris), Aug. *Res gestae* 12.2 (ara Pacis Augustae);

Varro *De ling. Lat.* V 164 (Volupiae sacellum), Festus 302-3L (sacellum Quirini), Tac. *Ann.* XII 24 (sacellum Larundae).

10. S. Weinstock, *Divus Julius* (Oxford 1971) 366, cf. 293.
11. M.H. Crawford, *Roman Republican Coinage* (Cambridge 1974) 273 (no. 242.1), 275 (no. 243.1). According to Mario Torelli in E.M. Steinby (ed.), *Lexicon Topographicum Urbis Romae* I (Rome 1993) 306, the hanging objects in C. Augurinus' design are not bells but *vittae*, and the beasts at the base not lions but griffins.
12. F. Coarelli, *Il foro romano: periodo arcaico* (Rome 1983) 172-5. The altar belongs to the fourth level of the Comitium, the column to the fifth: at *Journal of Roman Studies* 76 (1986) 307, I argue that the former may be late fifth or early fourth century, and the latter perhaps *c*.338 BC.
13. Festus 184L, cf. Dion. Hal. I 87.2, III 1.2; Coarelli, op. cit. 166-8.
14. Gellius *NA* IV 5.1-4, Plut. *Publ.* 16.7, *vir. ill.* 11.2; Coarelli, op. cit. 161f, 168f.
15. Pliny *Nat. Hist.* XXXIV 21; cf. XVIII 15 ('L. Minucius Augurinus', statue mentioned but no column).
16. Livy IV 12.8, 13.7, 16.2; Dion. Hal. XII 1.5-6, 1.11-12, 4.6. The text at Livy IV 16.2 should read 'L. Minucius boue aurato ⟨et statua⟩ extra portam Trigeminam est donatus'; Crévier's addition, or something like it, is essential, since the *bos auratus* was not a monument but a beast to be sacrificed (*TLL* II 1521.47-65).
17. Note, however, the interpretation of Torelli (loc. cit., n. 11 above): 'un togato in posa eroica di *adlocutio*(?), piede su roccia e mano sinistra recante un corto oggetto non facilmente determinabile.'
18. Livy X 9.2 (300 BC); cf. T. Mommsen, *Römische Forschungen* I (Berlin 1864) 65-8—the origin of the *cognomen* Augurinus?
19. T. Hölscher, 'Die Anfänge römische Repräsentationskunst', *Römische Mittheilungen* 85 (1978) 315-57, at 336f; so too E. Welin, *Studien zur Topographie des Forum Romanum* (Lund 1953) 162-70.
20. For the difference, cf. Crawford, op. cit. (n. 11) 196. Sceptres are shown at Crawford's plates 36.6 and 14, 39.3, etc; staffs (*scipiones*) at 20.1, 21.7-8, 23.12-13, with *Bulletin de correspondence hellénique* 28 (1904) plate 12.
21. As suggested by Torelli, loc. cit. (n. 11): 'the consul of 497 and 491'.
22. Torelli, loc. cit. (n. 11).
23. Scelerata: Festus 450L, Festus (Paulus) 451L. Agonensis: Festus (Paulus) 9L.
24. For the evidence, see F. Coarelli, *Il foro boario* (Rome 1988) 25-34, 42-50.
25. F. Coarelli, *Guida archeologica di Roma* (Milan 1974) 281 = *Roma* (Guide archeologiche Laterza, Bari 1980) 314; cf. op. cit. (n. 24) 241.
26. *Gnomon* 62 (1990) 730-2. The flight of C. Gracchus—from the Aventine through the Porta Trigemina to the Pons Sublicius (Val. Max. IV 7.2, *De vir. ill.* 65.5)—seems at first sight to be an argument in favour of Coarelli's position. In fact it is the opposite, since on his reconstruction the Porta Trigemina would surely have been guarded by D. Brutus' soldiers (cf. Oros. V 12.7). The Gracchans had to scramble down from the temple of Luna: the drop that was necessary ('desilit', *De vir. ill.* 65.5) evidently took them outside the Servian precinct, from where they doubled back *into* the city through the Porta Trigemina, to get to the bridge.

27. Livy XXXV 10.12, XLI 27.8; cf. G. Gatti, *Bull. Com.* 62 (1934) 123–49.
28. Livy XXXVIII 56.4 (Scipio tombs); XXX 38.10, XL 34.4, cf. Strabo VI 2.6 (C272), *Inscr. Ital.* XIII 2.134–5 (Venus Erycina, *ad/extra portam Collinam*).
29. R. Lanciani, *Forma urbis Romae* (1893–1901, repr. 1990), sheet 34.
30. *FUR* frr. 31a–c; Steinby, op. cit. (n. 11) 450, figs 150–1. Wrongly, I think, identified as the *centum gradus* (Tac. *Hist.* III 71.3), which were at the Tarpeian Rock on the *arx*: see F. Coarelli, *Il foro romano: periodo repubblicano e augusteo* (Rome 1985) 81 n.70.
31. The name of the gate at the Capitoline steps is not known: perhaps Porta Catularia, mentioned at Festus (Paulus) 39L?
32. See n. 18 above. For the problem of 'plebeian names' in the early *fasti*, see Andrew Drummond in *Cambridge Ancient History* VII.2 (ed. 2, Cambridge 1989) 173–6.
33. T.R.S. Broughton, *The Magistrates of the Roman Republic* I (New York 1951) xi. I argue the opposite case in *Liverpool Classical Monthly* 8.2 (Feb. 1983) 20f = *Roman Studies* (Liverpool 1987) 294.
34. Livy IX 44.14f; A. Degrassi in *Inscr. Ital.* XIII 1.542f.
35. Namely '. . . Caruetus' (Fasti Cap.) and L. Postumius (Diod. Sic. XI 91.1) respectively.
36. *Transitiones*: e.g. Dio V 22.2 (on 461–455 BC); see in general R.E.A. Palmer, *The Archaic Community of the Romans* (Cambridge 1970) 293–6, esp. 293 on the Minucii ('the entire story is a late fabrication'). Marcii: T. Mommsen, *Römische Forschungen* II (Berlin 1879) 149f; F. Münzer, *Römische Adelsparteien und Adelsfamilien* (Stuttgart 1920) 81.
37. Livy VIII 40.4: 'uitiatam memoriam funebribus laudibus reor *falsisque imaginum titulis*, dum familiae ad se quaeque famam rerum gestarum honorumque fallente mendacio trahunt.' For the arrangements in the *atrium*, see H.I. Flower, *Ancestor Masks and Aristocratic Power in Roman Culture* (Oxford 1996) 185–222.
38. Livy IV 16.3–4 ('falsum imaginis titulum'); Pliny *Nat. Hist.* XVIII 15, cf. XXXIV 21 (n. 15 above).
39. Broughton assumes that this L. Minucius was identical with the consul and *decemuir* L. Minucius P.f.M.n. Esquilinus Augurinus (so named in the Fasti Capitolini for 458; only the *cognomina* survive in the entry for 450). Pliny (*Nat. Hist.* XVIII 15) and Zonaras (VII 20) call him L. Minucius Augurinus, which may imply the identification; however, if Livy had known Minucius to be an ex-*decemuir*, he would hardly have made Cincinnatus refer, in this very episode, to the recent condemnation and exile of the *decemuiri* (Livy IV 15.4). See Mommsen, op. cit. (n. 36) 211f, rightly doubting the identification.
40. Cincius *FGrH* 810 F 4, followed by Piso fr. 4P: Dion. Hal. XII 4.2–6. See G. Forsythe, *The Historian L. Calpurnius Piso Frugi and the Roman Annalistic Tradition* (Lanham MD 1994) 69: 'Since Dionysius elsewhere never cites Cincius without mentioning Fabius Pictor as well . . ., it seems probable that Pictor's history did not include the sedition of Sp. Maelius, but Cincius was the first writer who took a current folk tale and anchored it in time based upon a documented grain shortage.' Ibid. 301–10 for Forsythe's commentary on the Piso fragment.

41. Plutarch also has this detail (*Brut.* 1.5).
42. Dion. Hal. XII 4.3, 4.6: γενομένης δὲ μηνύσεως ὑπὸ τοῦ Μηνυκίου . . . μήνυσιν ἀποδόντι Μηνυκίῳ.
43. Cic. *Cat.* I 3, *Mil.* 72, *De rep.* II 49, *De am.* 36 (all invoking the parallel of Scipio Nasica and Ti. Gracchus); *Phil.* II 114 (the *liberatores* and Caesar).
44. Cic. *Mil.* 72: 'annona leuanda iacturisque rei familiaris.'
45. Crawford, loc. cit (n. 11 above).
46. Piso, writing after 120 BC, may have made Minucius an eleventh tribune, honoured by the people for subsidising the price of grain (Pliny *Nat. Hist.* XVIII 15, p. 94 above).
47. Livy IV 13.7, cf. 7.12, 20.8, 23.2.
48. See most recently Andrew Lintott in *Cambridge Ancient History* IX (ed. 2, Cambridge 1994) 62–86, esp. 68–73 (Ti. Gracchus as 'tyrant'), 78–9 (C. Gracchus' corn-law). For Gracchan aspects of the Maelius story, especially in Piso, see Forsythe, op. cit. (n. 40) 302f.
49. Broughton, *MRR* I (n. 33 above) 521: M. Minucius Rufus *cos.* 110? [See now F. Zevi, *Mélanges de l'École française de Rome* 106 (1994) 1073–6, suggesting that the Porticus Minucia of 106 BC was deliberately placed at the site of the Gracchan corn distributions, and that Minucius was now claiming credit for them; also Coarelli, op. cit. (n. 5) 337–45, though differing from Zevi on the site of the portico.]
50. Livy IV 13–14, Dion. Hal. XII 2. Full references in Broughton, *MRR* I 56.
51. Livy IV 12.7 ('nam utrumque traditur'); R.M. Ogilvie, *A Commentary on Livy Books 1–5* (Oxford 1965) 552.
52. Dion. Hal. XII 2.3, 2.7–8; cf. Livy IV 14.4–6. Butchers' shops (later *argentariae* and *novae*) as *tabernae plebeiae*: Festus 258L, cf. Varro ap. Non. 853L, Livy XXVI 27.2; Coarelli, op. cit. (n. 30) 140–9.
53. Dion. Hal. XII 2.8; Ogilvie, op. cit. (n. 51) 555.
54. Cic. *Rosc. Am.* 89, Seneca *De prov.* 7, Firm. Mat. I 7.34; for its position, by the Vicus Iugarius and the later Basilica Iulia, see Festus 370–2L. The relevance of the Lacus Servilius to the Ahala story was first suggested by E. Pais, *Ancient Legends of Roman History* (London 1906) 210–12.
55. E. Gabba, *Athenaeum* 38 (1960) 218 n. 121 on Dion. Hal. V 74.4 (Macer fr. 10P), 77.4f (Sulla); also Gabba in *Tria Corda: scritti in onore di Arnaldo Momigliano* (Como 1983) 220f.
56. Cic. *De sen.* 56, with J.G.F. Powell, *Cicero, Cato maior de senectute* (Cambridge 1988) 219.
57. Cf. n. 43 above (Cicero on Ahala as a *privatus*); Broughton, *MRR* I 39 (Cincinnatus in 458). For a similar spelling out of details, cf. Cic. *De nat. deor.* II 7 (also 44 BC), with T.P. Wiseman, *Clio's Cosmetics* (Leicester 1979) 111.
58. I.e. Valerius Antias, if the argument at *Clio's Cosmetics* 113–21 is accepted.
59. Ogilvie, op. cit (n. 51) 551: a generous judgement.
60. Livy IV 15.2 ('uim parantem'), contrast 14.4–6; and at 15.1 Cincinnatus allows the possibility that Maelius was innocent of *regnum*.
61. Livy IV 12.8–11, 16.2; cf. Dion. Hal. XII 1.5–6 (appointed by Senate), Pliny *Nat. Hist.* XVIII 15 (honoured by people).
62. Livy IV 13.7: 'nihil enim constat.'

63. D. Gutberlet, *Die erste Dekade des Livius als Quelle zur gracchischen und sullanischen Zeit* (Beiträge zur Altertumswissenschaft 4, Hildesheim 1985).
64. Above, n. 19 (cf. n. 12).
65. Broughton, *MRR* I 57 n. 2; cf. n. 40 above.
66. Dion. Hal. XII 1.14 (μεμήνυται), 2.1 (ἐμηνύθη . . . τὸν μηνυτὴν; Zonaras VII 20 (τὸ μήνυμα); cf. n. 42 above.
67. Cic. *Rosc. Am.* 50, *Sest.* 72 ('ille Serranus ab aratro'), Virg. *Aen.* VI 844, Val. Max. IV 4.5, Pliny *Nat. Hist.* XVIII 20; Schol. Gron. 308St (C. Atilius Serranus), Serv. *ad Aen.* VI 844 ('Atilius quidam senator'), Schol. Pers. 1.74 (Cincinnatus!). Often identified as C. Atilius Regulus *cos.* 257, but wrongly: Valerius Maximus distinguishes the two.
68. Oros. IV 12.2, cf. Eutrop. III 3 '<Bu>bulco'. The Fasti Capitolini call him C. Atilius A.f.A.n. Bulbus, and deny him the triumph in 235 which Val. Max. IV 4.5 seems to imply. Cf. Val. Max. IV 4.4 on *bubulci* called from the plough to the consulship.
69. Cic. *Leg. agr.* II 64, *Sest.* 143, *Cael.* 39, *Pis.* 58, *Planc.* 60; Sen. *Contr.* II 1.8, Val. Max. IV 4.11, Quintilian VII 2.38, XII 2.30, Pliny *Paneg.* 13, Juv. II 154, XI 91, Apuleius *Apol.* 10.
70. Prisc. *Gramm.* II 135.23 'faber fabri Fabricius'. In only one of the thirteen passages in n. 69 (the first) is he called Luscinus; cf. Pliny *Nat. Hist.* XI 150 for the meaning of the *cognomen*. [On Fabricius and *faber*, see now J. Henderson, *Figuring Out Roman Nobility: Juvenal's Eighth Satire* (Exeter 1997) 45–6; the entire book is a commentary on speaking names.]
71. Crawford, op. cit. (n. 11) 333–5, no. 335.3.
72. *ILLRP* 35 = *CIL* I² 28; R. Wachter, *Altlateinischer Inschriften* (Bern 1987) 346f, 349–59.
73. Varro *De ling. Lat.* V 158 (*publice*), Ovid *Fasti* V 285–94 (*publica cura*) on the builders of the Clivus Publicius (L.M. Publicii Malleoli, according to Festus 276L); *ILLRP* 357 = *CIL* I² 834 for C. Poplicius Bibulus, honoured *populi iussu*. See Wiseman, op. cit. (n. 57) 92f.
74. Plut. *Quaest. Rom.* 4 (*Mor.* 264c-d) = Juba *FGrH* 275 F91; cf. Livy I 45.3–7, Val. Max. VII 3.1, *Vir. ill.* 7.10–14.
75. Broughton, *MRR* III (1986) 70.
76. Lucr. III 1034, Cic. *Balb.* 34, Virg. *Aen.* VI 842, Val. Max. III 5.1, Sil. It. VII 106; H.A.J. Munro, *T. Lucreti Cari de rerum natura libri sex* II (Cambridge 1864) 273f = ed. 4 (London 1920) 226f; [Henderson, op. cit. (n. 70) 142 n. 49.]
77. Livy IX 44.1, Fasti Capitolini.
78. Livy I 7.12–14, IX 29.9, Dion. Hal. I 40.4–5, Festus 270L; Plut. *Quaest. Rom.* 60 (*Mor.* 278f), Macrobius *Sat.* III 6.12–14, Servius auctus on *Aeneid* VIII 269, *Origo gentis R.* 8.3.
79. E.g. Cic. *Tusc.* IV 4 (Ap. Caecus' *carmen Pythagoreum*), Pliny *Nat. Hist.* XXXIV 26 (Pythagoras' statue in the Comitium, time of the Samnite wars), ps.-Epicharmus fr. 295 Kaibel (Pythagoras a Roman citizen).
80. Plut. *Aem. Paul.* 2.2, *Numa* 8.10, Festus (Paulus) 22L.
81. *Suda* s.v. 'Philoxenos', cf. *Grammaticae Romanae fragmenta* 443–6 Funaioli; Dion. Hal. I 33.4, Tac. *Ann.* XI 14. See E. Gabba in *Miscellanea di studi alessandrini in memoria di A. Rostagni* (Turin 1963) 188–94.

82. Eratosthenes ap. Schol. Plato *Phaedrus* 244b (Ruhnk p. 61), cf. Clem. Alex. *Strom.* I 108.3; Callimachus *Iambi* fr. 106–7 Pfeiffer.
83. Q. Publilius Philo *cos.* 339, 327, 320, 315, *cens.* 332; P. Sempronius Sophus *cos.* 304, *cens.* 300.
84. Plut. *Numa* 7.5 = Juba *FGrH* 275 F88 (πιλαμένας τινὰς ὄντας); Diomedes *Gramm. Lat.* I 475–6 Keil ('Bellonae, id est 'Ἐννοῦς, filio'). *Inire*: Servius on *Aeneid* VI 775, cf. Ovid *Fasti* II 441.
85. Livy X 19.17, Ovid *Fasti* VI 201–4, *CIL* XI 1827 = *ILS* 54; cf. Pliny *Nat. Hist.* XXXV 12 (misdated to 495 BC). Bellona as Enyo: Plut. *Sulla* 30.2, *Cic.* 13.4, Dio L 4.5, etc. A possible context for the 'warlike' Inuus is suggested in *Journal of Roman Studies* 85 (1995) 10–12.
86. Livy X 46.7, Pliny *Nat. Hist.* VII 213. It had two myrtle-trees in front of it, one for the patricians and the other for the plebeians (Pliny *Nat. Hist.* XV 120).
87. Livy X 9.2. This part of the argument is repeated from *Liverpool Classical Monthly* 16.8 (Oct. 1991) 118f.
88. Cn. Gellius fr. 7P (Solinus 1.7), Servius on *Aeneid* III 359; Crawford, op. cit. (n. 11) 377, no. 363 (coins of L. Marcius Censorinus, 82 BC). See M. Torelli, *Typology and Structure of Roman Historical Reliefs* (Ann Arbor 1982) 103–5, and Coarelli, op. cit. (n. 30) 91–111, suggesting that the statue of Marsyas in the Forum was set up by Cn. Marcius Censorinus in 295.
89. Cic. *De div.* I 89, cf. I 115, II 113; Livy XXV 12.3 (*uates inlustris*, prophecies consulted in 212 BC), Festus 162L, Festus (Paulus) 185L, Isid. *Orig.* VI 8.12.
90. Cic. *De div.* I 115, II 113; see nn. 71–3 above for the Publicii.
91. Fasti Capitolini: T. Genucius L.f.L.n. Augurinus *cos.* and X*vir* 451, M. Genucius Augurinus *cos.* 445, Cn. Genucius M.f.M.n. Augurinus *tr. mil. cos. pot.* 399. Minucii: pp. 97–8 above.
92. T.P. Wiseman, *Remus: a Roman Myth* (Cambridge 1995) 109f.
93. Broughton, *MRR* I 243 for the sources; cf. J. Nichol, *The Historical and Geographical Sources used by Silius Italicus* (Oxford 1936) 73–6, on 'the tendency to exalt Fabius'.
94. Cic. *Ad Att.* I 1.2, with D.R. Shackleton Bailey, *Cicero's Letters to Atticus* I (Cambridge 1965) 292.

Chapter 10

1. E.M. Steinby, 'Il lato orientale del Foro Romano: proposte di lettura', *Arctos* 21 (1987) 139–84, esp. 167–77, [and in *Lexicon Topographicum Urbis Romae* I A-C (Rome 1993) 167–8].
2. Pliny *Nat. Hist.* XXXVI 102, Tac. *Ann.* III 72, Appian *Bell. civ.* II 26, Dio XLIX 42.2, LIV 24.2.
3. Livy XL 51.43–6, Plut. *Caes.* 29.3; cf. Varro *De ling. Lat.* VI 4 ('in basilica Aemilia et Fuluia')—Fulvius' colleague was M. Aemilius Lepidus. [See now H. Bauer in *Lexicon Topographicum* I (n. 1 above) 173–5, 183–7.]
4. Steinby, op. cit. 143 ('un limite orientale del Foro mediorepubblicano'), 156 ('il limite orientale della piazza'), 179 ('al limite orientale del Foro').

5. Servius on *Aeneid* VIII 363: 'in radicibus Palatii finibusque Romani fori.' Basilica as extension of Regia: Steinby, op. cit. 175 on Appian *Bell. civ.* II 148.
6. Livy XL 51.5; Varro fr. 121 Funaioli (Donatus *ad Eun.* 256), Festus (Paulus) 42L, 112L (giving names of censors), Plut. *Quaest. Rom.* 54; Varro *De ling. Lat.* V 146–7, 152. See F. Coarelli, *Il foro romano: periodo repubblicano e augusteo* (Rome 1985) 151–2, [and C. Morselli in E.M. Steinby (ed.), *Lexicon Topographicum Urbis Romae* II D-G (Rome 1995) 298].
7. Varro *Men.* 456B (Nonius 149L); Dion. Hal. V 49.1, Plut. *Publ.* 10.2. Publicola's house was close to that of Tullus Hostilius (Cic. *De rep.* II 53), which was on the site of the temple of the Penates (Varro in Nonius 852L), which was above the *macellum* (Varro in Donatus *ad Eun.* 256). [See now F. Coarelli in *Lexicon Topographicum* II (n. 6 above) 209–10.]
8. G. Fuchs, 'Zur Baugeschichte der Basilica Aemilia in republikanischer Zeit', *Römische Mittheilungen* 63 (1956) 14–25.
9. Pliny *Nat. Hist.* XXXV 13—the only reference to the Basilica Aemilia in all our literary sources.
10. Cic. *Ad Att.* IV 16.6 ('in aduentum Caesaris'), 16.7 ('Britannici belli exitus exspectatur').
11. Plut. *Caes.* 29.2–3. The sum (from Caesar's Gallic booty) equals about 20% of the entire treasury of Ptolemaic Cyprus (Plut. *Cato min.* 38.1).
12. Plut. *Rom.* 2.3; L.R. Taylor, *The Voting Districts of the Roman Republic* (Rome 1960) 45 and Map 1.
13. Ilia: Fabius Pictor *FGrH* 809 F 4a (Plut. *Rom.* 3.3, Dion. Hal. I 76.3, 77.1, 79.4), Ennius *Ann.* frr. 56, 60 Sk. Servilia: *Anthologia Palatina* III 19. For Cicero (*De div.* I 40), quoting Ennius, she is 'Vestalis illa'.
14. Val. Max. I 1.7, Dion. Hal. II 68.3–5, Prop. IV 11.53–4; compare Tuccia, Attus Navius, Q. Claudia ('mira sed et scaena testificata', Ovid *Fasti* IV 326).
15. Sil. It. VIII 293–7, Festus (Paulus) 22L.
16. Stemma (partly conjectural) in G.V. Sumner, *The Orators in Cicero's Brutus* (Toronto 1973) 66.
17. Plut. *Numa* 8.10, *Aem. Paul.* 2.2, Festus (Paulus) 22L; M. Gaggiotti, *Analecta Romana Instituti Danici* 14 (1985) 65–6.
18. Plut. *Numa* 21.2, q.v. also for protests at the invention of these legendary genealogies—perhaps by Cn. Gellius in polemic with Piso: E. Gabba, *Entretiens Hardt* 13 (1967) 159–61.
19. Livy XXV 1.12 (consular candidate in 215), XXXVII 4.5 (praetor in 190); *ILS* 949 (son of Paullus Lepidus *cos.* 34?). 'Regillus Lepidi filius' (Cic. *Ad Att.* XII 24.2) is variously identified: see Shackleton Bailey's commentary ad loc., and Sumner, op. cit. (n. 16) 164 (son of *cos.* 137? 78? 77?).
20. Val. Max. VI 6.1, Tac. *Ann.* II 67.2 (cf. Goodyear's commentary ad loc.), Justin XXX 2.8, 3.4; D.C. Braund, *Papers of the British School at Rome* 51 (1983) 30–3.
21. Livy XXXV 10.11–12, XLI 27.8; see A. Boethius in Boethius and Ward-Perkins, *Etruscan and Roman Architecture* (Harmondsworth 1970) 107–8, and E. Nash, *Pictorial Dictionary of Ancient Rome* (London 1968) II

238–40. W. Reiter, *Aemilius Paullus, Conqueror of Greece* (London 1988) 109, absurdly calls it 'a modest building programme'.

22. (a) *CIL* XV 7150 ('nauis harenaria quae seruit in Aemilianis') must refer to a riverside location; (b) Suet. *Claud.* 18.1 (Claudius at the Diribitorium during a fire in the Aemiliana) must refer to the Campus Martius area; Varro *De re rust.* III 2.6, Tac. *Ann.* XV 40 and *CIL* VI 37811 are more likely to refer to (b) than to (a). F. Coarelli, *Il foro boario* (Rome 1988) 147–55, makes a heroic effort to attribute all the references to the same place, but in vain: see *Gnomon* 62 (1990) 733.

23. Livy XXXVII 58.3–4.

24. Livy XXXIX 2.10. The road from Bononia to Aquileia attributed to him by Strabo (V 217) is the result of a confusion: T.P. Wiseman, *Athenaeum* 67 (1989) 418–19.

25. See Festus 332L, distinguishing it from the aspirated Greek *Rhegium*; cf. Cic. *Ad fam.* XII 5.2 (*Regium Lepidi*), Phlegon *FGrH* 257 F 37.20, 37.45 (πόλεως βασιλείας).

26. Livy XL 51.4 (179), XXXV 21.5 (192 flood), Plut. *Numa* 9.3, ps.Aethicus *Grammatici Latini minores* 83 Riese; Coarelli, op. cit. (n. 22) 139–47. Pons Aemilius: Juv. 6.32, Hist. Aug. *Heliogabalus* 17.2, calendar *fasti* on 17 August ('Portuno ad pontem Aemilium').

27. Livy XL 52.4–6, Macrobius *Sat.* I 10.10; *Grammatici Latini* VI 265K (Caesius Bassus) for the inscription.

28. Livy XLV 40.6, Plut. *Aem. Paul.* 34.1, Florus I 28.13; cf. Pol. I 1.5.

29. See n. 5 above. Lacus: Minucius Felix *Octavius* 7.3, Florus I 28.15; Steinby, op. cit. (n. 1) 168–9.

30. Festus 282L, Livy X 23.3, Macrobius *Sat.* III 6.10; Coarelli, op. cit. (n. 22) 164–78.

31. Cic. *De nat. deor.* II 61 (temples of Mens and Fides), Strabo V 217, *De vir. ill.* 72.8; E. Fentress, *Papers of the British School at Rome* 52 (1984) 72–6 for the milestones.

32. Martial VI 85.6 etc (one of the Augustan *regiones*).

33. Hor. *Ars poetica* 32–3, with Porphyrio ad loc.: 'Aemilii Lepidi ludus gladiatorius fuit, quod nunc Polycleti balineum est.'

34. R. Syme, *Athenaeum* 61 (1983) 12 = *Roman Papers* IV (Oxford 1988) 233, whence the title of chapter 8 of *The Augustan Aristocracy* (Oxford 1986).

35. Basilica: n. 9 above. L. Paullus ('Paullus Lepidus' on his coins) was praetor and consul four years earlier than his brother M. Lepidus. 'Scipio Lepidi f.': Orosius V 22.17.

36. Sall. *Hist.* I 55.26–7M, 77.6M.

37. Val. Max. VII 7.5; on Mamercus and the 'lightweight' Manius Lepidus (consul in 66), see G.V. Sumner, *Journal of Roman Studies* 54 (1964) 41–8.

38. Dio XXXVII 21.2 (trophy of the *oikoumene*), Plut. *Pomp.* 45, Diod. Sic. XL 4, Pliny *Nat. Hist.* VII 97; see M.H. Crawford, *Journal of Roman Studies* 66 (1976) 216 on the new standards set by Pompey's achievement.

39. M.H. Crawford, *Roman Republican Coinage* (Cambridge 1974) I 441, 443–4 (nos. 415, 419).

40. Thus Vell. Pat. I 9.3, Plut. *Aem. Paul.* 4.8: triumph *ex praetura* in 189, not in the *Fasti Capitolini*.

41. Nepos *Atticus* 18.4 (cf. 18.2 'ut ex eo clarorum uirorum propagines possimus cognoscere'). Cornelius Scipio may be Q. Metellus Scipio *cos.* 52, or more probably P. Scipio Salvitto *cos.* 35: see (respectively) F. Münzer, *Hermes* 40 (1905) 93–100, and R. Billows, *American Journal of Ancient History* 7.1 (1982) 53–68, esp. 61.
42. Cic. *Vat.* 28. For the position of the Fornix Fabianus, see Coarelli, op. cit. (n. 6) 172–3.
43. *ILLRP* 392. The survival of the Fornix Fabianus after the construction of the Augustan arch north of Divus Iulius is a problem faced neither by Coarelli nor by Steinby. Perhaps Augustus' arch incorporated the Fornix and its inscriptions?
44. Hercules Pompeianus: Vitruvius III 3.5, Pliny *Nat. Hist.* XXXIV 57. Venus Victrix: Tertullian *De spect.* 10, Tiro in Gellius X 1.7 (Victoria), Pliny *Nat. Hist.* VIII 20. Curia Pompeii: Pliny *Nat. Hist.* XXXV 59, Asconius 52C, Plut. *Brut.* 14.2 etc. Pompey's house: Plut. *Pomp.* 40.5; L. Richardson jr, *American Journal of Archaeology* 91 (1987) 123–6.
45. I owe the suggestion to Nicholas Purcell, and am grateful to him for allowing me to use it. Argiletum: Cic. *Ad Att.* XII 32.2 (rents), Martial I 3.1, 117.8–11, II 17.3. Macellum: Livy XL 51.5 and n. 6 above. Carinae: see N. Terrenato in E. Herring, R. Whitehouse and J. Wilkins (eds), *Papers of the Fourth Conference of Italian Archaeology* vol. 4 (London 1992) 31–47, esp. 35–6.
46. Pliny *Nat. Hist.* VII 97 for the Minerva temple and its inscription. For *tabernarii* (Cic. *Flacc.* 18), *turba forensis* (Cic. *De or.* I 118) etc, see P.J.J. Vanderbroek, *Popular Leadership and Collective Behavior in the Late Roman Republic* (Amsterdam 1987) 87–8 and passim (see index, s.v. 'artisans/shopkeepers').
47. For the date, see L.R. Taylor, *Athenaeum* 42 (1964) 17–18; T.R.S. Broughton, *The Magistrates of the Roman Republic* III (Atlanta 1986) 9.
48. Livy XLIV 16.10–11; [see now I. Iacopi in *Lexicon Topographicum* I (n. 1 above) 187–8]. *Tabernae veteres*: Plaut. *Curculio* 480, Pliny *Nat. Hist.* XXXV 25, 113; cf. Catullus 37.1–2.
49. Cic. *Mil.* 24 ('singulari uirtute civis . . . homo ad conseruandam rem p. natus'), *Vat.* 25 ('quem ciuem, quem uirum!'), cf. *Ad Q.f.* II 4.1, *Ad fam.* XV 14.5 on 'Paullus noster'.
50. Cic. *Ad fam.* VIII 10.3 (Caelius, November 51), *Ad Att.* VI 1.7 (February 50), with Shackleton Bailey's commentary ad locc.
51. Crassus: Plut. *Crass.* 16.2, *Comp. Nic. Crass.* 4. Caesar: Caes. *De bell. Gall.* VII 63–76.
52. Curia: Cic. *De fin.* V 2 (dramatic date 79 BC), Pliny *Nat. Hist.* XXXIV 26, cf. Dio XLIV 5.2. Basilica Porcia: Plut. *Cato min.* 5.1 etc. Concord and Basilica Opimia: Cic. *Sest.* 140, Varro *De ling. Lat.* V 156, Appian *Bell. civ.* I 26, Plut. *C. Gracc.* 17.6; see N. Purcell, *Journal of Roman Archaeology* 2 (1989) 161–2, who very plausibly identifies the 'Tabularium' portico as the Basilica Opimia.
53. Suet. *Iul.* 44.1, 'theatrum summae magnitudinis Tarpeio monti accubans'— not to be confused with the Caesarian project later completed as the Theatre of Marcellus (Dio XLIII 49.2). For the Tarpeian Rock, see Coarelli,

op. cit. (n. 6) 80–6; for the logic of a theatre in the Forum, see T.P. Wiseman in I.M. Barton (ed.), *Roman Public Buildings* (Exeter 1989) 151–5.

54. The Curia and the adjoining Basilica Porcia were burnt down at Clodius' funeral in 52 (Asconius 33C). Faustus: Dio XL 50.2–3.
55. Plut. *Ant.* 6.4, Caes. *De bell. civ.* II 21.5, Dio XLIII 1.1–3.
56. Dio XLIV 5.2, cf. Sall. *Hist.* I 55.20M; [see now E. Tortorici in *Lexicon Topographicum* II (n. 6 above) 245–6]. The Felicitas temple is presumably under the baroque church of S. Martina near the arch of Septimius Severus.
57. Appian *Bell. civ.* II 148 (pyre), IV 12 (Paullus), Dio XLVII 18.4 (Divus Iulius), LIII 23.2 (Saepta).
58. Dio XLIX 42.2 (34 BC), LIV 24.2–3 (14 BC), Tac. *Ann.* III 72.1; P. Zanker, *Forum Romanum* (Tübingen 1972), [and N. Purcell in *Lexicon Topographicum* II (n. 6 above) 336–42].
59. R. Syme, *The Augustan Aristocracy* (Oxford 1986) 104–40 with stemmata 4 and 5, and *Athenaeum* 65 (1987) 7–26 = *Roman Papers* VI (Oxford 1991) 247–68.
60. Vell. Pat. II 88 (put down by Maecenas).
61. Tac. *Ann.* I 12.2 ('M. Lepidum dixerat capacem sed aspernantem'), Dio LIX 22.6 (Gaius' heir). See Propertius IV 11, with Billows, op. cit. (n. 41) 59–60, for the continued resonance of the 'Paulli Maximi Africani'.
62. L. Paullus: Suet. *Aug.* 19.1, with Syme, *Augustan Aristocracy* ch. 9. M. Lepidus: Seneca *Epist.* 4.7, Suet. *Gaius* 24.3, *Claud.* 9.1, Dio LIX 22.6, Josephus *Ant. Jud.* XIX 20, 49.
63. Pliny *Nat. Hist.* XXXVI 102, Statius *Silvae* I 1.30. Cf. Propertius III 3.8 (supposedly on the subject matter of Ennius' *Annales*): 'regiaque Aemilia uecta tropaea rate.'

Chapter 11

1. See J.M. Davidson, *Eminent Radicals in and out of Parliament* (London 1880) 168–78; C. Kent, in *Biographical Dictionary of Modern British Radicals II: 1830–1870* (Brighton 1984) 53–8; R. Harrison, *Before the Socialists: Studies in Labour and Politics 1861–1881* (London 1965) 251–345: 'The Positivists: a Study of Labour's Intellectuals'. There will be a biography of him in the *New Dictionary of National Biography* (publication scheduled for 2004).
2. E.g. 'Trades Unions', *Westminster Review* 20 (July-Oct. 1861) 510–42; 'The Trades Union Commission', *Fortnightly Review* 8.1 (July 1867) 1–18; 'The International Working Men's Association', *Fortnightly Review* 14.5 (Nov. 1870) 517–35. Beesly was a regular contributor to the *Bee-Hive* weekly ('A Journal of General Intelligence, Advocating Industrial Interests'), which was the mouthpiece of the Trades Council. See Royden Harrison, 'Professor Beesly and the Working-Class Movement', in A. Briggs and J. Saville (eds), *Essays in Labour History in Memory of G.D.H. Cole* (London 1960) 205–41.
3. R. Harrison, 'E.S. Beesly and Karl Marx', *International Review of Social*

History 4 (1959) 21–58 and 208–38, quoting (at p. 32) a letter in *Christian Socialist*, March 1884.

4. Kent, op. cit. (n. 1 above) 54; cf. Roy Jenkins, *Gladstone* (London 1995) 4: 'the best working rule I have been able to devise is to multiply all nineteenth-century values by a factor of fifty in order to turn them into late-twentieth-century terms.' Beesly himself (see n. 5) describes his university income as 'insignificant'; he clearly had private means.

5. Beesly in W.P. Ker, *Notes and Materials for the History of University College, London* (London 1898) 36–7. I am very grateful to Michael Crawford for tracking down this item for me.

6. Convenient summaries in Harrison, opp. citt. (n. 1) 251–4, (n. 2) 206–10.

7. *Westminster Review* 19 (Jan.-April 1861) 305–36, quotations from pp. 320 and 336. The review is unsigned.

8. Ibid. 310–11.

9. Ibid. 324.

10. Ibid. 326–7.

11. Ibid. 327.

12. 'The Republican Triumph', *Bee-Hive* 185 (29 April 1865) 4, q.v. for the death of Lincoln: 'Since the great Julius fell under the daggers of the Roman aristocrats, perhaps no death so sad has thrown a gloom over the world.' For Beesly's splendid speech at John Bright's rally of working-class support for Emancipation (St James' Hall, 26 March 1863), see Harrison, op. cit. (n. 1) 69–77.

13. M.S. Vogeler, *Frederic Harrison: the Vocations of a Positivist* (Oxford 1984) 58.

14. Letter to Engels, 19 August 1865: Karl Marx, Friedrich Engels, *Werke* Band 31 (Berlin 1965) 145.

15. 'Catiline as a Party Leader', *Fortnightly Review* 1.2 (1 June 1865) 167–84; 'Cicero and Clodius', ibid. 5.4 (1 July 1866) 421–44; 'The Emperor Tiberius', ibid. 8.6 (Dec. 1867) 635–48 and 9.1 (Jan. 1868) 14–30. Reprinted as *Catiline, Clodius and Tiberius* (London 1878, repr. New York 1924): 'Catiline', 1–37; 'Clodius', 38–83; 'Tiberius', 84–148. Page references below give the original pagination first.

16. R. Syme, *The Roman Revolution* (Oxford 1939) ix: 'It has not been composed in tranquillity ... [T]he theme, I firmly believe, is of some importance.' See H. Galsterer in K.A. Raaflaub and M. Toher (eds), *Between Republic and Empire: Interpretations of Augustus and his Principate* (Berkeley 1990) 1–20, esp. 12 on Syme's use of 'revolution'.

17. 'Catiline' 168 = 3–4.

18. Aubert de Vertot d'Aubeuf, *Histoire des révolutions arrivées dans le gouvernement de la République romaine* (Paris 1719, 7th ed. 1778); *The History of the Revolutions that happened in the Government of the Roman Republic* (London 1720, 6th ed. 1770). The *Discours préliminaire* begins: 'L'amour de la liberté a été le premier objet des Romains dans l'établisse-ment de la république, et la cause ou le prétexte des révolutions dont nous entreprenons d'écrire l'histoire. Ce fut cet amour de la liberté qui fit proscrire la royauté, qui diminua l'autorité du consulat, et qui en suspendit le titre en différentes occasions.'

NOTES TO PAGES 125–129

19. N. Hooke, *The Roman History, from the Building of Rome to the Ruine of the Commonwealth* (London 1738–71) I iii, 115 (Decemvirs and Tarquins respectively); T. Gordon, *The Works of Sallust* (London 1744) 6, rendering 'Sed ea tempestate' (Sall. *Cat.* 7.1) as 'Upon this Revolution, . . .'
20. Hooke, op. cit. ii-iii.
21. Reprinted in G. Claes, *The Politics of English Jacobinism: Writings of John Thelwall* (Penn State 1995) 389–500; see 488–9 on the 'band of Ruffian Senators' (Hooke's phrase) who 'extinguished Roman liberty in the blood of [Tiberius] Gracchus'.
22. Hooke, op. cit. (n. 19) II 560. Cf. Thelwall (Claes, op. cit. 489 n.): 'Genuine Republican Rome expired with the Gracchi. The atrocious contests that ensued, between Sylla and Marius, and Caesar and Pompey, were mere struggles of individual ambition—or at least of *Monarchic and Aristocratic factions.*'
23. 'Catiline' 170 = 8 (133 BC as 'the commencement of the revolution') and 171 = 9: 'The Roman revolution was inaugurated by the Gracchi. Never had a good cause more noble champions.' The fourth book of Mommsen's *History of Rome* (1856, English trans. 1866), covering the period from Ti. Gracchus to Sulla, is entitled 'Die Revolution'.
24. Ibid. 168 = 4, 170–1 = 9.
25. Kent, op. cit. (n. 1) 54; Beesly, 'England and the Sea', in *International Policy: Essays on the Foreign Relations of England* (London 1866) 153–222 = (ed. 2, London 1884) 103–49, quotation from 196 = 131; *Hansard*, Commons 3 May 1867 (3rd series, 186.1929–33).
26. 'The Emperor Tiberius' (n. 15 above) 28 = 144.
27. 'Catiline' 171 = 10. Cf. 172 = 12 on Sulla, 'too fond of ease and self-indulgence to care for empire'.
28. Ibid. 171–2 = 9–11.
29. Ibid. 175 = 18–19, quoting Sall. *Cat.* 37.1. (In fact, Sallust's very sweeping analysis includes at 38.3 the assertion that ideology counted for nothing, and that the people's champions were no less motivated by lust for power than those of the Senate.)
30. Ibid. 176–8 = 20–24. This is the context of the phrase Marx noticed: 'Our dull littérateurs have adopted [these libels] as serious facts, rather than confess how little we really know of ancient history beyond its broad features' (177 = 23).
31. Ibid. 181 = 30.
32. Ibid. 176 = 19.
33. Ibid. 180 = 28.
34. Ibid. 180 = 29 on Cic. *Mur.* 51, 'quem omnino uiuum illinc exire non oportuerat'.
35. Ibid. 181 = 30 on Cic. *Cat.* I 4–6 and 12 (Beesly's note gives the false reference 'IV 12').
36. Ibid. 182 = 32 on Sall. *Cat.* 35.5, 'plura quom scribere uellem, nuntiatum est uim mihi parari'.
37. Letter to Beesly in 1864, quoted by Harrison, op. cit. (n. 1) 280.
38. G. Dutton, *The Hero as Murderer* (Sydney 1968, a sympathetic but not uncritical biography of Eyre) 214–307.

39. Ibid. 308–64.
40. 'The Trial of Mr Eyre', *Bee-Hive* 253 (18 August 1866) 4.
41. See n. 15 above.
42. 'Cicero and Clodius' 421 = 39–40.
43. Ibid. 421–2 = 41; cf. n. 8 above.
44. Cf. ibid. 436 = 71: 'My aim is not to persecute the memory of an individual, but to set the Roman Revolution in a clear light, and strip off the false colours with which the anecdote-mongers have bedaubed it.' The same point, and the same capitals, at 441 = 82, and 'The Emperor Tiberius' 635 = 86.
45. 'Catiline' 183 = 34–5, 184 = 36.
46. 'Cicero and Clodius' 432–3 = 64–5 (Cic. *Ad Att.* I 16.11, 'sine ulla pastoricia fistula'); cf. 422 = 42, 'the lower orders of Rome, who had loved and trusted Catiline, exhibited a constant and determined hostility to the man who had hunted their hero to death to please the oligarchy'.
47. Ibid. 434 = 67.
48. Ibid. 440 = 80; Cic. *Post red. in Sen.* 28, *Pis.* 36 ('uos diribitores, uos custodes fuisse tabularum').
49. Ibid. 435 = 69–70; Cic. *Post red. ad Quir.* 8.
50. Ibid. 435 = 70 n. 1; cf. Plut. *Cic.* 31.1; W. Forsyth, *Life of Marcus Tullius Cicero* (London 1864) I 198.
51. Ibid. 422 = 42.
52. Ibid. 440 = 79–80.
53. See n. 40 above.
54. 'The Emperor Tiberius' (n. 15 above) 635–6 = 86–7.
55. Ibid. 637 = 90; cf. also 20 = 126–7.
56. See Harrison, op. cit. (n. 2) 228f, who quotes Beesly's comment to a fellow-Positivist: 'There will be little harmony between us and Bright henceforth, I fear.'
57. 'The Emperor Tiberius' 642 = 101 n. 1; contrast 645 = 105 n. 2 on Velleius, with his 'freedom and heartiness of style'.
58. Ibid. 26–9 = 139–47, quotation from 27 = 141–2.
59. Davidson, op. cit. (n. 1) 176: he had urged the unions to 'ferret out any member guilty of a breach of the law and drag him to justice'. Cf. Harrison, op. cit. (n. 1) 279.
60. *The Times* 4 July 1867 p. 9; Harrison, op. cit. (n. 2) 226–7.
61. Harrison, op. cit. (n. 3) 38–9.
62. See for instance R. Harrison (ed.), *The English Defence of the Commune 1871* (London 1971) 37–117.
63. 'Cicero and Clodius' 441 = 82.

Chapter 12

Versions of this paper were given at seminars in Oxford (1993) and at the Victoria University of Wellington, New Zealand (1996); I am very grateful for helpful suggestions made on both occasions, and for those of Prof. A.J. Woodman on the typescript.

1. Sir Keith Thomas, in conversation with the author, 1993.
2. *Proceedings of the British Academy* 84 (1994) 560. Bowersock was even more laconic in *Proceedings of the American Philosophical Society* 135 (1991) 121: 'Original books on Ovid and the Arval Brothers were followed by a massive and long-awaited work, *The Augustan Aristocracy*, published in 1986.' Cf. F. Millar in *Dictionary of National Biography 1986–1990* (Oxford 1996) 444: 'a work of remarkable complexity, interest, and novelty.'
3. Keith Feiling in *The Observer*, quoted on the cover of the 1960 paperback. And that judgement has lasted: see for instance F.G.B. Millar in *Journal of Roman Studies* 71 (1981) 146 ('*The Roman Revolution*, on re-reading, does seem to me a work of art unmatched among major historical works'), and loc. cit. n. 2 above ('As a work of literature, and as an exercise in intellectual and stylistic control, it has no equal in the historiography of Rome, and few in that of any period or area'). The essays of H. Galsterer, Z. Yavetz and J. Linderski, in K.A. Raaflaub and M. Toher (eds), *Between Republic and Empire: Interpretations of Augustus and his Principate* (Berkeley 1990) 1–20, 21–41, 42–53, provide eloquent testimony to the lasting impact of *The Roman Revolution*.
4. *Emory University Quarterly* 18 (1962) 140 = *Roman Papers* VI (Oxford 1991) 96. Cf. *Journal of Roman Studies* 34 (1944) 92 = *Roman Papers* I (Oxford 1979) 149, on M. Gelzer's *Caesar der Politiker und Staatsmann*: 'The author is not arguing a thesis; and remembering that history is narrative, not research, disputation, and the passing of judgements, he lets the facts speak for themselves.'
5. *The Roman Revolution* (Oxford 1939) vii, the Preface. Henceforth, I shall omit the place of publication in citing Syme's books: with the exception of *Sallust* (University of California Press, Berkeley and Los Angeles, distributed in the UK by Cambridge UP), they were all published by the Clarendon Press, Oxford.
6. *Tacitus* (1958) v, the Preface.
7. A.N. Sherwin-White, *Journal of Roman Studies* 49 (1959) 140. Cf. Millar, loc. cit. (n. 2 above): 'the most original and creative of his works, the infinitely complex and fruitful two-volume work on *Tacitus*.'
8. *Sallust* (1964) 3: 'Who was Sallust?' Compare 'Who was Tacitus?', *Harvard Library Bulletin* 11 (1957) 185–98 = *Roman Papers* VI (1991) 43–54.
9. *Sallust* (1964) v, the Preface.
10. Pointed out to me by Christopher Pelling in 1993. I certainly hadn't noticed, and I wonder how many readers do. The groups are: 1–3, 4–7, 8–10, 11–14, 15–17, 18–20, 21, 22–26(?), 27–29, 30 (the 22/23 sequence comes at the turn of the page).
11. A.R. Birley, in *Roman Papers* VI (1991) v, the Editor's Preface.
12. A.R. Birley, in *Anatolica* (1995) xvii, the Editor's Introduction: the chapters were to be '?Caesar in the East', 'Antonius and the Vassals', 'The Policy of Augustus', 'Strabo on the House of Herod', and 'Eurycles'.
13. *Roman Papers* VI (1991) xi, 'Prologue'—the preface to the Italian edition of *Colonial Elites*.
14. *The Augustan Aristocracy* (1986) v, the first Preface.
15. Cf. *Emperors and Biography* (1971) vii.

16. Tac. *Ann.* III 24.2: *Tacitus* (1958) 368–71, 427, *Historia* 23 (1974) 483f = *Roman Papers* III (1984) 939f, *History in Ovid* (1978) 197f; full statement in *Historiographia Antiqua* (Louvain 1977) 231–63 = *Roman Papers* III (1984) 1014–42. The idea is doubted by A.J. Woodman and R.H. Martin, *The Annals of Tacitus, Book 3* (Cambridge 1996) 230.
17. Cic. *Phil.* XI 36.
18. Suet. *Tib.* 3.1; for Syme on Tiberius, see especially *Historia* 23 (1974) 481–96 = *Roman Papers* III (1984) 937–52.
19. Tac. *Ann.* III 54.1; see Woodman and Martin, op. cit. (n. 16) 390 for parallels (their first Livy reference should be to XXXII 20.3). Greek tyrants typically suppressed such groups: Aristotle *Pol.* VI 1313b, cf. D. Kelly in I. Worthington (ed.), *Voice into Text: Orality and Literacy in Ancient Greece* (Leiden 1996) 152f.
20. Tac. *Ann.* I 12; cf. *Tacitus* (1958) 380–2, on the *capaces imperii*.
21. *Sallust* (1964) 4, cf. 3, 'imagination demands its rights, or a little licence—and scholarship has a plain duty to extend the debatable frontiers of knowledge'.
22. *Tacitus* (1958) v, the Preface.
23. *Sitzungsberichte der Bayerische Akademie der Wissenschaften, phil.-hist. Klasse* (1974, Heft 7) 6 = *Roman Papers* III (1984) 914.
24. *Fictional History Old and New: Hadrian* (Oxford 1986) = *Roman Papers* VI (1991) 157–81.
25. Op. cit. 10 = 165.
26. *Tacitus* (1958) ix, opening the Prologue.
27. Tac. *Ann.* I 1.1; deliberate verse doubted (surely wrongly) by F.R.D. Goodyear, *The Annals of Tacitus* I (Cambridge 1972) 89f, q.v. for bibliography.
28. *The Augustan Aristocracy* (1986) 38–40, cf. Tac. *Ann.* I 9–10.
29. A. Momigliano, *New York Review of Books* (18 July 1974) 34 = *Sesto contributo alla storia degli studi classici e del mondo antico* (Rome 1980) 81. Reviews: *Journal of Roman Studies* 30 (1940) 75, *Gnomon* 33 (1961) 55, *English Historical Review* 84 (1969) 566, ibid. 88 (1973) 114 = *Secondo contributo...* (Rome 1960) 407, *Terzo contributo...* (Rome 1966) 739, *Quinto contributo...* (Rome 1975) 104, *Sesto contributo...* (Rome 1980) 714.
30. *The Roman Revolution* (1939) viii, 'pessimistic and truculent'. Sallust: 'sombre and pessimistic' (*Harvard Studies in Classical Philology* 64 [1959] 75 = *Roman Papers* I [1979] 452), 'grim and truculent', (*Sallust* [1964] 256), 'truculent, censorious, and subversive' (*Ten Studies in Tacitus* [1970] 130). Compare also *Roman Papers* I (1979) 971 on Sallust and Tacitus as pessimistic historians ('they find that there is work to be done; that is to say, the writing of history') with *Journal of Roman Studies* 58 (1968) 145 = *Roman Papers* II (1979) 711: 'one uses what one has, and there is work to be done.'
31. *History in Ovid* (1978) 225. Cf. *Roman Papers* I (1979) 970, on Gibbon: 'the middle thirties may mark a decisive turn in the life of a man or in the destiny of a writer.' Syme was 36 when *The Roman Revolution* was published (and the Second World War began).

32. *Tacitus* (1958) 546, 362f.
33. *Greece and Rome* 28 (1981) 41 = *Roman Papers* III (1984) 1365.
34. *Greeks Invading the Roman Government* (Stephen J. Brademas Lecture, Brookline Mass. 1982) 28 = *Roman Papers* IV (1988) 19.
35. Op. cit. (n. 24) 9 = 164.
36. Ibid. 23, 24 = 179, 180.
37. Ibid. 24 = 180, n.73 (referring also to R. Brentano, *The Historian's Workshop* [New York 1970] 26); A. Powell, *Hearing Secret Harmonies* (*A Dance to the Music of Time* vol. 12, 1975) 84.
38. A. Powell, *Books Do Furnish a Room* (*A Dance...* vol. 10, 1971) 229.
39. Loc. cit. (n. 7 above).
40. Cf. *Ammianus and the Historia Augusta* (1968) ch. 21, 'Other Frauds'; *Emperors and Biography* (1971) ch. 17, 'Fiction and Credulity'; *Historia Augusta Papers* (1983) ch. 1, 'Fraud and Imposture'.
41. Loc. cit. (n. 34 above).
42. A. Powell, *Temporary Kings* (*A Dance* . . . vol. 11, 1973) 219.

Appendix A

1. So Mommsen omitted all these splendid stories from his history of Rome, and rightly too, for Schwegler's attempts to extract nuggets of historical gold from the accumulated mass of these stories, however praiseworthy in themselves, have not been very successful.
2. [B.G. Niebuhr, *Römische Geschichte* I (Berlin 1811) 177–80, on Cato *Origines* fr. 118P (Cic. *Tusc.* I 2.3, IV 2.3, *Brut.* 75) and Varro *De vita populi Romani* fr. 84R (Nonius 107–8L).]
3. Schwegler in the first volume of his history of Rome (*Römische Geschichte* [Tübingen 1853], 54 nn. 3–4) has listed the supporters and the opponents of Niebuhr's theory, although Macaulay's essay now means the list should be augmented.
4. [See pp. 2–5 above on the work of Ribbeck (1881), Ranke (1883), Meiser (1887), Trieber (1888) and Schöne (1893).]
5. Livy V 21.8, on the conquest of Veii: 'Inseritur huic loco fabula ... sed in rebus tam antiquis si quae similia ueri sint pro ueris accipiantur, satis habeam: haec ad ostentationem scaenae gaudentis miraculis aptiora quam ad fidem neque adfirmare neque refellere operae pretium est.' Dionysius *Ant. Rom.* III 18, referring to the duel between the Horatii and the Curiatii: ἀπαιτούσης δὲ τῆς ὑποθέσεως καὶ τὸν τρόπον διεξελθεῖν τῆς μάχης ἀκριβῶς, καὶ τὰ μετὰ ταύτην γενόμενα πάθη θεατρικαῖς ἐοικότα περιπετείαις μὴ ῥᾳθύμως διελθεῖν. Ibid. IX 22, in the narrative of the defeat of the Fabii: μύθοις γὰρ δὴ ταῦτά γε καὶ πλάσμασιν ἔοικε θεατρικοῖς. Ibid. I 84, in the narrative of the rescue of Romulus and Remus: ἕτεροι . . . καὶ τῆς λυκαίνης τὸ τιθασὸν, ἣ τοὺς μαστοὺς ἐπεῖχε τοῖς παιδίοις ὡς δραματικῆς μεστὸν ἀτοπίας διασύρουσιν. Plutarch *Romulus* 8: ὕποπτον μὲν ἐνίοις ἐστὶ τὸ δραματικὸν καὶ πλασματῶδες, οὐ δεῖ δὲ ἀπιστεῖν τὴν τύχην ὁρῶντας οἵων ποιημάτων δημιουργός ἐστι.

6. [The authors and plays referred to are as follows. Italian: Alfieri, Vittorio (1749–1803), *Virginia* (1777), *Brutus* (1786/1788); Aretino, Pietro (1492–1556), *Orazia*; Bianchi, Giovanni Antonio (1686–1768), *Virginia* (1732); Costi (unidentified), *Brutus*; Crescenzo, Nicolò, *Coriolano* (1727); Delfino, Giovanni (1617–1699), *Lucrezia*; Gigli, Girolamo (1660–1722), *Gli Orazi e Curiazi*; Gravina, Gian Vincenzo (1664–1718), *Servio Tullio* (1712), *Appio Claudio* (1712); Martelli, Lodovico (1503–?1530), *Tullia* (1533); Martello, Pier Iacopo (1665–1727), *Quinto Fabio*; Pansuti, Saverio (?-1730), *Orazia* (1719), *Brutus* (1723), *Virginia* (1725). Spanish: Pastor, Juan (unidentified), *Lucretia*; Cueva, Juan de la (?1550–?1610), *Tragedia de la muerte de Virginia y Appio Claudio* (1580), *Comedia de la libertad de Roma por Mucio Cévola*. French: Corneille, Pierre (1606–1684), *Horace* (1640); Voltaire (François-Marie Arouet, 1694–1778), *Brutus* (1730). English: Shakespeare, William (1564–1616), *Coriolanus* (1608); anon., *The Four Sons of Fabius* (1580). German: Freytag, Gustav (1816–1895), *Die Fabier* (1859).]

7. In his work *Die griechischen Tragödie* (Part 3 p. 1356) Welker rightly says: 'It is obvious that during the Republic tragedy was the supreme genre of serious poetry.' His remarks at this point are the best comment that has been made on the value of Roman tragedy in general.

8. In any case we will regard the *Persians* and the *Capture of Miletus* as forerunners only in a certain sense, and certainly not as models for the Roman *praetexta*. The source for Naevius is certainly Euripides, and he can hardly have known the *Capture of Miletus*.

9. No other creation of the Roman spirit has been so pitilessly obliterated as Roman tragedy. Of the many Roman tragedians who must have existed we know of only 36 at the most, and the majority of them only by their names; and of plays we know at most only 150 titles. That would make about four works per tragedian. But the ancient tragedians were known to be particularly fertile, and even more so in the case of the Romans because they were mainly translators; so just one or two could have composed 150 plays.

10. [Tac. *Dial.* 2–3.]

11. [Details in A. Klotz, *Scaenicorum Romanorum fragmenta* I: *Tragicorum fragmenta* (Munich 1953) 358–72. See also E.H.Warmington, *Remains of Old Latin* II: *Livius Andronicus, Naevius, Pacuvius and Accius* (Loeb Classical Library, London 1936). Referred to below as 'Klotz' and 'Warmington'.]

12. [Thomas Babington Macaulay, *Lays of Ancient Rome* (London 1842) 7.]

13. [A. Schöne, *Das historische Nationaldrama der Römer: die Fabula praetexta* (Kiel 1893).]

14. [A slip for 'Pomponius'; Cassius wrote a *Brutus* (Varro *De ling. Lat.* VI 7, VII 72).]

15. Schöne, op. cit. (n. 13) 5f, 12f; O. Ribbeck, *Rheinisches Museum* 36 (1881) 321.

16. In this context one cannot appeal to the detailed nature of the Greek stories, such as that of Herakles. These Greek sagas owe their loving

217

execution, and their completeness even to the smallest detail, to artists who were consciously creative, the later epic writers and dramatists. Rather, they prove that our Roman saga of Romulus and Remus also owes its finished form to the poet's art.

17. This proof of identity is not very artistic; but even Aeschylus, one of the princes of dramatic art, has Electra recognise her brother by his footprints.

18. *Romulus* 8: ὧν τὰ πλεῖστα καὶ Φαβίου λέγοντος, καὶ τοῦ Πεπαρηθίου Διοκλέους, ὅς δοκεῖ πρῶτος ἐκδοῦναι Ῥώμης κτίσιν. Ibid. 3: τοῦ δὲ πίστιν ἔχοντος λόγου μάλιστα καὶ πλείστους μάρτυρας τὰ μὲν κυριώτατα πρῶτος εἰς τοὺς Ἕλληνας ἐξέδωκε Διοκλῆς ὁ Πεπαρήθιος ᾧ καὶ Φάβιος Πίκτωρ ἐν τοῖς πλείοτοις ἐπηκολούθηκε.

19. The fact that Callias made use of Roman tradition is shown by the correct form of Romulus' name - the earlier Greeks usually have 'Romus', 'Romanus' etc - and the name Latinus. Schwegler has collected the innumerable different foundation stories (*Röm. Gesch.* I part 1).

20. Before Diocles there is not the slightest trace of the detailed story which was to become so well known. Even Aristotle follows other narratives. Then with Diocles our story suddenly appears, fully-fledged.

21. The setting is similar in Euripides' *Andromache*; there the stage represents the palace of Neoptolemus opposite the temple of Thetis, in front of which Andromache sits by the altar, seeking asylum. In Terence's *Self-Tormentor* the scene is set in the country, between the houses of Chremes and Menedemus.

22. 'Rex Veiens regem salutat Vibe Albanum Amulium
comiter senem sapientem. contra redhostis?—min salust?' [Klotz 360, Warmington 138.]

23. 'Cedo, qui rem uestram publicam tantam amisistis tam cito?' [Klotz 360, Warmington 110.]

24. 'Proueniebant oratores nouei, stulti adulescentuli' (Ribbeck, *Tragic. fragm.* 278). [Klotz 360, Warmington 110. Note that both the last two lines are cited by Cicero from Naevius *Ludus*. Reich accepts the emendation *Lupus*, as does Klotz; Warmington takes the lines as from a comedy. See now J.G.F. Powell, *Cicero, Cato Maior de senectute* (Cambridge 1988) 145–6, who suggests *Lydus*, presumably a comedy.]

25. This explains why, when Faustulus later carries the vessel, the *gnorisma*, through the gateway, the gates were under close guard because of the danger of war.

26. In a very similar way Orestes in Euripides' *Iphigeneia* (cf. lines 303–321) is taken prisoner by the Tauric herdsmen.

27. Dionysius *Ant. Rom.* I 81: τῷ δράσαντι δεινὰ τὸ ἀντιπαθεῖν οὐ πρὸς ἄλλου τινὸς μᾶλλον ἤ τοῦ πεπονθότος ὀφείλεται. What we have set out here as the herdsman's speech is given in narrative form in Dionysius I 79.12–14, 81.1–3, and in Plutarch *Romulus* 7. But Dionysus expressly says later (I 31) that the herdsmen accused Remus before Amulius, listed his misdemeanours and displayed their injuries. We therefore have reason to suppose that the preceding narrative was taken from the speech of the leader of the herdsmen.

28. Plutarch *Romulus* 7, Dionysius *Ant. Rom.* I 81.
29. These words are another example of tragic irony, because recognition is about to follow.
30. Up to this point, the content of the first scene can be found mostly in direct speech in Plutarch *Rom.* 7 and Dionysius I 81. Then Dionysius says that Numitor now informs Remus how Amulius dethroned him, made Silvia a Vestal, and imprisoned her after her disgrace. So these facts, which are told in chronological order by the historian (Dionysius I 76–78, Plutarch *Rom.* 3), come into this speech in our drama. I have changed indirect into direct speech here.
31. Deep and truly tragic compassion must seize the audience at the sight of this old man, so cruelly injured and now so helpless. But it is already becoming clearer that Remus and Romulus are old Numitor's grandsons, thought to be dead, and that the work of vengeance is beginning.
32. Dionysius I 82.
33. Dionysius I 82.
34. Faustulus has come hurrying to the city with the vessel, fearing that Numitor will not believe what Romulus says without proof of his identity.
35. This refers to the declaration of war on the Veientes, mentioned at the beginning [n. 25 above].
36. Dionysius I 82–3.
37. Dionysius I 83.
38. That Diocles used this drama, which was staged shortly before he wrote his κτίσις Ῥώμης, as a historical source, need not surprise us in a historian of that epoch, especially a Greek who knew little of Roman matters. When king Agamemnon or Orestes or Ajax or Odysseus, or any other hero famed in saga, bestrode the stage and played out his fate, the spectator, filled with religious awe, would fully believe that he had seen a true piece of history, even while recognizing that a poet had shaped it. So Diocles will have been very happy to find in Naevius' drama such a clear and detailed account of what was only hinted at in meagre and contradictory fashion in the other foundation stories.
39. ['Complex plots' (μῦθοι πεπλεγμένοι): Aristotle *Poetics* 10, 13, 18 (1452a12–20, 1452b30–3, 1455a33–4).]
40. [See n. 15 above.]

Appendix B

1. See T.J. Cornell and A. Drummond, in *Cambridge Ancient History* VII.2 (ed.2, Cambridge 1989) 347–50 and 625–7.
2. O. Hirschfeld, *Wiener Studien* 3 (1881) 101–2 = *Kleine Schriften* (Berlin 1913) 443.
3. Suet. *Tib.* 1.1, etc; T.P. Wiseman, *Clio's Cosmetics* (Leicester 1979) 59–61.
4. Hirschfeld, op. cit. 102 = 443.

5. F. Coarelli, in *Spectacles sportifs et scèniques dans le monde étrusco-italique* (Coll. de l'École française de Rome 172, 1993) 214–5 = *Il Campo Marzio dalle origini alla fine della repubblica* (Rome 1997) 103–4.
6. Op. cit. 217 = 105–6.
7. Cf. S. Weinstock, *Divus Julius* (Oxford 1971) 191–7; I.M.LeM. DuQuesnay, in *Papers of the Liverpool Latin Seminar 1976* (Arca 2, Liverpool 1977) 39–43.
8. Coarelli, op. cit. (n. 5) 221–4 = 110–13, 225–6 = 113–5.
9. Coarelli, op. cit. 223 = 111, following Hirschfeld.
10. Plut. *Publ.* 9.6 ὡς ἔνιοι λέγουσι, 14.3 ἔνιοι δέ φασι.
11. Coarelli, op. cit. 222 = 111.

Index

221

Valerius Maximus, on Secular games
82–3
Valerius Publicola, P.   76, 79, 80–8, 108,
165–7
sons of 86–7
Valesius, legendary Sabine   83
Varro, M. Terentius, antiquarian author
9, 11, 18, 108, 165, 166
on origins of drama   x, 14
on *fabulae praetextae*   15
on Nonae Caprotinae   3, 8–11
on gods in drama   19, 22, 24, 73
on Secular Games   166
Veii, capture of   2, 5
Velia   xii, 108–9
Velleius Paterculus, C., historian   144,
146, 147
Venus, on stage   21
Vercingetorix, Gallic leader   110, 119
Veturia, mother of Coriolanus   88, 89
Via Minucia   90

Viae Aemiliae   112–3, 114
Vibe of Veii   159–60
Vibius Pansa, C.   62
Victoria, on stage   20, 33
Vindicius, loyal slave   81
Virgil (P. Vergilius Maro)   62, 66, 82
Virginia, tragic heroine   5, 153, 154
Virtus, on stage   20, 33
Vitellii, legendary traitors   80–1, 89
Volcanal   91, 93
Volcanalia   68

Walsh, P.G.   43
Wright, Henry B.   6–7, 31

Yourcenar, Marguerite   148, 149

Zevi, Fausto   81
Zorzetti, Nevio   12–13, 14
Zosimus, on altar of Dis   83, 167